FIFTH EDITION

GRAMMAR in CONTEXT

SANDRA N. ELBAUM

The cover photo shows the
MacArthur Causeway over
Biscayne Bay in Miami,
Florida.

HEINLE
CENGAGE Learning™

Australia • Brazil • Japan • Korea • Mexico • Singapore • Spain • United Kingdom • United States

HEINLE
CENGAGE Learning

Grammar in Context 3A, Fifth Edition
Student Book
Sandra N. Elbaum

Publisher: Sherrise Roehr

Acquisitions Editor: Tom Jefferies

Development Editor: Sarah Sandoski

Senior Technology Development Editor:
  Debie Mirtle

Director of Global Marketing: Ian Martin

Director of US Marketing: Jim McDonough

Product Marketing Manager: Katie Kelley

Marketing Manager: Caitlin Driscoll

Content Project Manager: Andrea Bobotas

Senior Print Buyer: Susan Spencer

Project Manager: Chrystie Hopkins

Production Services: Nesbitt Graphics, Inc.

Interior Design and Cover Design:
  Muse Group, Inc.

Library of Congress Control Number: 2009936999

ISBN 13: 978-1-4240-8092-2

ISBN 10: 1-4240-8092-4

Heinle
20 Channel Center Street
Boston, Massachusetts 02210
USA

Cengage Learning is a leading provider of customized learning solutions with office locations around the globe, including Singapore, the United Kingdom, Australia, Mexico, Brazil, and Japan. Locate our local office at international.cengage.com/region

Cengage Learning products are represented in Canada by Nelson Education, Ltd.

Visit Heinle online at **elt.heinle.com**

Visit our corporate website at **www.cengage.com**

Printed in China
5 6 7 8 9 10 — 15 14 13

Contents

Lesson 3

Lesson 4

Lesson 5

Lesson 6

Lesson 7

Lesson 8

Lesson 9

Lesson 10

Grammar Unreal Conditions—Present; Real Conditions vs.
Unreal Conditions; Unreal Conditions—Past; Wishes 417

Context Science or Science Fiction? 417

READING Time Travel 418

10.1 Unreal Conditions—Present 419

10.2 Implied Conditions 427

READING Traveling to Mars 429

10.3 Real Conditions vs. Unreal Conditions 430

READING Life 100 Years Ago 432

10.4 Unreal Conditions—Past 434

READING Science or Wishful Thinking? 437

10.5 Wishes 438

10.6 Wishing for a Desired Change 444

SUMMARY 449

EDITING ADVICE 450

EDITING QUIZ 450

TEST/REVIEW 452

EXPANSION 457

Appendices

A. Noncount Nouns AP1

B. Uses of Articles AP3

C. The Verb *Get* AP9

D. Gerund and Infinitive Patterns AP11

E. Verbs and Adjectives Followed by a Preposition AP15

F. Direct and Indirect Objects AP16

G. Spelling and Pronunciation of Verbs AP17

H. Capitalization Rules AP20

I. Plural Forms of Nouns AP21

J. Metric Conversion Chart AP23

K. Comparative and Superlative Forms AP26

L. Glossary of Grammatical Terms AP29

M. Alphabetical List of Irregular Verb Forms AP34

N. Map of the United States of America AP36

Index

Acknowledgments

Many thanks to Dennis Hogan, Sherrise Roehr, and Tom Jefferies from Heinle Cengage for their ongoing support of the *Grammar in Context* series. I would especially like to thank my development editor, Sarah Sandoski, for her patience, sensitivity, keen eye to detail, and invaluable suggestions.

And many thanks to my students at Truman College, who have increased my understanding of my own language and taught me to see life from another point of view. By sharing their observations, questions, and life stories, they have enriched my life enormously.

This new edition is dedicated to the millions of displaced people in the world. The U.S. is the new home to many refugees, who survived unspeakable hardships in Burundi, Rwanda, Sudan, Burma, Bhutan, and other countries. Their resiliency in starting a new life and learning a new language is a tribute to the human spirit.—*Sandra N. Elbaum*

Heinle would like to thank the following people for their contributions:

Elizabeth A. Adler-Coleman
Sunrise Mountain High School
Las Vegas, NV

Dorothy Avondstondt
Miami Dade College
Miami, FL

Judith A. G. Benka
Normandale Community College
Bloomington, MN

Carol Brutza
Gateway Community College
New Haven, CT

Lyn Buchheit
Community College of Philadelphia
Philadelphia, PA

Charlotte M. Calobrisi
Northern Virginia Community College
Annandale, VA

Gabriela Cambiasso
Harold Washington College
Chicago, IL

Jeanette Clement
Duquesne University
Pittsburgh, PA

Allis Cole
Shoreline Community College
Shoreline, WA

Fanshen DiGiovanni
Glendale Community College
Glendale, CA

Antoinette B. d'Oronzio
Hillsborough Community College-Dale Mabry Campus
Tampa, FL

Rhonda J. Farley
Cosumnes River College
Sacramento, CA

Jennifer Farnell
University of Connecticut American Language Program
Stamford, CT

Gail Fernandez
Bergen Community College
Paramus, NJ

Irasema Fernandez
Miami Dade College
Miami, FL

Abigail-Marie Fiattarone
Mesa Community College
Mesa, AZ

John Gamber
American River College
Sacramento, CA

Marcia Gethin-Jones
University of Connecticut American Language Program
Stamford, CT

Kimlee Buttacavoli Grant
The Leona Group, LLC
Phoenix, AZ

Shelly Hedstrom
Palm Beach Community College
Lake Worth, FL

Linda Holden
College of Lake County
Grayslake, IL

Sandra Kawamura
Sacramento City College
Sacramento, CA

Bill Keniston
Normandale Community College
Bloomington, MN

Michael Larsen
American River College
Sacramento, CA

Bea C. Lawn
Gavilan College
Gilroy, CA

Rob Lee
Pasadena City College
Pasadena, CA

Oranit Limmaneeprasert
American River College
Sacramento, CA

Linda Louie
Highline Community College
Des Moines, WA

Melanie A. Majeski
Naugatuck Valley Community College
Waterbury, CT

Maria Marin
De Anza College
Cupertino, CA

Michael I. Massey
Hillsborough Community College-Ybor City Campus
Tampa, FL

Marlo McClurg-Mackinnon
Cosumnes River College
Sacramento, CA

Michelle Naumann
Elgin Community College
Elgin, IL

Debbie Ockey
Fresno, CA

Lesa Perry
University of Nebraska at Omaha
Omaha, NE

Herbert Pierson
St. John's University
Queens, NY

Dina Poggi
De Anza College
Cupertino, CA

Steven Rashba
University of Bridgeport
Bridgeport, CT

Mark Rau
American River College
Sacramento, CA

Maria Spelleri
State College of Florida Manatee-Sarasota
Venice, FL

Eva Teagarden
Yuba College
Marysville, CA

Colin S. Ward
Lone Star College-North Harris
Houston, TX

Nico Wiersema
Texas A&M International University
Laredo, TX

Susan Wilson
San Jose City College
San Jose, CA

A word from the author

My parents immigrated to the U.S. from Poland and learned English as a second language. Born in the U.S., I often had the task as a child to explain the intricacies of the English language. It is no wonder that I became an English language teacher.

When I started teaching over forty years ago, grammar textbooks used a series of unrelated sentences with no context. I knew instinctively that there was something wrong with this technique. It ignored the fact that language is a tool for communication, and it missed an opportunity to spark the student's curiosity. As I gained teaching experience, I noticed that when I used interesting stories that illustrated the grammar, students became more motivated, understood the grammar better, and used it more effectively.

In 1986, I published the first edition of *Grammar in Context* and have continued to search for topics that teach grammar in contexts that are relevant to students' lives. The contexts I've chosen each tell a story: practical ones about technology (eBay and Freecycle), interesting people, whether well-known or not, recent events that made history (Hurricane Katrina), science (travel to Mars), and more. Whether the task is a fill-in grammar exercise, a listening activity, an editing exercise, an interactive conversation activity, or free writing, the context is reinforced throughout the lesson.

I hope you enjoy the new edition of *Grammar in Context!*

Sandra N. Elbaum

In memory of
Meyer Shisler
Teacher, Scholar, Inspiration

Welcome to *Grammar in Context,*
Fifth Edition

Grammar in Context presents grammar in interesting contexts that are relevant to students' lives and then recycles the language and context throughout every activity. Learners gain knowledge and skills in both the grammar structures and topic areas.

The new fifth edition of *Grammar in Context* engages learners with updated readings, clear and manageable grammar explanations, and a new full-color design.

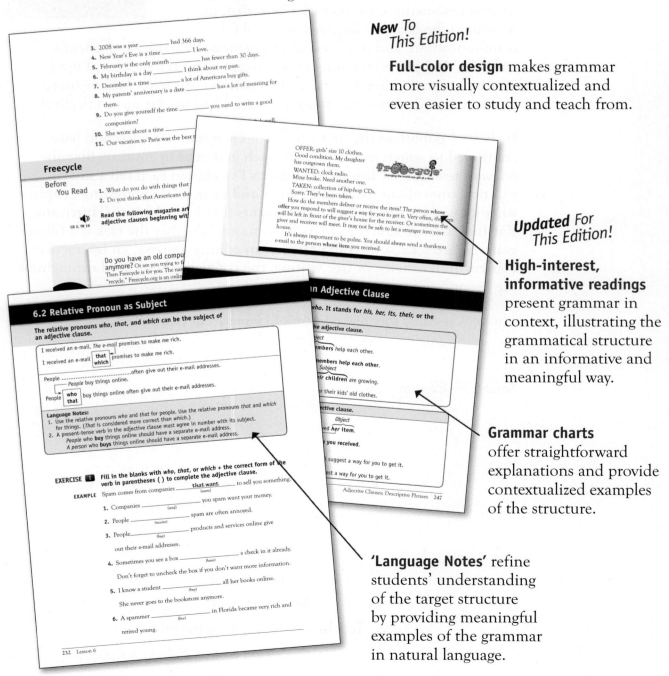

New To This Edition!

Full-color design makes grammar more visually contextualized and even easier to study and teach from.

Updated For This Edition!

High-interest, informative readings present grammar in context, illustrating the grammatical structure in an informative and meaningful way.

Grammar charts offer straightforward explanations and provide contextualized examples of the structure.

'Language Notes' refine students' understanding of the target structure by providing meaningful examples of the grammar in natural language.

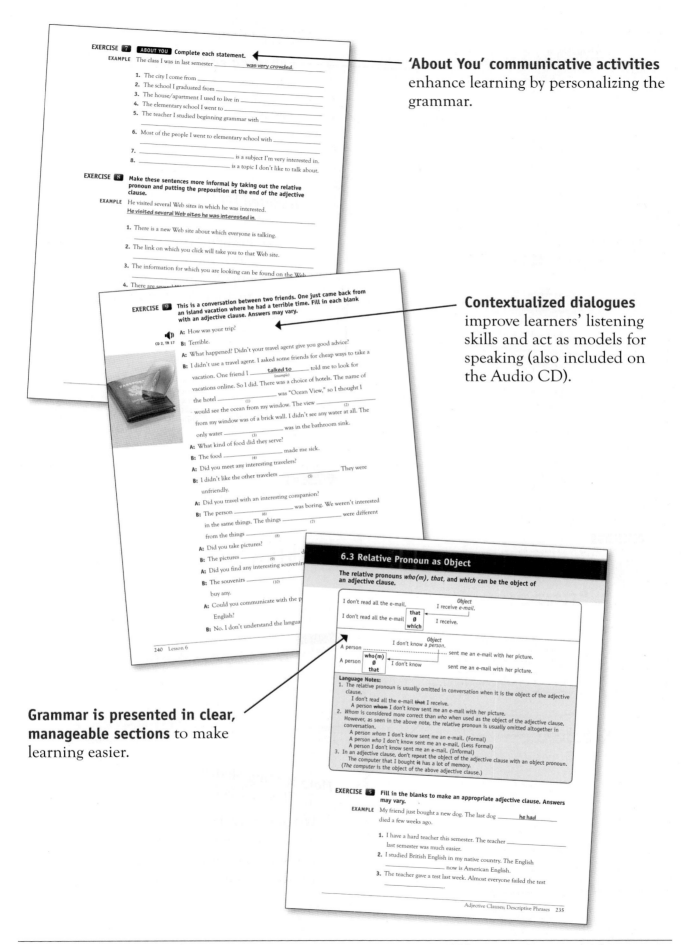

'About You' communicative activities enhance learning by personalizing the grammar.

Contextualized dialogues improve learners' listening skills and act as models for speaking (also included on the Audio CD).

Grammar is presented in clear, manageable sections to make learning easier.

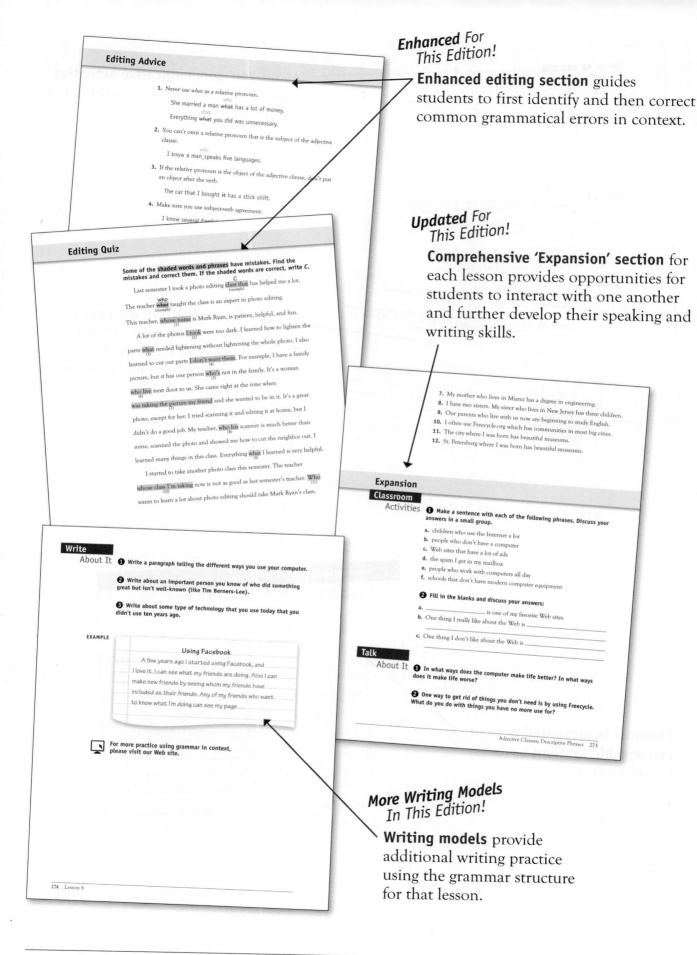

Editing Advice

1. Never use *what* as a relative pronoun.

   She married a man ~~what~~ has a lot of money.
   (who)

   Everything ~~what~~ you did was unnecessary.
   (that)

2. You can't omit a relative pronoun that is the subject of the adjective clause.

   I know a man ~~who~~ speaks five languages.

3. If the relative pronoun is the object of the adjective clause, don't put an object after the verb.

   The car that I bought ~~it~~ has a stick shift.

4. Make sure you use subject-verb agreement.

   I know several Engli...

Enhanced For This Edition!

Enhanced editing section guides students to first identify and then correct common grammatical errors in context.

Editing Quiz

Some of the shaded words and phrases have mistakes. Find the mistakes and correct them. If the shaded words are correct, write *C*.

Last semester I took a photo editing class that has helped me a lot.
(example)

The teacher what taught the class is an expert in photo editing.
(example)

This teacher, whose name is Mark Ryan, is patient, helpful, and fun.
(1)

A lot of the photos I took were too dark. I learned how to lighten the
(2)

parts what needed lightening without lightening the whole photo. I also
(3)

learned to cut out parts I don't want them. For example, I have a family
(4)

picture, but it has one person who's not in the family. It's a woman
(5)

who live next door to us. She came right at the time when
(6)

was taking the picture my friend and she wanted to be in it. It's a great
(7)

photo, except for her. I tried scanning it and editing it at home, but I

didn't do a good job. My teacher, who his scanner is much better than
(8)

mine, scanned the photo and showed me how to cut the neighbor out. I

learned many things in this class. Everything what I learned is very helpful.
(9)

I started to take another photo class this semester. The teacher

whose class I'm taking now is not as good as last semester's teacher. Who
(10) *(11)*

wants to learn a lot about photo editing should take Mark Ryan's class.

Updated For This Edition!

Comprehensive 'Expansion' section for each lesson provides opportunities for students to interact with one another and further develop their speaking and writing skills.

7. My mother who lives in Miami has a degree in engineering.
8. I have two sisters. My sister who lives in New Jersey has three children.
9. Our parents who live with us now are beginning to study English.
10. I often use Freecycle.org which has communities in most big cities.
11. The city where I was born has beautiful museums.
12. St. Petersburg where I was born has beautiful museums.

Expansion

Classroom Activities

❶ Make a sentence with each of the following phrases. Discuss your answers in a small group.

a. children who use the Internet a lot
b. people who don't have a computer
c. Web sites that have a lot of ads
d. the spam I get in my mailbox
e. people who work with computers all day
f. schools that don't have modern computer equipment

❷ Fill in the blanks and discuss your answers:

a. _____ is one of my favorite Web sites.
b. One thing I really like about the Web is _____
c. One thing I don't like about the Web is _____

Talk

About It

❶ In what ways does the computer make life better? In what ways does it make life worse?

❷ One way to get rid of things you don't need is by using Freecycle. What do you do with things you have no more use for?

Adjective Clauses; Descriptive Phrases 273

Write

About It ❶ Write a paragraph telling the different ways you use your computer.

❷ Write about an important person you know of who did something great but isn't well-known (like Tim Berners-Lee).

❸ Write about some type of technology that you use today that you didn't use ten years ago.

EXAMPLE

Using Facebook

A few years ago I started using Facebook, and I love it. I can see what my friends are doing. Also I can make new friends by seeing whom my friends have included as their friends. Any of my friends who want to know what I'm doing can see my page ...

For more practice using grammar in context, please visit our Web site.

More Writing Models In This Edition!

Writing models provide additional writing practice using the grammar structure for that lesson.

274 Lesson 6

Additional resources for each level

FOR THE STUDENT:

New To This Edition!

- **Online Workbook** features additional exercises that learners can access in the classroom, language lab, or at home.
- **Audio CD** includes dialogues and all readings from the student book.
- Student Web site features a review unit and additional practice: http://elt.heinle.com/grammarincontext.

FOR THE TEACHER:

New To This Edition!

- **Online Lesson Planner** is perfect for busy instructors, allowing them to create and customize lesson plans for their classes, then save and share them in a range of formats.

Updated For This Edition!

- **Assessment CD-ROM with Exam*View*®** lets teachers create and customize tests and quizzes easily and includes many new contextualized test items.
- **Teacher's Edition** offers comprehensive teaching notes including suggestions for more streamlined classroom options.
- Instructor Web site includes a printable Student Book answer key.

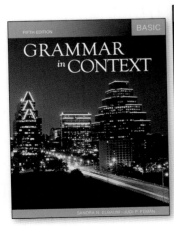
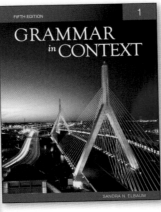

Grammar

The Present Perfect Tense

The Present Perfect Continuous Tense[1]

Context

Jobs

[1]The present perfect continuous is sometimes called the present perfect progressive.

Cover Letter and Job Résumé

Before You Read

1. Do you have a résumé?

2. Do you have a job now? What do you do?

 CD 1, TR 01

Read the following cover letter and résumé. Pay special attention to the present perfect and present perfect continuous tenses.

6965 Troy Avenue
Chicago, Illinois 60659
773-555-1946
dmendoza99@e*mail.com

Mr. Ray Johnson, General Manager
Paradise Hotel
226 West Jackson Boulevard
Chicago, Illinois 60606

Dear Mr. Johnson:

I would like to apply for the job of hotel office manager at the Paradise Hotel.

I come from Mexico City, where my family owns a hotel. I worked in the family business part-time when I was in high school. After high school, I studied hotel and restaurant management at the National University of Mexico. I came to the U.S. in 1998 because I wanted to continue my education and learn about managing larger hotels. Since I came to the U.S., I **have worked** in several American hotels. Over the years my English **has improved**, and I now consider myself bilingual. I am fluent in both Spanish and English, and this is a plus in the hotel business. I **have** also **studied** French and can speak it fairly well. I **have been** a U.S. citizen for the past five years.

I received my bachelor's degree from the University of Illinois in 2002 and my master's degree from Northwestern University in 2004. For the past few years, I **have been working** at the Town and Country Hotel. As you can see from my résumé, I **have had** a lot of experience in various aspects of the hotel business. Now that I have my degree in business administration, I am ready to assume[2] more responsibilities.

If you **have** already **filled** the manager's position, I would like you to consider me for any other position at your hotel. I **have** always **loved** the hotel business, and I know I can be an asset[3] to your hotel.

Enclosed is my résumé for your review. Thank you for considering my application. I look forward to meeting with you soon.

Sincerely,

Daniel Mendoza

Daniel Mendoza

---

[2]*Assume* means *take on* or *accept.*
[3]To be an *asset* to a company means to have a talent or ability that will help the company.

DANIEL MENDOZA

6965 Troy Avenue
Chicago, Illinois 60659
773-555-1946
dmendoza99@e*mail.com
www.mendozahotel.com

SUMMARY: Hotel professional with proven management skills and successful experience in improving operations, upgrading properties, building teams, and improving customer relations.

PROFESSIONAL EXPERIENCE

- Developed sales/marketing plans geared towards business travelers
- Handled customer relations, correspondence, and communication
- Coordinated, organized, and supervised front desk operations and food service
- Assisted guests and groups in planning tours and arranging transportation, restaurant accommodations, and reservations
- Designed and maintained hotel Web site
- Managed hotel bookkeeping

EMPLOYMENT HISTORY

2007–Present	Town and Country Hotel, Front Office Manager	Chicago, IL
2002–2007	Mid-Town Hotel, Bookkeeper (part-time)	Evanston, IL
1998–2002	Travel Time Hotel, Front Desk Clerk (part-time)	Champaign, IL
1994–1998	Hotel Mendoza, Front Desk Clerk	Mexico City, Mexico

TECHNICAL PROFICIENCIES

- Microsoft Office (Word, Excel, Access, PowerPoint); Quicken; Photoshop; Dreamweaver; Flash; Fireworks; FrontPage; HTML

EDUCATION

- Master of Science: Business Administration, Northwestern University, 2004
- Bachelor of Science: Business Administration, University of Illinois, 2002
- Degree in Hotel Management: National University of Mexico, 1998

PROFESSIONAL AFFILIATIONS

- Travel & Tourism Research Association (TTRA)
- Association of Travel Marketing Executives (ATME)
- International Association of Convention & Visitor Bureaus (IACVB)

EXERCISE **1** **True or False. Based on the cover letter and résumé, decide if the statement is true (T) or false (F).**

EXAMPLES Daniel has worked for his parents.   T

Daniel has worked in California.   F

1. Daniel has never worked in a factory.
2. Daniel has had experience with computers.
3. He has been in the U.S. for less than two years.
4. He has included information about his education.
5. He has studied a foreign language.
6. He has had experience in several hotels.
7. He has already met with Mr. Johnson.
8. He has included his age and marital status in his résumé.

1.1 The Present Perfect Tense—Forms

Affirmative

Subject	*Have*	Past Participle	Complement	Explanation
I	have	been	in the U.S. for a year.	To form the present perfect tense, use: *I, you, we, they, there,* or a plural noun + *have* + past participle.
You	have	had	a lot of experience.	
We	have	written	a job résumé.	
They	have	seen	the application.	
My parents	have	given	me encouragement.	
There	have	been	many interviews.	

Subject	*Has*	Past Participle	Complement	Explanation
My sister	has	been	a doctor for two years.	To form the present perfect tense, use: *he, she, it, there,* or a singular noun + *has* + past participle.
She	has	had	a lot of experience.	
My father	has	visited	me in the U.S.	
It	has	been	hard to find a job.	
There	has	been	a lot of unemployment.	

Negative

Subject	*Have/ Has*	*Not*	Past Participle	Complement	Explanation
He	has	not	found	a job.	To form the negative, put *not* between the auxiliary verb (*has/have*) and the past participle.
Mr. Johnson	has	not	seen	the résumé yet.	
We	have	not	had	an interview.	
I	have	not	applied	for a job.	

With an Adverb

Subject	*Have/ Has*	Adverb	Past Participle	Complement	Explanation
You	have	never	worked	in a factory.	You can put an adverb between the auxiliary verb (*have/has*) and the past participle.
We	have	always	wanted	to learn English.	
They	have	already	found	a job.	
He	has	just	had	an interview.	
The manager	has	probably	interviewed	a lot of people.	

EXERCISE 2 Read the following student composition. Underline all present perfect tense verbs.

Looking for a Job

I am looking for a job. I <u>have been</u> an electrical engineer for the past eight years. I arrived in the U.S. a few months ago, so I have not had much experience with American job interviews. I don't think my English is a problem because I have studied English since I was a child. In my country, I found a job right after I graduated from college. I stayed at the same job until I came here. The process of finding a job in the U.S. is a bit different. To learn about this process, I have used the Internet. I have also taken a course at a nearby college on how to prepare for an interview. So far, I have had three interviews, but I have not done well on them. I hope that each interview will help me do better on the next one, and soon I hope to find a good job.

1.2 The Past Participle

The past participle is the third form of the verb. We use it to form the present perfect tense.

Regular Verbs—Past and past participle are the same.

FORMS			EXPLANATION
Base Form	**Past Form**	**Past Participle**	The past participle of regular verbs ends in
work	worked	worked	-ed. The past form and the past participle
improve	improved	improved	of regular verbs are the same.

Irregular Verbs—Past and past participle are the same.

FORMS			EXPLANATION
Base Form	**Past Form**	**Past Participle**	The past participle of many irregular verbs
have	had	had	is the same as the past form.
buy	bought	bought	
leave	left	left	
make	made	made	
put	put	put	

Irregular Verbs—Past and past participle are different.[4]

BASE FORM	PAST FORM	PAST PARTICIPLE
become	became	become
come	came	come
run	ran	run
blow	blew	blown
draw	drew	drawn
fly	flew	flown
grow	grew	grown
know	knew	known
throw	threw	thrown
swear	swore	sworn
tear	tore	torn
wear	wore	worn
break	broke	broken
choose	chose	chosen
freeze	froze	frozen
speak	spoke	spoken
steal	stole	stolen
begin	began	begun
drink	drank	drunk
ring	rang	rung
sing	sang	sung
sink	sank	sunk
swim	swam	swum
bite	bit	bitten
drive	drove	driven
hide	hid	hidden
ride	rode	ridden
rise	rose	risen
write	wrote	written
be	was/were	been
do	did	done
eat	ate	eaten
fall	fell	fallen
forget	forgot	forgotten
forgive	forgave	forgiven
get	got	gotten
give	gave	given
go	went	gone
lie	lay	lain
mistake	mistook	mistaken
prove	proved	proven (or proved)
see	saw	seen
shake	shook	shaken
show	showed	shown (or showed)
take	took	taken

[4]Note: For an alphabetical list of irregular past tenses and past participles, see Appendix M.

EXERCISE 3   Fill in the blanks with the past participle of the verb shown.

EXAMPLE   shake ___shaken___

1. eat _____	**16.** write _____
2. go _____	**17.** grow _____
3. read _____	**18.** begin _____
4. drive _____	**19.** be _____
5. work _____	**20.** study _____
6. see _____	**21.** ride _____
7. believe _____	**22.** hide _____
8. swim _____	**23.** look _____
9. drink _____	**24.** leave _____
10. steal _____	**25.** fall _____
11. find _____	**26.** feel _____
12. listen _____	**27.** choose _____
13. think _____	**28.** lose _____
14. live _____	**29.** do _____
15. make _____	**30.** understand _____

EXERCISE 4   Fill in the blanks with the correct form of the verb in parentheses ( ) to form the present perfect tense.

EXAMPLE   Daniel ___has sent___ three résumés this week.
(send)

1. He _____ several interviews.
(have)

2. Mr. Johnson _____ a letter from Daniel.
(get)

3. There _____ many applicants for the job.
(be)

4. Daniel's parents _____ in the hotel business.
(always/be)

5. Daniel _____ from college.
(already/graduate)

6. I _____ Daniel's résumé.
(read)

7. Daniel _____ as a programmer.
(never/work)

8. He _____ his résumé to many companies.
(send)

9. The company _____ 20 applicants so far.
(interview)

1.3 The Present Perfect—Contractions

EXAMPLES	EXPLANATION
I've had a lot of experience. **It's** been hard to find a job. **There's** been a change in my plans.	We can make a contraction with subject pronouns and *have* or *has*. I have = I've He has = He's You have = You've She has = She's We have = We've It has = It's They have = They've There has = There's
My father**'s** taught me a lot about the hotel business. The manager**'s** had many job applications.	Most singular nouns can contract with *has*.
I **haven't** had experience in the restaurant business. Mr. Johnson **hasn't** called me.	Negative contractions: have not = haven't has not = hasn't

Language Note: The *'s* in *he's, she's, it's,* and *there's* can mean *has* or *is*. The verb form following the contraction will tell you what the contraction means.
  He**'s** working. = He **is** working.
  He**'s** worked. = He **has** worked.

EXERCISE 5 **Contract *have* or *has* with the subject for affirmative statements. Use *hasn't* or *haven't* for negative statements.**

EXAMPLE You _ve_____ already sent your application.

1. I _____ applied for many jobs.

2. We _____ seen Daniel's résumé.

3. His father _____ never come to the U.S.

4. It _____ been hard for Daniel to find a job.

5. Daniel _____ had several jobs so far.

6. Mr. Johnson (not) _____ looked at all the résumés.

7. They (not) _____ made a decision yet.

1.4 The Present Perfect—Question Formation

Compare affirmative statements and questions.

Wh- Word	Have/ Has	Subject	Have/ Has	Past Participle	Complement	Short Answer
		He	has	had	hotel experience.	
	Has	he		had	restaurant experience?	No, he hasn't.
Where	**has**	he		had	hotel experience?	In Mexico and the U.S.
		You	have	worked	in the U.S.	
	Have	you		worked	in Mexico?	Yes, I have.
How long	**have**	you		worked	in the U.S.?	For six years.
		Someone	has	read	the résumé.	
	Who		has	read	the résumé?	
		Something	has	happened.		
	What		has	happened?		

Compare negative statements and questions.

Wh- Word	Haven't/ Hasn't	Subject	Haven't/ Hasn't	Past Participle	Complement
		He	hasn't	found	a job yet.
Why	**hasn't**	he		found	a job?
		You	haven't	seen	my résumé.
Why	**haven't**	you		seen	my résumé?

EXERCISE **6** **Read the job interview with Daniel. Write the missing words in the blanks.**

CD 1, TR 02

A: I've ___looked at___ your résumé. I see you work in a hotel.
    (example)

B: Yes, I do.

A: How long _____ you _____ this job?
           (1)   *(2)*

B: I' _____ had this job for several years. But I
        (3)

_____ a lot of experience in the hotel business.
        (4)

In fact, my parents own a hotel in Mexico.

A: How long _____ your parents _____ a hotel?
                         (5)   (6)

B: Most of their lives.

A: _____ you seen your parents recently?
       (7)

B: My mother _____ _____ to the U.S. a few times to see me.
                      (8)   (9)

But my father _____ never _____ here because someone
                      (10)   (11)

has to stay at the hotel all the time. He's _____ me
                                        (12)

many times, "When you are an owner of a business, you don't have

time for vacations." But I don't want to be an owner now. I just want a

job as a manager. _____ you filled the position yet?
                         (13)

A: No, I haven't. I' _____ already _____ several
                 (14)   (15)

people and will interview a few more this week. When we make our

decision, we'll let you know.

1.5 Uses of the Present Perfect Tense—An Overview

EXAMPLES	EXPLANATION
Daniel **has been** in the U.S. since 1998. He **has had** his present job for several years. He **has** always **loved** the hotel business.	The action started in the past and **continues** to the present.
He **has sent** out 20 résumés so far. He **has had** three interviews this month.	The action **repeats** during a period of time that started in the past and continues to the present.
Mr. Johnson **has received** Daniel's letter. He **hasn't made** his decision yet. **Has** Daniel ever **worked** in a restaurant? Daniel **has studied** French, and he speaks it fairly well.	The action occurred at an **indefinite time** in the past. It still has importance to a present situation.

EXERCISE 7 Fill in the blanks with appropriate words to complete each statement. In some cases, answers may vary. (Refer to the résumé and cover letter on pages 2–3.)

EXAMPLE Daniel has included ___his phone number___ in his résumé.

1. Daniel has been _____ since 1998.

2. He has had his job at the Town and Country Hotel for _____.

3. He has studied at _____ universities.

4. He has never worked in _____.

5. He has had a lot of experience in _____.

6. In his résumé, he has not included _____.

7. So far, he has worked in _____ hotels.

8. He hasn't _____ a job yet.

9. Why _____ a job yet?

10. _____ ever organized group transportation?

11. Daniel has _____ a hotel bookkeeper.

12. _____ finished his master's degree yet?
    Yes, he _____.

13. How long _____ a member of a travel association?
    He's been a member for several years.

14. How many times _____ worked with business travelers?

15. He has lived in _____ cities in Illinois. He has never _____ in New York.

16. He has _____ French and speaks it fairly well.

1.6 The Present Perfect with Continuation from Past to Present

We use the present perfect tense to show that an action or state started in the past and continues to the present.

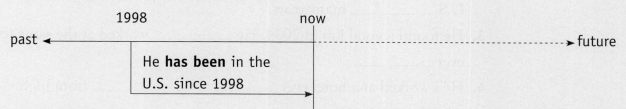

EXAMPLES	EXPLANATION
a. Daniel *has been* a U.S. citizen **for two years.** b. His parents *have been* in the hotel business **all their lives.** c. He *has had* his job **for the past few years.**	a. Use *for* + amount of time. b. Omit *for* with an expression beginning with *all*. c. You can say *for the past / last* + time period.
Daniel *has been* in the U.S. **since 1998.** I *have been* a citizen **since last March.**	Use *since* + date, month, year, etc. to show when the action began.
He *has had* a car **since he** *came* **to the U.S.** He *has wanted* to manage hotels **ever since he** *was* **a teenager.**	Use *since* or *ever since* to begin a clause that shows the start of a continuous action. The verb in the *since* clause is in the simple past tense.
Daniel went to Chicago in 2002. He *has been* there **ever since.** His father started to work in the hotel when he was twenty years old. He *has worked* there **ever since.**	You can put *ever since* at the end of the sentence. It means "from the past time mentioned to the present."
How long *have* you *been* in the U.S.? **How long** *has* your family *owned* a hotel?	Use *how long* to ask an information question about length of time.
Daniel *has* **always** *loved* the hotel business. I *have* **always** *wanted* to start my own business. I *have* **never** *worked* in a restaurant. Daniel *has* **never** *written* to Mr. Johnson **before.**	We use the present perfect with *always* and *never* to show that an action began in the past and continues to the present. We often use *before* at the end of a *never* statement.

EXERCISE 8   Fill in the blanks to complete the sentences. Not every sentence needs a word.

EXAMPLE   I'_ve___ been in the U.S. for three years.

1. Daniel has _____ in Chicago _____ 2004.

2. How _____ has he been in the U.S.? He' _____ been in the U.S. _____ many years.

3. He found a good job in 2004. He _____ worked at the same job ever _____.

4. He's worked at a hotel ever _____ he _____ from high school.

5. His parents have lived in Mexico _____ all their lives.

6. Daniel has had his apartment for the _____ ten months.

7. _____ you always worked in a hotel?

8. _____ long have you had your job?

9. Daniel _____ been in the U.S. since he _____ from college.

10. He's wanted to manage a hotel _____ since he was a child.

EXERCISE 9   **ABOUT YOU** Make statements with *always*.

EXAMPLE   Name something you've always thought about.

I've always thought about my future.

1. Name something you've always disliked.

2. Name something you've always liked.

3. Name something you've always wanted to own.

4. Name something you've always wanted to do.

5. Name something you've always believed in.

EXERCISE 10   **ABOUT YOU** Write four true sentences telling about things you've always done or ways you've always been. Share your answers with the class.

EXAMPLES   I've always worked very hard.

I've always been very thin.

1. _____

2. _____

3. _____

4. _____

EXERCISE 11 **ABOUT YOU** Make statements with *never*.

EXAMPLE   Name a machine you've never used.

I've never used a sewing machine.

1. Name a food you've never tried.
2. Name something you've never drunk.
3. Name something you've never owned.
4. Name something you've never done.
5. Name something your teacher has never done in class.
6. Name a job you've never had.

EXERCISE 12 **ABOUT YOU** Write four true sentences telling about things you've never done but would like to. Share your answers with the class.

EXAMPLES   I've never gone to Paris, but I'd like to.

I've never flown in a helicopter, but I'd like to.

1. _____
2. _____
3. _____
4. _____

1.7 Negative Statements with *Since*, *For*, and *In*

We can use *since*, *for*, and *in* with negative statements.

EXAMPLES	EXPLANATION
Daniel hasn't worked in Mexico **since** 1998.	He worked in Mexico until 1998. He stopped in 1998.
Daniel hasn't seen his parents **for** three years. OR Daniel hasn't seen his parents **in** three years.	He saw his parents three years ago. That was the last time. In negative statements, you can use either *for* or *in*.
Language Note: We often say *in ages* to mean "in a long time." Hi Daniel! I haven't seen you **in ages**!	

ABOUT YOU **Name something.**

EXAMPLES   Name something you haven't eaten in a long time.

I haven't eaten fish in a long time.

1. Name someone you haven't seen in a long time.
2. Name a place you haven't visited in a long time.
3. Name a food you haven't eaten in a long time.
4. Name a subject you haven't studied since you were a child.
5. Name a game you haven't played since you were a child.
6. Name something you haven't had time to do since you started to study English.

1.8 The Present Perfect vs. the Simple Present

EXAMPLES	EXPLANATION
I **am** in the U.S. now. I **have been** in the U.S. *for* two years.	The simple present refers only to the present time. The present perfect with *for*, *since*, *always*, or *never* connects the past to the present.
He **has** a car. He **has had** his car *since* March.	
I love my job. I **have** *always* **loved** my job.	
I **don't like** to wake up early. I **have** *never* **liked** to wake up early.	

EXERCISE 14   **Fill in the blanks to complete the following conversations. Some answers may vary.**

EXAMPLES   **A:** Do you have a computer?

B: Yes, I do.

A: How long _____have you_____ had your computer?

B: I _____'ve had_____ my computer for three years.

1. **A:** Do you have a car?

   B: Yes, I do.

   A: How long _____ your car?

   B: I _____ my car for six months.

2. **A:** Is your sister married?

   B: Yes, she is.

   A: How long _____ married?

   B: She _____ since 2005.

3. **A:** Do you have a bike?

   B: Yes, I _____.

   A: How long _____ your bike?

   B: I _____ my bike _____ the past

   _____.

4. **A:** Do you want to learn English?

   B: Of course I do.

   A: _____ long _____ to learn

   English?

   B: I _____ to learn English ever since I

   _____ a child.

5. **A:** Does your mother have a driver's license?

   B: Yes, she _____.

   A: How _____ her driver's license?

   B: She _____ her driver's license since

   _____.

6. **A:** _____ Ms. Foster your teacher?

   B: Yes, she is.

   A: How long _____ your teacher?

   B: For _____.

7. **A:** Does your school have a computer lab?

   B: Yes, it _____.

   A: _____ long _____ a

   computer lab?

   B: It _____ a computer lab since

   _____.

8. **A:** Do you know your friend Mark very well?

   B: Yes, I _____.

   A: How long _____ each other?

   B: We _____ each other ever _____

   we _____ in elementary school.

   (continued)

9. A: _____ your son _____ a laptop?

B: Yes, he _____.

A: How long _____?

B: He bought one when he started going to college and he

_____ it ever _____.

10. A: Does your mother like to dance?

B: Yes, she _____.

A: _____ she always _____ to dance?

B: Yes. She's always liked to dance. But my father

_____ never _____ to dance.

EXERCISE 15 **Read each statement about your teacher. Then ask your teacher a question beginning with the words given. Include *always* in your question. Your teacher will answer.**

EXAMPLE You're a teacher. Have you ___*always been a teacher?*___

No. I was a nurse before I became a teacher. I've only been a teacher for five years.

1. You teach grammar. Have you _____

2. You work with ESL students. Have you _____

3. You're a teacher at this school. Have you _____

4. You think about grammar. Have you _____

5. English is easy for you. Has English _____

6. Your last name is _____. Has your last name ____
_____

7. You live in this city. Have you _____

8. You like teaching. Have you _____

EXERCISE 16 **ABOUT YOU** **Ask a present tense question. Another student will answer. If the answer is *yes*, ask *Have you always . . .?***

EXAMPLE **A:** Are you interested in learning English?
B: Yes, I am.
A: Have you always been interested in learning English?
B: Yes. I've been interested in learning English since I was a small child.

1. Are you a good student?

2. Do you wear glasses?

3. Do you like to travel?

4. Are you interested in politics?

5. Do you like American movies?

6. Are you an optimist?

7. Do you think about your future?

8. Do you live in an apartment?

9. Are you a friendly person?

10. Do you use credit cards?

11. Do you work hard?

12. Do you want a college degree?

Where Have All the Jobs Gone?

Before
You Read

1. Do you know anyone who has lost a job?

2. Do you think some jobs are more secure than others? Which ones?

CD 1, TR 03

Read the following magazine article. Pay special attention to the present perfect and present perfect continuous tenses.

Have you ever **called** an American company for service and **gotten** an answer from someone in another country? Many American companies **have been moving** customer service and technology jobs overseas. Using workers in other countries is called "outsourcing." India, the Philippines, and China are the leading countries used in outsourcing. Why these countries? Because they have a high level of information technology (IT) workers who are fluent in English.

Why **has** this shift[5] **occurred**? By using lower wages[6] overseas, U.S. companies can cut labor costs. In addition, service is available to customers 24 hours a day by phone or online.

[5]A *shift* is a change.
[6]*Wages* means pay for doing a job.

(continued)

The Present Perfect Tense; The Present Perfect Continuous Tense   **19**

Years ago, American companies started using foreign labor for manufacturing jobs. But college-educated workers thought they had nothing to worry about. Then companies started to move call centers abroad[7] to cut costs. But more and more of the jobs going abroad today go to highly skilled, educated people.

Many American workers who **have been working** at the same company for years are losing their jobs. Many educated workers **have had** to take jobs for lower pay or get more training or education. While U.S. companies **have been benefiting** from outsourcing, American workers **have been losing**. While some American workers in some fields **have become** more insecure about their jobs, educated, skilled workers abroad **have become** more confident.

The U.S. government **has been studying** the impact of outsourcing on the American economy.

1.9 The Present Perfect Continuous

Forms

Subject	Have/ Has	Been	Present Participle	Complement
I	have	been	working	in a call center.
Workers	have	been	losing	their jobs.
You	have	been	getting	more job experience.
Companies	have	been	moving	jobs overseas.
The U.S.	has	been	studying	the effects of outsourcing.
Daniel	has	been	working	at a hotel.
He	has	been	living	in the U.S.

Language Notes:
1. To form the negative, put *not* between *have* or *has* and *been*.
    You **have *not* been** studying.   She **has *not* been** working hard.
2. We can make contractions for negative forms.
    have not = haven't   has not = hasn't

[7]*Abroad* means beyond the boundaries of one's country.

Uses

EXAMPLES	EXPLANATION
I **have been working** at the same job *since* 2007. American companies **have been using** workers in foreign countries *for* many years.	We use the present perfect continuous to talk about an action that started in the past and continues to the present. We use *for* and *since* to show the time spent at an activity.
He **has been working** as a programmer for the past few years. <div align="center">OR</div>He **has worked** as a programmer for the past few years.	With some verbs, we can use either the present perfect or the present perfect continuous with actions that began in the past and continue to the present. There is very little difference in meaning.
He's working now. → He **has been working** for the past eight hours.	If the action is still happening, use the present perfect continuous, not the present perfect.
I **have** *always* **worked** as a programmer. I **have** *never* **had** another career.	Do not use the continuous form with *always* and *never*.
Americans **have become** insecure about their jobs. I **have had** my job for ten years.	We do not use a continuous tense with nonaction verbs. *Wrong:* Americans *have been becoming* insecure. *Wrong:* I *have been having* my job for ten years. (See Language Notes below for a list of nonaction verbs.)
Action: I **have been thinking** *about* starting a new career. Nonaction: I **have** always **thought** *that* an educated person can find a good job.	*Think* can be an action or nonaction verb, depending on its meaning. *Think about* = action verb *Think that* = nonaction verb
Nonaction: Daniel **has had** a lot of experience in hotels. Action: Daniel **has been having** problems finding a job.	*Have* is usually a nonaction verb. However, *have* is an action verb in these expressions: *have a problem, have a hard time, have a good time, have difficulty, have trouble.*

Language Notes:
1. The following are usually nonaction verbs.

like	want	know	own	see	think (that)
love	need	believe	understand	hear	care (about)
hate	prefer	cost	remember	seem	have (for possession)

2. When used as sense-perception verbs, the following are nonaction verbs.

smell	taste	feel	look	sound

EXERCISE 17 **Fill in the blanks with the present perfect continuous form of the verb in parentheses ( ).**

EXAMPLE   Bob __has been working__ as a programmer for the past ten years.
            (work)

1. His company _____ jobs to India since 2005.
                       (send)

2. He and his coworkers _____ about losing their jobs.
                              (worry)

3. Bob _____ classes for the past two years to get retrained.
          (take)

4. He _____ a lot of articles about outsourcing.
         (read)

5. He _____ on his résumé for the past two days.
         (work)

6. His friends _____ him to see a job counselor.
                   (advise)

EXERCISE 18 **Fill in the blanks in the following conversations. Some answers may vary.**

EXAMPLE   A: Do you _____play_____ a musical instrument?

B: Yes. I play the guitar.

A: How long _____have_____ you _____been playing_____ the guitar?

B: I _'ve been playing_ the guitar since I _____was_____ 10 years old.

1. A: Do you work with computers?

   B: Yes, I do.

   A: How long _____ you _____ with computers?

   B: I _____ with computers since 2004.

2. A: _____ your father study English?

   B: Yes, he does.

   A: How long _____ he been _____ English?

   B: He _____ since he _____ to the U.S.

3. A: Does your teacher have a lot of experience?

   B: Yes, she _____.

   A: How long _____ teaching English?

   B: She _____ English for 20 years.

4. A: Do you wear glasses?

   B: Yes, I _____.

   A: How long _____ glasses?

   B: I _____ glasses since I _____ in high school.

5. A: _____ your parents live in this city?

   B: Yes, they _____.

   A: How long _____ in this city?

   B: For _____.

6. A: Is your roommate preparing to take the TOEFL[8] test?

   B: Yes, he _____.

   A: How long _____ to take this test?

   B: Since _____.

7. A: _____ you studying for your chemistry test?

   B: Yes, I _____.

   A: How long _____ for your chemistry test?

   B: I _____ all week.

8. A: _____ your roommate using the computer now?

   B: Yes, he _____.

   A: How long _____ it?

   B: He started to use it when he woke up and _____ it ever _____.

9. A: _____ it raining now?

   B: Yes, it _____.

   A: How long _____?

   B: It _____ since _____.

10. A: _____ she talking about her children again?

   B: Yes, she _____.

   A: How long _____ about them?

   B: For the past _____.

---

[8]The *TOEFL*™ is the Test of English as a Foreign Language. Many U.S. colleges and universities require foreign students to take this test.

EXERCISE 19   **ABOUT YOU**   Fill in the blanks to make a true statement about the present. Then make a statement that includes the past by changing to the present perfect continuous form with *for* or *since*.

EXAMPLE   I'm studying ___French.___

I've been studying French for two semesters.

1. I work in / as _____

_____

2. I live _____

_____

3. I attend _____

_____

4. I'm trying to _____

_____

5. I'm wearing _____

_____

6. The teacher is explaining _____

_____

7. I'm thinking about _____

_____

8. I'm using _____

_____

9. I'm studying _____

_____

10. We're using _____

_____

1.10 The Present Perfect Tense vs. the Simple Past Tense

EXAMPLES	EXPLANATION
How long **have** you **had** your current car? I've **had** my current car *for* three months. *How long* **have** you **been working** at your current job? I've **been working** at my current job *for* two years.	Use *how long* and *for* with the present perfect tense or present perfect continuous tense to include the present.
How long **did** you **have** your last car? I **had** my last car *for* six years. *How long* **did** you **work** at your last job? I **worked** at my last job *for* five years.	Use *how long* and *for* with the simple past tense when you are not including the present.
When **did** you **come** to the U.S.? I **came** to the U.S. a few years *ago*.	A question that asks *when* usually uses the simple past tense. A sentence that uses *ago* uses the simple past tense.
I **came** to this city on January 15. I **have been** in this city since January 15. I **have been living** in this city since January 15.	Use the simple past tense to refer to a past action that does not continue. Use the present perfect (continuous) tense to show the continuation of an action from past to present.

EXERCISE 20 **ABOUT YOU** Fill in the blanks with the simple past, the present perfect, or the present perfect continuous, using the words in parentheses ( ). Another student will answer the question.

EXAMPLES How long ___have you had___ your present computer?
                   (you/have)

When ___did you buy___ your computer?
        (you/buy)

1. How long _____ your last computer?
            (you/own)

2. How long _____ at this school?
            (you/study)

3. How long _____ at your last school?
            (you/study)

4. How long _____ in this city?
            (you/be)

5. How long _____ at your last address?
            (you/live)

6. How long _____ your dictionary?
            (you/have)

7. When _____ your dictionary?
        (you/buy)

8. When _____ for this class?
        (you/register)

(continued)

9. When _____?

(the semester/begin)

10. When _____ today?

(the teacher/arrive)

EXERCISE 21 Two friends meet on the street. Fill in the blanks in their conversation below. Use the present perfect, the present perfect continuous, or the simple past. Fill in any other necessary words.

CD 1, TR 04

A: Hi, Ivan. I ___**haven't seen**___ you _____ ages.

(example: not/see)   (1)

Where _____?

(2 you/be)

B: I _____ for a job for the last few weeks.

(3 look)

A: What _____ to your old job?

(4 happen)

B: My company is outsourcing, and I _____ laid off last

(5 get)

month. I'm getting depressed. I _____ a paycheck

(6 not/have)

_____ four weeks.

(7)

A: Don't lose hope. You're young and educated and healthy.

B: I know. But jobs here are disappearing, even for educated people.

A: That's true. Look at me. I _____ to be an actor, but

(8 always/want)

I _____ tables in a restaurant for the last three

(9 wait)

years. My friend, Ron, has a degree in accounting, and he

_____ a taxi for the _____ two years.

(10 drive)   (11)

B: At least you're earning some money now. For the last month, I

_____ money but I _____ any.

(12 spend)   (13 not/earn)

A: If you want, I can ask my boss if there are any openings for a

waitperson in the restaurant.

B: I _____ in a restaurant, and I don't really want to.

(14 never/work)

A: It would just be temporary, until you can find a computer job.

B: Temporary? Like your job? You _____ from

(15 graduate)

college three years ago, and you _____ tables

(16 wait)

ever _____.

(17)

A: But I _____ up hope of being a famous actor.

(18 never/give)

1.11 The Present Perfect with Repetition from Past to Present

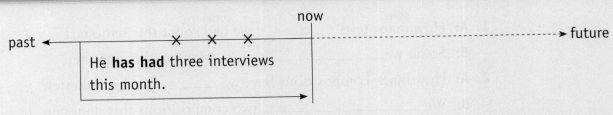

past ← — He **has had** three interviews this month. — now — — — → future

EXAMPLES	EXPLANATION
Daniel is looking for a job. He **has had** three interviews *this month*. Mr. Johnson **has interviewed** two people *today*.	We use the present perfect tense to talk about the repetition of an action in a time period that includes the present. The time period is open, and there is a possibility for more repetition to occur. Open time periods include: *today, this week, this month, this year, this semester*.
My company is sending some jobs to India. It **has sent** 50 jobs to India *so far*. *Up to now* 50 workers in my company **have lost** their jobs.	*So far* and *up to now* mean "including this moment." We use these expressions with the present perfect to show that another repetition may occur. These expressions can come at the beginning or the end of the sentence.
Daniel **has worked** at *several* hotels. You **have had** *a lot of* experience with computers. I **have learned** *many* new skills at my job. Daniel **has had** *four* jobs so far.	We can use *several, many, a lot of,* or a number to show repetition from past to present.
How many interviews **have** you **had** this year? *How much* money **have** you **spent** on career counseling so far? I **haven't spent** *any* money *at all* on career counseling.	We can ask a question about repetition with *how many* and *how much*. A negative statement with *"any . . . at all"* means the number is zero.
We**'ve studied** two lessons so far.	Do not use the continuous form for repetition. *Not: We've been studying* two lessons so far.

EXERCISE 22 **Fill in the blanks in the following conversations.**

EXAMPLE A: How many pages have we ___done___ in this book so far?

B: We __'ve__ done 27 pages so far.

1. A: How many tests _____ we had so far this semester?

   B: So far we _____ two tests this semester.

2. A: How many compositions have we _____ this semester?

   B: We _____ two compositions this semester.

3. A: How many times have you _____ absent this semester?

   B: I _____ absent one time this semester.

4. A: How many times _____ the teacher been absent this semester?

   B: The teacher _____ absent at all this semester.

5. A: How _____ lessons _____ the teacher _____ so far?

   B: She _____ only one lesson so far.

6. A: How _____ time has the teacher _____ on the present perfect?

   B: He _____ about three hours on the present perfect.

7. A: How _____ students _____ the computer lab today?

   B: More than 100 students _____ the computer lab so far today.

8. A: How _____ exercises _____ so far?

   B: We _____ done about 22 exercises so far.

EXERCISE 23 **ABOUT YOU** **Write a statement to tell how many times you have done something in this city. (If you don't know the exact number, you may use *a few*, *several*, or *many*.)**

EXAMPLES live in / apartment(s)

I've lived in one apartment in this city.

get lost / time(s)

I've gotten lost a few times in this city.

1. have / job(s)

   _____

2. have / job interview(s)

   _____

3. have / out-of-town visitor(s)

_____

4. buy / car(s)

_____

5. attend / school(s)

_____

6. live in / apartment(s)

_____

7. go downtown / time(s)

_____

EXERCISE 24 **ABOUT YOU** Ask a question with _How much . . . ?_ or _How many . . . ?_ and the words given. Talk about today. Another student will answer.

EXAMPLES   coffee / have

A: How much coffee have you had today?
B: I've had three cups of coffee today.

glasses of water / drink

A: How many glasses of water have you drunk today?
B: I haven't drunk any water at all today.

1. tea / have
2. juice / drink
3. cookies / eat
4. glasses of water / have
5. times / check your e-mail
6. miles / walk or drive
7. money / spend
8. text messages / receive
9. text messages / send
10. photos / take
11. times / use your dictionary

1.12 The Present Perfect Tense vs. the Simple Past Tense with Repetition

EXAMPLES	EXPLANATION
How many interviews **have** you **had** *this month*? I **have had** two interviews *so far this month*. How many times **have** you **been** absent *this semester*? I **have been** absent twice *so far*.	To show that there is possibility for more repetition, use the present perfect. *This month* and *this semester* are not finished. *So far* indicates that the number given may not be final.
How many interviews **did** you **have** *last month*? I **had** four interviews *last month*. How many times **were** you absent *last semester*? I **was** absent four times *last semester*.	To show that the number is final, use the simple past tense with a past time expression (*yesterday, last week, last year, last semester,* etc.).
Compare: a. I **have seen** my counselor twice *this week*. b. I **saw** my counselor twice *this week*. a. I **have made** five phone calls *today*. b. I **made** five phone calls *today*.	With a present time expression (such as *today, this week,* etc.), you may use either the present perfect or the simple past tense. a. The number may not be final. b. The number seems final.
Compare: a. My grandfather died in 1998. He **had** several jobs in his lifetime. b. My father is a programmer. He **has had** five jobs so far.	a. If you refer to the experiences of a deceased person, you must use the simple past tense because nothing more can be added to that person's experience. b. A living person can have more of the same experience.
Compare: a. In my country, I **had** five jobs. b. In the U.S., I **have had** two jobs.	a. To talk about a closed phase of your life, use the simple past tense. For example, if you do not plan to live in your native country again, use the simple past tense to talk about your experiences there. b. To talk about your experiences in this phase of your life, you can use the present perfect tense.

EXERCISE 25 CD 1, TR 05 In the conversation below, fill in the blanks with the correct form of the verb in parentheses ( ).

A: I'm very frustrated about finding a job. I _____ **have sent** _____ out
(*example: send*)

100 résumés so far. And I _____ dozens of phone calls
(*1 make*)

to companies.

B: Have you _____ (2 have) any answers to your letters and calls?

A: Yes. Last week I _____ (3 have) six interviews. But so far, nobody

_____ (4 offer) me a job.

B: You should call those companies.

A: I know I should. But this week, I _____ (5 be) very busy

getting career counseling. I _____ (6 see) my counselor

several times in the past few weeks.

B: Has your counselor _____ (7 give) you any advice about looking

for a job?

A: Yes. Last week she _____ (8 give) me a lot of advice. But looking

for a job is so strange in the U.S. I feel like I have to sell myself.

B: Don't worry. You _____ (9 not/have) much work experience in

the U.S. so far. I'm sure you'll get used to the process of finding a job.

A: I don't know. I _____ (10 talk) to a lot of other people

looking for work. Even though English is their native language, they

_____ (11 not/have) much luck either.

B: _____ (12 it/be) easy for you to find a job when you lived

in your native country?

A: In my native country, I _____ (13 never/have) this problem. After I

_____ (14 graduate) from college, I _____ (15 find) a job

immediately and _____ (16 work) in the same place for many years.

B: In the U.S., people change jobs often. Take me, for example.

I _____ (17 have) six jobs, and I'm only 28 years old.

A: I'm 40 years old. But when I lived in my native country,

I _____ (18 have) the same job for ten years. And

I _____ (19 live) in the same apartment for many years until I

came to the U.S. My parents _____ (20 live) in the same

apartment from the time they got married until the time they died.

B: Get used to it! Life today is about constant change.

The *Occupational Outlook Handbook*

1. Have you ever seen a counselor about finding a job?

2. What careers interest you? What are some jobs you wouldn't want to have?

CD 1, TR 06

Read the following conversation between a college student (S) and her counselor (C). Pay special attention to the present perfect tense and the present perfect continuous tense.

C: I see you're majoring in art. **Have** you **thought** about a career yet for your future?

S: I've **thought** about it, but I'm still not sure what I'm going to do when I graduate. I've always **loved** art, but my parents are worried that I won't be able to make a living as an artist. Lately **I've been thinking** about changing majors.

C: What major **have** you **been considering**?

S: Graphic design or commercial art.

C: **Have** you **taken** any courses in these fields?

S: I've already **taken** a course in graphic design. But I don't know much about the future of this career. Are there a lot of jobs for graphic artists?

C: **Have** you ever **used** the *Occupational Outlook Handbook*?

S: No, I **haven't.** I've never even **heard** of it. What is it?

C: It's a government publication that gives you a lot of information about jobs in the U.S. You can find it in the library or on the Internet. If you look up "graphic designer" in this publication, it will tell you the nature of the work, where the jobs are, what salary you can expect, what kind of training you need, what the future will be for graphic designers, and much more.

S: Thanks for the information. Can I come back and see you in a few weeks after I have a chance to check out the *Occupational Outlook Handbook*?

C: Yes, please come back.

(A few weeks later)

C: Hi. **Have** you **looked** at the *Occupational Outlook Handbook* yet?

S: Yes. Thanks for telling me about it. **I've looked** at many jobs in the art field, but so far I **haven't decided** on anything yet. But I have some ideas.

C: **Have** you **talked** to your parents lately? **Have** you **told** them that you're planning on changing majors?

S: Oh, yes. They're very happy about it. They don't want me to be a starving artist.[9]

1.13 The Present Perfect Tense with Indefinite Past Time—An Overview

We use the present perfect tense to refer to an action that occurred at an indefinite time in the past and that still has importance to a present situation.

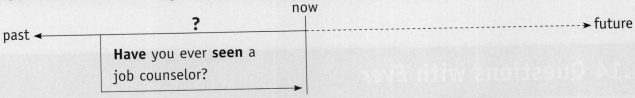

QUESTIONS	SHORT ANSWERS	EXPLANATION
Has she *ever* **visited** a counselor? **Have** you *ever* **used** the *Occupational Outlook Handbook*? **Have** you *ever* **taken** an art history course?	Yes, she **has.** No, I never **have.** No, I **haven't.**	A question with *ever* asks about any time between the past and the present. Put *ever* between the subject and the main verb in a question.
Have you **decided** on a major *yet*? **Has** she **told** her parents about her decision *yet*?	No, not *yet.* Yes, she *already* has.	*Yet* and *already* refer to an indefinite time in the near past. There is an expectation that an activity took place a short time ago.
Have you **talked** to your parents *lately*? **Have** you **seen** your counselor *recently*?	No, I **haven't.** Yes, I **have.**	Questions with *lately* and *recently* refer to an indefinite time in the near past.

[9]A *starving artist* is an artist who does not make enough money to support him or herself.

EXERCISE **26** **Read the following conversation. Underline the present perfect tense and circle the present perfect continuous tense.**

EXAMPLE **A:** There's going to be a job fair at the college next week. <u>Have</u> you ever <u>gone</u> to one?

B: What's a job fair?

A: Representatives from different companies come to one place. You can meet these people, find out about their companies, and give them your résumé. Lately I've been going to a lot of job fairs. And I've been looking for jobs online. I've just rewritten my résumé too. I haven't found a job yet, but I'm hopeful.

B: But you have a good job as an office manager.

A: I'm going to quit in two weeks. I've already given my employer notice. I've worked there for two years, and I haven't had a raise yet. I've realized that I can make more money doing something else. I've talked to a career counselor and I've taken a test to see what I'm good at. I've also taken more courses to upgrade my skills.

B: Have you decided what you want to do?

A: Yes. I've decided to be a legal assistant.

1.14 Questions with *Ever*

EXAMPLES	EXPLANATION

Have you *ever* **seen** a job counselor?
  Yes, I **have**. I**'ve seen** a job counselor a few times.
Have you *ever* **used** the Internet to find a job?
  Yes, I**'ve used** the Internet many times.
Have you *ever* **worked** in a restaurant?
  No, I never **have**.
	We use *ever* to ask a question about any time in the past.

Have you *ever* **written** a résumé?
  a. Yes, I **have**.
    OR
  b. Yes. I **wrote** my résumé two weeks ago.
Has he *ever* **taken** a design course?
  a. Yes. He **has taken** several design courses.
    OR
  b. Yes. He **took** one last semester.
	You can answer an *ever* question with the present perfect or the simple past.
	a. Use the **present perfect** to answer with no reference to time.
	b. Use the **simple past** to answer with a definite time (*last week, last semester, last Friday, two weeks ago*, etc.).

EXERCISE 27 **ABOUT YOU** Ask a question with *Have you ever . . . ?* and the words given. Use the past participle of the verb. Another student will answer. If the answer is *yes*, ask for more specific information. To answer with a specific time, use the simple past tense. To answer with a frequency response, use the present perfect tense.

EXAMPLE   eat a hot dog

A: Have you ever eaten a hot dog?
B: Yes, I have.
A: When did you eat a hot dog?
B: I ate one at a picnic last summer.

1. find money on the street
2. go to a garage sale
3. meet a famous person
4. study art history
5. bake bread
6. be on television
7. win a contest or a prize
8. lend money to a friend
9. lose your keys
10. break an arm or a leg
11. go to a football game
12. go to court
13. hear of[10] Martin Luther King Jr.
14. eat in a Vietnamese restaurant
15. order products over the Internet
16. get lost in this city
17. tell a lie
18. go to Canada
19. travel by train
20. eat pizza
21. act in a play
22. see a play in this city
23. eat Chinese food
24. see a job counselor
25. go camping
26. use a scanner

EXERCISE 28   Work with a partner. Use *ever* to write four questions to ask your teacher. Your teacher will answer.

EXAMPLES   Have you ever eaten raw fish?

Have you ever written a poem?

1. _____

2. _____

3 _____

4. _____

[10]*Hear of* means to recognize a name.

EXERCISE **29**   **Fill in the blanks with the present perfect tense or the simple past tense to complete each conversation. Sometimes part of the verb (phrase) has already been supplied.**

1. **A:** Have you ever ___studied___ algebra?
   (example)

   B: Yes. I studied it in high school.

   A: I like math a lot. Do you?

   B: No, I _____ never_____ math.

2. **A:** Have you ever _____ to Canada?

   B: No, I never have. But I would like to go there some day.

   A: _____ you ever gone to Mexico?

   B: Yes. I _____ there two years ago.

3. **A:** Have you ever broken your arm or leg?

   B: Yes. I _____ my leg when I was ten years old. I was climbing a tree.

   A: Which leg _____ you _____?

   B: I broke my left leg.

4. **A:** _____ your parents ever come here to visit you?

   B: No, they never _____. But last year my brother _____ to visit me for three weeks.

5. **A:** _____ you ever _____ an Italian movie?

   B: No, I haven't. But I _____ seen many French movies.

   A: I _____ never _____ a French movie.

6. **A:** _____ you ever _____ to the public library in this city?

   B: Yes. I _____ gone there many times. Last Monday I _____ there and checked out a novel by Mark Twain. I've never _____ Mark Twain's books in English.

   A: _____ you ever _____ his books in translation?

   B: Oh, yes. In high school, I _____ two of his novels in Spanish.

EXERCISE 30 **ABOUT YOU** Interview a student who has a job. Ask a question with *Have you ever . . . ?* and the words given.

EXAMPLE ask your boss for a raise

A: Have you ever asked your boss for a raise?
B: No, I never have.

1. get job counseling at this school
2. use the Internet to find a job
3. fill out a job application online
4. use the *Occupational Outlook Handbook*
5. go to a state employment office
6. use a résumé writing service
7. take courses to train for a job
8. read a book about finding a job
9. attend a job fair
10. use a computer on a job
11. work in a restaurant
12. have a problem with a coworker
13. work for a family member
14. work in a hotel
15. think about owning your own business
16. be unemployed
17. quit a job

1.15 Yet, Already

Use *yet* with the present perfect tense with an expected action. Use *already* for a recent action at an indefinite time.

EXAMPLES	EXPLANATION
I **have talked** to my job counselor *already*. I **have** *already* **talked** to my job counselor.	For an affirmative statement, use *already*. You can put *already* at the end of the verb phrase or between the auxiliary verb and the main verb.
I **haven't written** my résumé *yet*. The counselor **hasn't answered** my e-mail *yet*.	For a negative statement, use *yet*. Put *yet* at the end of the verb phrase.

Have you **talked** with your counselor *yet*?
    No, I **haven't**.
Have you **written** your résumé *yet*?
    No, **not** *yet*.
Have you **filled** out the application *yet*?
    Yes, I *already* **have**.
	For questions, use *yet*. You can use *yet* in a negative answer. You can use *already* in an affirmative answer.

Has he **found** a job *yet*?
    Yes, he **found** a job *two weeks ago*.
Have you **gotten** a raise *yet*?
    Yes, I **got** a raise *last month*.
	You can answer a *yet* question with a specific time. If you do so, you must use the simple past tense.

Language Note: You often hear the simple past tense in questions and negatives with *yet* and statements with *already*. There is no difference in meaning between the present perfect and the simple past tense.

>   **Have** you **eaten** dinner *yet?* = **Did** you **eat** dinner *yet?*
>   No, I **haven't eaten** dinner yet. = No, I **didn't eat** dinner yet.
>   I **have eaten** dinner *already*. = I **ate** dinner *already*.

EXERCISE **31** **Ask a student who has recently moved here questions with the words given and *yet*. The student who answers should use the simple past tense if the answer has a specific time.**

EXAMPLE go downtown

A: Have you gone downtown yet?
B: Yes. I went downtown three weeks ago.

1. buy a map of this city

2. find an apartment

3. get a library card

4. use public transportation

5. visit any museums

6. meet any of your neighbors

EXERCISE 32 Ask a question with the words given and *yet*. The student who answers should use the simple past tense if the answer has a specific time.

EXAMPLES the teacher / take attendance

A: Has the teacher taken attendance yet?
B: Yes, he has. He took attendance at the beginning of the class.

the teacher / return the homework

A: Has the teacher returned the homework yet?
B: No, he hasn't. OR No, not yet.

1. we / have an exam
2. we / study modals
3. you / learn the irregular past tense forms
4. the teacher / learn the students' names
5. you / learn the other students' names
6. the teacher / teach the past perfect tense

EXERCISE 33 Daniel is preparing for his job interview. He has made a list of things to do. He has checked those things he has already done. Make sentences about Daniel's list using the present perfect tense with *yet* or *already*.

EXAMPLES ___✓___ prepare his résumé
He has already prepared his résumé.

_____ send his suit to the cleaner's
He hasn't sent his suit to the cleaner's yet.

1. __✓__ buy a new tie
2. __✓__ wash his white shirt
3. _____ iron his white shirt
4. __✓__ get a haircut
5. __✓__ rewrite his résumé
6. _____ take his résumé to a copy center
7. __✓__ see a job counselor
8. _____ put his papers in his briefcase
9. __✓__ send for his transcripts
10. __✓__ get letters of recommendation

EXERCISE **34** **Fill in the blanks to complete each conversation.**

EXAMPLE   A: Have you bought your textbook yet?

B: No. I ___haven't___ bought it yet.

1. A: Have you _____ dinner yet?

   B: No, I haven't. I _____ lunch at 2:30, so I'm not hungry now.

2. A: _____ your sister gotten married yet?

   B: Yes. She _____ married two weeks ago. She _____ a beautiful wedding.

   A: Has she _____ back from her honeymoon yet?

   B: Yes. She _____ back last Thursday.

3. A: Have your parents _____ an apartment yet?

   B: No. They _____ found one yet. They're still looking.

4. A: I'm going to rent the movie *Spider-Man*. Have you _____ it yet?

   B: Yes, I _____ it a couple of years ago, but I'd like to see it again.

5. A: What are you going to do during summer vacation?

   B: I haven't _____ about it yet. It's only April.

   A: I've already _____ plans. I'm going to Mexico. I _____ my ticket last week.

6. A: Has the movie _____ yet? I want to buy some popcorn before it begins.

   B: Shhh! It _____ ten minutes ago.

7. A: Do you want to go to the museum with me on Saturday?

   B: Sorry. I _____ already _____ other plans for Saturday.

8. A: _____ your brother _____ back from Mexico yet?

   B: No, he hasn't. We're expecting him to arrive on Tuesday.

9. A: I'd like to talk to the teacher, please.

   B: I'm sorry. She's already _____ for the day.

   A: But she told me to call her before four o'clock and it's only 3:30.

   B: She _____ at two o'clock because her son was sick.

10. A: Is that a good book?

    B: Yes, it is. I haven't _____ it yet, but when I finish it, you can have it.

1.16 Questions with *Lately* and *Recently*

Questions with *lately* and *recently* ask about an indefinite time in the near past. We can answer a *lately* or *recently* question with the present perfect tense or the simple past tense.

EXAMPLES	EXPLANATION

Have you **seen** your parents *lately*?
    No, I **haven't**.
Have you **gotten** a raise *recently*?
    No. I **haven't gotten** a raise *recently*.
	When the answer is *no*, we usually use the present perfect tense.

Have you **had** any interviews *lately*?
    Yes. I **had** an interview *last week*.
Have you **seen** a job counselor *recently*?
    Yes. I **saw** one *two days ago*.
	When the answer is *yes*, we usually give a specific time and use the simple past tense.

EXERCISE 35   **ABOUT YOU** Ask a *yes/no* question with the words given. Another student will answer. A past tense statement may be added to a *yes* answer.

EXAMPLE   go swimming recently

A: Have you gone swimming recently?
B: Yes, I have. I went swimming yesterday.

1. write to your family lately
2. go to the library recently
3. go to the zoo lately
4. see any good movies lately
5. receive any letters lately
6. be absent lately
7. have a job interview lately
8. read any good books recently
9. make any international calls lately
10. take any tests recently

EXERCISE 36   **Work with a partner. Write three questions to ask your teacher about what he or she has done lately. Your teacher will answer.**

EXAMPLE   Have you taken a vacation lately (or recently)?

1. _____
2. _____
3. _____

EXERCISE 37 **Fill in the blanks with the correct verb forms.**

EXAMPLE   **A:** Have you ___gotten___ a letter from your parents lately?
(get)

   B: Yes. I ___got___ a letter from them yesterday.

1. A: Have you _____ any pictures lately?
(take)

   B: No, I _____. My camera is broken.

2. A: Have you _____ any good movies lately?
(see)

   B: Yes. I _____ a great movie last weekend.

3. A: Have you _____ for a walk lately?
(go)

   B: Yes. I _____ for a walk yesterday.

4. A: Have you _____ yourself a gift lately?
(buy)

   B: Yes. I _____ myself a new CD player last week.

5. A: Have you _____ a good conversation with a friend lately?
(have)

   B: No. I _____ time to talk with my friends lately.

6. A: Have you _____ the art museum lately?
(visit)

   B: No. I _____ never _____ the art museum.

7. A: Have you _____ the laundry lately?
(do)

   B: Yes. I _____ it this morning.

8. A: Have you _____ to any parties lately?
(go)

   B: No, I _____. I've been too busy lately.

9. A: Have you _____ any compositions lately?
(write)

   B: Yes. I _____ a composition last night.

10. A: Have you _____ any good books lately?
(read)

   B: No, I _____. I'm too busy with my schoolwork.

1.17 The Present Perfect Continuous Tense with Ongoing Activities

EXAMPLES	EXPLANATION
Many American companies **have been sending** jobs abroad. American companies **have been benefiting** from outsourcing. Lately I **have been thinking** about changing majors. My English **has been improving** a lot lately.	We use the present perfect continuous to show that an activity has been ongoing or in progress from a time in the near past to the present. Remember, do not use the continuous form with nonaction verbs: She **has been** absent a lot lately.

EXERCISE 38 **ABOUT YOU** Fill in the blanks with *have* or *haven't* to tell about your experiences lately. (You may add a sentence giving more information.)

EXAMPLE   I __haven't__ been reading a lot lately.
I haven't had much time.

1. I _____ been getting a lot of sleep recently.
2. I _____ been getting together with my friends lately.
3. I _____ been watching the news a lot lately.
4. I _____ been studying a lot lately.
5. I _____ been learning a lot about English grammar lately.
6. I _____ been worrying a lot lately.
7. I _____ been looking for a job recently.
8. I _____ been watching a lot of TV recently.
9. I _____ been sending a lot of text messages lately.
10. I _____ been spending a lot of money recently.
11. I _____ been absent a lot lately.
12. I _____ been using a computer a lot lately.

EXERCISE 39 **ABOUT YOU** Fill in the blanks to make true statements about yourself.

EXAMPLES   ___My pronunciation___ has been getting better.
___My eyesight___ has been getting worse.

1. _____ has been improving.
2. _____ has been getting worse.
3. _____ has been increasing.

(continued)

4. _____ has been helping me with my studies.

5. _____ has been making me tired.

1.18 The Present Perfect Tense with No Time Mentioned

EXAMPLES	EXPLANATION
A: I'm changing my major. **B: Have** you **told** your parents about it? **A:** The job situation is bad these days. **B:** I know. Many workers **have lost** their jobs. **A:** Her uncle has a taxicab business. **B:** Really? **Has** he **made** a lot of money in his business? **A:** Are there a lot of call centers in India? **B:** Yes, there are. A lot of jobs **have moved** overseas.	We can use the present perfect to talk about the past without any reference to time. The time is not important or not known or imprecise. Using the present perfect, rather than the past, shows that the past is relevant to a present situation or statement.

EXERCISE 40   **ABOUT YOU** Fill in the blanks to make a true statement about yourself.

EXAMPLE   I've eaten _____*pizza*_____, and I like it a lot.

1. I've visited _____, and I would recommend it to others.

2. I've tried _____, and I like this food a lot.

3. I've seen the movie _____, and I would recommend it to others.

4. The teacher has said that _____, but some of us forget.

5. I've studied _____, and it has really helped me a lot.

6. I've had a lot of experience with _____ and can help you with it, if you need me to.

EXERCISE **41** **ABOUT YOU** Place a check mark (✓) next to the work-related experiences you've had. Then at the bottom, write three more things you've done at your present or former job. Write things that would impress an interviewer.

1. _____ I've worked on a team.

2. _____ I've taken programming courses.

3. _____ I've had experience talking with customers on the phone.

4. _____ I've worked overtime when necessary to finish a project.

5. _____ I've worked and gone to school at the same time.

6. _____ I've helped my family financially.

7. _____ I've given oral presentations.

8. _____ I've done research.

9. _____ I've created a Web site.

10. _____ I've done physical labor.

11. _____ I've been in charge of a group of workers.

12. _____ I've traveled as part of my job.

13. _____

14. _____

15. _____

EXERCISE **42** Fill in the blanks with the present perfect tense (for no time mentioned) or the simple past tense (if the time is mentioned). Use the verb in parentheses ( ). Answers may vary.

CD 1, TR 07

I ___**have had**___ many new experiences since I moved
(example: have)

here. I _____ some foods for the first time in my
(1 try)

life. I _____ pizza, but I don't like it much.
(2 eat)

Yesterday, I _____ Chinese food for the first
(3 try)

time and thought it was delicious.

I _____ a lot of new people and have some new
(4 meet)

friends. I _____ some new behaviors. For example,
(5 see)

there's a guy in my math class who wears torn jeans every day. Yesterday

I _____ him if he needs money for new clothes, but he
(6 ask)

just laughed and said, "Torn clothes are in style."

(continued)

I _____ some interesting places. I
(7 visit)

_____ to the art museum and the science museum.
(8 go)

I _____ a boat ride on a nearby river. I
(9 take)

_____ to the top of the tallest building.
(10 even/go)

I _____ about looking for a job. I
(11 learn)

_____ résumés and I _____ job
(12 write)   (13 have)

interviews. I _____ to job fairs. I _____
(14 go)   (15 even/use)

the Internet for my job search. Last week I _____
(16 go)

to see a job counselor at my college, and she _____
(17 give)

me some help with interviewing techniques.

1.19 The Present Perfect Tense vs. the Present Perfect Continuous Tense with No Time Mentioned

We can use both the present perfect tense and the present perfect continuous tense with no time mentioned.

EXAMPLES	EXPLANATION
a. My counselor **has helped** me with my résumé. b. My family **has been helping** me a lot.	The (a) examples are present perfect. They refer to a single occurrence at an indefinite time in the past.
a. I **have applied** for a job in New York. b. I **have been applying** for jobs all over the U.S.	The (b) examples are present perfect continuous. They refer to an ongoing activity that is not finished. The activity is still in progress.
a. **Have** you **used** the Internet in your job search lately? b. I've **been using** the Internet a lot lately.	

EXERCISE 43   **Check (✓) the sentence or clause that best completes the idea.**

EXAMPLE   I can't concentrate. The people in the next apartment . . .

_____ have made a lot of noise.

__✓__ have been making a lot of noise.

1. My boss has been sick all week.

_____ She's stayed in bed.

_____ She's been staying in bed.

2. My friend is unhappy.

____ She has just lost her job.

____ She has been losing her job.

3. She lost her job three weeks ago. She hasn't had much free time
   lately because . . .

____ she has looked for a new job.

____ she has been looking for a new job.

4. My résumé writing skills have been improving a lot because . . .

____ I have practiced with my counselor.

____ I have been practicing with my counselor.

5. At first my sister planned to move, but she found a job here. So . . .

____ she has changed her mind.

____ she has been changing her mind.

6. I meet new people everywhere: in my neighborhood, at my job, at
   school.

____ I have met new people.

____ I have been meeting new people.

7. Now I can buy a new computer because I . . .

____ have found a job.

____ have been finding a job.

8. Every week I put 20 percent of my salary in the bank. I hope
   I'll have enough to buy a new TV soon.

____ I have saved my money.

____ I have been saving my money.

9. I'm going to become an engineer.

____ I have made my decision.

____ I have been making my decision.

10. I need to finish my résumé soon.

____ I've worked very hard on it.

____ I've been working very hard on it.

EXERCISE 44 **Fill in the blanks with the simple past, the present perfect, or the present perfect continuous tense of the verb in parentheses ( ). In some cases, more than one answer is possible.**

EXAMPLE   I _____worked_____ as a cashier when I was in high school.
                        (work)

1. I think I'm qualified for the job of driver because I

   _____ as a driver before.
         (work)

2. I _____ as a pilot many years ago. My job as a pilot
         (work)

   _____ me away from home much of the time.
         (take)

3. I don't like the sight of blood, so I _____ about
                                              (never/think)

   becoming a doctor.

4. I'm a hair stylist. I _____ people's hair for six years.
                              (cut)

5. I'm afraid of the interview process because I

   _____ a job interview before.
         (never/have)

6. Many years ago, I _____ as a kindergarten
                           (work)

   teacher. Now I have my own day-care center.

7. I'm a car mechanic. I _____ a mechanic for three
                              (be)

   years. I _____ a lot of experience working with
              (have)

   American cars, but I _____ much experience with
                              (not/have)

   foreign cars.

8. I'm 62 years old and I like my job as a lab technician, but lately I

   _____ a lot about retirement.
         (think)

9. When I was in my native country, I _____ an
                                              (be)

   engineer, but now I'm a salesperson.

10. People _____ me why I want to be a funeral

(often/ask)

director when I graduate.

11. Lately I _____ the Internet a lot to get

(use)

information about jobs.

Summary of Lesson 1

Compare the simple present and the present perfect tenses.

SIMPLE PRESENT	PRESENT PERFECT
She **has** a job. She **is** a lab technician.	She **has had** her job for six months. She **has been** a lab technician since May.

Compare the present continuous and the present perfect continuous tenses.

PRESENT CONTINUOUS	PRESENT PERFECT CONTINUOUS
He **is working** now. She **is using** the Internet now.	He **has been working** for three hours. She **has been using** it for two hours.

Compare the simple past and the present perfect tenses.

SIMPLE PAST	PRESENT PERFECT
Daniel **worked** in Mexico City from 1994 to 1998.	He **has worked** in the U.S. since 1998.
He **found** a job in 2004.	He **has had** his present job since January 2004.
He **bought** his car when he came to Chicago.	He **has had** a car since he came to Chicago.
When **did** he **come** to Chicago?	How long **has** he **been** in Chicago?
He **had** three interviews last month.	He **has had** two interviews this month.
He **studied** business in college.	He **has studied** French and speaks it well.
He **went** to New York in July.	He **has gone** to Los Angeles many times.
Did you **go** to the job fair last week?	**Have** you ever **gone** to a job fair?

Compare the present perfect and the present perfect continuous tenses.

PRESENT PERFECT	PRESENT PERFECT CONTINUOUS
Ron **has worked** as a programmer for the past five years. *(This sentence has the same meaning as the one on the right.)*	Ron **has been working** as a programmer for the past five years. *(This sentence has the same meaning as the one on the left.)*
I **have lived** in three American cities. *(This sentence refers to a repetition from past to present.)*	I **have been living** in this city for the past two years. *(This sentence shows a continuation from past to present.)*
How many apartments **have** you **had** in this city? *(This question asks about a repetition from past to present.)*	How long **have** you **been living** in your current apartment? *(This question asks about a continuation from past to present.)*
Dan **has studied** French. *(This sentence shows only past activity, with no indication of a continuation.)*	The U.S. government **has been studying** the effect of outsourcing. *(This sentence shows an activity that is still in progress.)*
I **have thought** about changing majors. *(This sentence tells about an indefinite time in the past.)*	I **have been thinking** a lot about my future. *(In this sentence, the phrase "a lot" indicates that this activity is still in progress.)*

Editing Advice

1. Don't confuse the *-ing* form and the past participle.

   I've been ~~taken~~ *taking* English courses for several years.

   Have you ever ~~being~~ *been* to Texas?

2. Don't confuse *for* and *since*.

   He's been in Chicago ~~since~~ *for* three years.

3. Use the simple past, not the present perfect, with a specific past time and in questions and statements with *when*.

   He ~~has written~~ *wrote* a book five years ago.

   She ~~has~~ bought a car when she ~~has~~ found a job.

   When ~~has he gotten~~ *did he get* his driver's license?

4. Use the present perfect (continuous), not the present tense, if the action started in the past and continues to the present.

have been
I'm working in a factory for six months.

have *had*
How long do you have your computer?

5. Don't use the continuous form for repetition.

eaten
How many times have you been eating pizza?

6. Use the simple past in a *since* clause.

came
He's had three jobs since he has come to the U.S.

7. Use the correct word order.

never been
He has been never late to class.

ever eaten
Have you eaten ever Chinese food?

8. Use *yet* in negative statements. Use *already* in affirmative statements.

yet
I haven't finished the book already.

already
I've finished the book yet.

9. Use *how long* for a question about length of time. Don't include the word *time*.

How long time have they been working in a restaurant?

10. If the main verb is *have*, be sure to include the auxiliary verb *have* for the present perfect.

has
He had his job since March.

Editing Quiz

Two women, Karen (K) and Lucy (L), meet by chance in a shopping mall. Here's their conversation. Some of the shaded words and phrases have mistakes. Find the mistakes and correct them. If the shaded words are correct, write *C*.

L: Hi, Karen. I ~~haven't seen~~ ^{*C*} you since high school. How are you? Tell me
(example)
about your life. What ~~you have~~ **have you** been doing lately?
(example)   *(1)*

K: Well, I got married after high school.
(2)

L: Really? How long time have you being married?
(3)   *(4)*

K: For about four years. And I've had a baby six months ago.
(5)   *(6)*

L: That's wonderful. Did you marry your high-school boyfriend, Steve?

K: Oh, no. I haven't seeing Steve since we've been in high school. I married
(7)   *(8)*
Robert Kanter. You've met him never. What about you? What
(9)
you have been doing since high school? Did you marry your old
(10)
boyfriend, Greg?

L: Oh, no. I haven't seen Greg since four years. I'm not married. I
(11)   *(12)*
haven't meet the right guy yet. I started college right after high school. I
(13)   *(14)*   *(15)*
graduated last year with a degree in teaching.
(16)

K: That's great! I've always have a great respect for the teaching profession.
(17)
Where do you teach?

L: I've had many interviews for teaching jobs, but I haven't find one
(18)   *(19)*
yet. But I been working at a day-care center since the last three
(20)   *(21)*   *(22)*
months. I was so happy when I've found this job. I was worried that I'd
(23)
never find a job.

K: Are you still living in Ridgeland?

L: No. I'm living in Oakwood since I graduated from college. Here's my
  (24)   (25)   (26)

phone number. Call me when you have more time and we can talk.

K: Thanks. I'd love to.

Lesson 1 Test/Review

PART **1** **Fill in the blanks with the simple present, simple past, present perfect, or present perfect continuous tense of the verb in parentheses ( ). In some cases, more than one answer is possible.**

A: Hi, Ben. I ___haven't seen___ you in a long time. How
                    (example: not/see)

___have you been___?
(example: you/be)

B: I'm okay. But I _____ a job now, so I feel
                        (1 not/have)

pretty depressed about it. I _____ for a job for the
                              (2 look)

past three months, but so far I _____ any success.
                                  (3 not/have)

A: My best friend _____ from college last year, and
                       (4 graduate)

he _____ a job yet. A lot of American jobs
     (5 not/find)

_____ in recent years. Many jobs
  (6 disappear)

_____ to India and other countries.
  (7 go)

B: That's terrible. My family _____ to the U.S. last
                                   (8 come)

year to find better jobs, but it's not easy anymore.

A: But it's not impossible. _____ the
                               (9 you/ever/use)

Occupational Outlook Handbook?

B: No, I never _____.
                   (10 have)

A: You can find it on the Web. It lists information about professions in

the U.S. My counselor _____ me about it when I
                        (11 tell)

_____ taking courses. I _____ a
  (12 start)   (13 have)

good job now. I _____ as a dental assistant.
                 (14 work)

B: How long _____ at that job?
                 (15 you/work)

(continued)

The Present Perfect Tense; The Present Perfect Continuous Tense   53

A: Since I _____ my certificate two years ago. I don't
(16 get)

have to worry about outsourcing. You can't look in people's mouths

from another country.

B: You're lucky to have such a good job.

A: It's not luck. I _____ this job carefully before I started
(17 choose)

taking courses. And I _____ hard when I was
(18 study)

in the dental program. Now when I _____ to work
(19 go)

every day, I _____ good because I'm helping people
(20 feel)

and making good money. Also I _____ good benefits.
(21 have)

In addition, I _____ two salary increases so far.
(22 get)

B: That's wonderful! _____ about becoming a dentist?
(23 you/ever/think)

Dentists make good money.

A: I _____ about it, but I don't want to spend so much
(24 think)

time studying for a new career. It takes a long time to become a dentist.

And you need to study a lot of science. I _____
(25 never/be)

very good in science.

B: Well, when you have time, will you show me how to find the

Occupational Outlook Handbook online?

A: I'd be happy to.

Expansion

Classroom Activities

❶ Walk around the room. Find one person who has done each of these things. Write that person's name in the blank.

a. _____ has been exercising a lot lately.

b. _____ has been watching a lot of TV lately.

c. _____ has never gone to an art museum.

d. _____ has traveled to more than five countries.

e. _____ has never owned a car.

f. _____ hasn't bought the textbook yet.

g. _____ has been in this city for less than six months.

h. _____ has just found a job.

i. _____ has worked in a restaurant.

j. _____ has never used public transportation in this city.

k. _____ has eaten raw fish.

l. _____ has worked out in a gym several times this month.

m. _____ has never shopped online.

n. _____ has never sent a text message.

o. _____ has been looking for a job.

❷ Role Play: Find a partner. Pretend that one of you is looking for a job and the other one is the interviewer. Ask and answer questions about your experience, education, interests, talents, etc. Here are some sample questions that interviewers sometimes ask:

- Why did you leave your last job?
- Why are you applying for this position?
- Where would you like to be five years from now?
- What are your strengths?
- What are your weaknesses?
- Why should we hire you?
- How many years experience have you had in this field?
- Have you had experience with computers?

③ Game—True-True-False: Form a small group. On a piece of paper, write two unusual things you have done in the past. Write one false statement about your past. (Use the present perfect with no mention of time.) Read your statements to the other members of your group. Your classmates have to guess which is the false statement.

EXAMPLES   I've flown in a helicopter.

I've worked on a farm.

I've met the president of my native country.

④ Fill in the blanks and discuss your answers.

a. I've learned _____ from my experiences in the U.S.

b. I've thought a lot about _____.

c. Most people in my native country have never _____.

d. In the U.S., it's been hard for me to _____.

Talk
About It

① How is looking for a job in the U.S. different from looking for a job in other countries?

② How is the work environment in your present job different from the work environment in a previous job you had?

③ In other countries, how do people usually select a career? Are there career counselors to help people make a decision?

④ Have you ever used the Internet to search for jobs? Has it been helpful?

⑤ In your native country, do high school students ever have a part-time job? If so, what kinds of jobs do they do?

6 Look at the following list of jobs. Which ones do you think are interesting and why? What do you think are some good or bad aspects of these jobs?

airplane pilot   funeral director   librarian
architect   gardener   musician
bus driver   immigration officer   newspaper reporter
circus clown   lawyer   police officer
firefighter   letter carrier   veterinarian

Write
About It

1 Write about a career that you think is interesting. Explain why you think this career is interesting.

2 Write about a job you would never want to have. Tell why.

3 Write an article giving advice to somebody looking for a job.

4 Write about your past work experience.

EXAMPLE

My Job Experience

I've been in the U.S. for only five years, but I have already had several jobs. When I arrived, I didn't know much English and I started to work as a dishwasher in a restaurant. I didn't like this job and quit after four months…

 For more practice using grammar in context, please visit our Web site.

Grammar

The Passive Voice

Participles Used as Adjectives

Get + **Participles and Adjectives**

Context

Hollywood

2.1 The Passive Voice—An Overview

We use the passive voice when the subject of the sentence is the receiver of the action.

EXAMPLES	EXPLANATION
Popcorn **is sold** in movie theaters. Old movies **were filmed** in black and white. Many movies **have been made** in Hollywood.	Passive verb = a form of *be* + past participle
subject verb object Active: The children **saw** the movie. subject verb by agent Passive: The movie **was seen** *by* the children.	Compare active and passive. The object of the active sentence (*movie*) is the subject of the passive sentence. If the agent of the action (the person who performs the action) is mentioned, it follows *by*.

The Oscars

Before You Read

1. Who is your favorite actor? Who is your favorite actress?

2. What movies have you seen recently?

CD 1, TR 08

Read the following magazine article. Pay special attention to verbs in the passive voice.

Did You **Know?**

Walt Disney has won the most Oscars ever: 26.

The Academy Awards **are given** out every year to recognize outstanding work of movie actors, directors, and others who are part of the movie-making industry. These awards, called Oscars, **are presented** in a formal ceremony in Hollywood. Several people **are nominated** in specific categories, such as Best Movie, Best Actor, Best Music, and Best Costumes. One nominee **is chosen** to receive an award in each category.

When the awards ceremony started in 1929, 15 awards **were presented** and the ceremony **was attended** by only 250 people. Tickets cost $10, and anyone who could afford a ticket could attend. Today about two dozen Oscars **are presented**. Tickets **are** no longer **sold** to the general public; invitations **are sent** only to people involved in making the movies and to their guests. Today the awards **are presented** in the 3400-seat Kodak Theatre in Hollywood.

Until 1941, the winners' names **were** already **known** before the ceremony and **published** in newspapers the night before the ceremony. Now the winners' names

are placed in sealed envelopes and the envelopes **are** not **opened** until the night of the ceremony.

Since 1953, Oscar night **has been televised** and **broadcast** all over the world. This show **is seen** by hundreds of millions of people. Viewers watch as their favorite movie stars arrive looking beautiful and hopeful.

2.2 The Passive Voice—Form

Compare active voice and passive voice in different tenses.

Tense	Active	Passive = *Be* + Past Participle
Simple Present	A committee **chooses** the winner.	The winner **is chosen** by a committee.
Present Continuous	They **are presenting** an award now.	An award **is being presented** now.
Future	They **will pick** the best movie. They **are going to pick** the best movie.	The best movie **will be picked**. The best movie **is going to be picked**.
Simple Past	They **announced** the winner's name.	The winner's name **was announced**.
Past Continuous	They **were interviewing** the winners.	The winners **were being interviewed**.
Present Perfect	They **have chosen** the best movie.	The best movie **has been chosen**.
Modal	You **can see** the movie on DVD.	The movie **can be seen** on DVD.

Language Notes:
1. Both the active voice and the passive voice can be used with different tenses and with modals. The tense of the passive sentence is shown in the verb *be*. Use the past participle with every tense.
2. If two verbs in the passive voice are connected with *and*, do not repeat *be*.

The Oscar ceremony **is televised *and* seen** by millions of people.

(continued)

EXAMPLES	EXPLANATION
Before 1941, the winners' names **were** *already* **known** before the ceremony. Today the winners **are** *never* **announced** ahead of time.	An adverb can be placed between the auxiliary verb and the main verb.
Affirmative: The movie **was filmed** in the U.S. **Negative:** It **wasn't filmed** in Canada. *Yes/No* **Question:** **Was** it **filmed** in Hollywood? **Short Answer:** No, it **wasn't**. *Wh-* **Question:** Where **was** it **filmed**? **Subject Question:** Which movie **was filmed** in Canada?	Observe affirmative statements, negative statements, and questions with the passive voice. Never use *do*, *does*, or *did* with the passive voice. (*Wrong:* The movie **didn't** filmed in Canada.)
Active: She saw **him**. **Passive:** **He** was seen *by* **her**. **Active:** **They** helped **us**. **Passive:** **We** were helped *by* **them**.	Notice the difference in pronouns in an active sentence and a passive sentence. After *by*, the object pronoun is used.

EXERCISE 1 Read the following sentences. Decide if the underlined verb is active (A) or passive (P).

EXAMPLES   The actress <u>received</u> an Oscar.   A

The actress <u>was given</u> an Oscar.   P

1. The actress <u>wore</u> a beautiful gown.
2. Halle Berry <u>presented</u> an Oscar.
3. Halle Berry <u>has been seen</u> in many movies.
4. The director <u>has been nominated</u> many times.
5. Old movies <u>were filmed</u> in black and white.
6. Many actors <u>live</u> in California.
7. Many movies <u>are made</u> in Hollywood.
8. The names of the winners <u>will be printed</u> in tomorrow's newspaper.
9. The actress <u>thanked</u> all the people who helped her win.
10. The actress <u>was driven</u> to the ceremony in a white limousine.
11. Hollywood <u>was built</u> at the beginning of the twentieth century.
12. Hollywood <u>has become</u> the movie capital of the U.S.

EXERCISE 2 Fill in the blanks with the passive voice of the verb in parentheses.
Use the tense or modal given.

EXAMPLE (simple present: *give*)

The best actor ___is___ ___given___ an Oscar.

1. (simple present: *see*)

   The awards ceremony _____ _____ by millions of people.

2. (future: *choose*)

   Which actor _____ _____ _____ next year?

3. (modal: *can / see*)

   The movie _____ _____ _____ at many theaters.

4. (present perfect: *make*)

   Many movies _____ _____ _____ about World War II.

5. (simple past: *give*)

   Kate Winslet _____ _____ the best actress award in 2009.

6. (present continuous: *show*)

   A good movie _____ _____ _____ at a theater near
   my house.

7. (simple past: *make*)

   Star Wars _____ _____ in 1977.

8. (present perfect: *show*)

   The movie _____ _____ _____ on TV many times.

9. (present perfect: *give*)

   Over 2,000 Academy Awards _____ _____ _____ out
   since 1929.

10. (simple past: *give*)

    In 1929, only one award _____ _____ to a woman.

11. (simple past: *add*)

    When _____ sound _____ to movies?

    It _____ _____ in 1927.

12. (simple present: *often / make*)

    Movies _____ _____ _____ in Hollywood.

13. (present perfect: *film*)

    How many movies _____ _____ _____ in black and
    white?

The Passive Voice; Participles Used as Adjectives; *Get* + Participles and Adjectives   **63**

2.3 Passive Voice and Active Voice—Uses

EXAMPLES	EXPLANATION
Compare: **Active:** The man **ate** the fish. **Passive:** The man **was eaten** by the fish.	When the verb is in the active voice, the subject performs the action. When the verb is in the passive voice, the subject receives the action.
A. **Active:** I **see** the Academy Awards ceremony every year. **Passive:** The Academy Awards ceremony **is seen** by millions. **B.** **Active:** **Do** you **know** the winners' names? **Passive:** The winners' names **are not known** until the night of the ceremony. **C.** **Active:** The Academy **presents** awards to the best actors and directors. **Passive:** The awards **are presented** every year.	The active voice focuses on the person who does the action. The passive voice focuses on the receiver or the result of the action. Sometimes the passive voice mentions the agent, the person who does the action (A). Sometimes it is not necessary to mention the agent (B and C).

EXERCISE 3 Write an active sentence and a passive sentence for each subject. Choose an appropriate tense.

EXAMPLE   *Active:* The test ___has 12 questions.___

Passive: The test ___will be given in a large auditorium.___

1. *Active:* My textbook _____

Passive: My textbook _____

2. *Active:* My best friend _____

Passive: My best friend _____

3. *Active:* Some students _____

Passive: Some students _____

4. *Active:* I_____

Passive: I_____

5. Active: Actors _____

    Passive: Actors _____

6. Active: Movies _____

    Passive: Movies _____

2.4 The Passive Voice Without an Agent

The passive voice is used more frequently without an agent than with an agent.

EXAMPLES	EXPLANATION
The invitations **have been sent** out. The winners' names **are placed** in envelopes.	The passive voice is used when it is not important to mention who performed the action.
A. Active: *Someone* **stole** my wallet. Passive: My wallet **was stolen** last week. **B.** Active: *Someone* **told** me that you like movies. Passive: I **was told** that you like movies.	The passive voice is used when we do not know the agent (A) or when we prefer not to mention the agent (B).
a. One person **is chosen** to receive the award. b. Oscar night **has been televised** since 1953.	The passive voice is used when the agent is obvious and doesn't need to be mentioned. a. It is obvious that the Academy chooses the winner. b. It is obvious that TV stations have televised Oscar night.
Compare Active (A) and Passive (P): A: *You* **can rent** DVDs at many stores. P: DVDs **can be rented** at many stores. A: *They* **sell** popcorn in movie theaters. P: Popcorn **is sold** in movie theaters.	In conversation, the active voice is often used with the impersonal subjects *people, you, we,* or *they.* In more formal speech and writing, the passive is used with no agent.

EXERCISE 4 **Fill in the blanks with the passive voice of the verb in parentheses ( ). Choose an appropriate tense.**

EXAMPLE Hollywood _____ was built _____ in the early 1900s.
                             (build)

    1. Most American movies _____ in Hollywood.
                                      (make)

    2. Let's get some popcorn. It's fresh. It _____ right now.
                                                  (make)

(continued)

3. Movie listings _____ in the newspaper.
   (can/find)

4. Children _____ to see some movies.
   (not/allow)

5. Hurry! The winners _____ in ten minutes.
   (announce)

6. In 1929, only fifteen Oscars _____.
   (present)

7. Before 1941, the winners' names _____ in
   (publish)

   newspapers the night before the ceremony.

8. A new theater _____ near my house at this time.
   (build)

9. We can't get into the movie theater because all the tickets

   _____ already.
   (sell)

10. Did you see the movie *Harry Potter*? Where _____ it

    _____?
    (film)

11. I went to the lobby to buy popcorn, and my seat _____.
    (take)

12. No one knows why the award _____ "Oscar."
    (call)

13. *Slumdog Millionaire* _____ as the best film of 2009.
    (choose)

14. In a movie theater, coming attractions[1]_____
    (show)

    before the feature film begins.

15. Sound _____ to movies in 1927.
    (add)

16. The Kodak Theatre, where the awards _____
    (present)

    each year, _____ in 2001.
    (build)

---

[1]*Coming attractions* are short previews of new movies. Theaters show coming attractions to get your interest in
returning to the theater to see a new movie.

2.5 The Passive Voice with an Agent

Sometimes the passive voice is used with an agent.

ACTIVE	PASSIVE
Active: Steven Spielberg **has made** many movies. **Passive:** Many movies **have been made** by Steven Spielberg. **Active:** Ralph Lauren **designs** many of the actresses' gowns. **Passive:** Many of the actresses' gowns **are designed** by Ralph Lauren.	When the sentence has a strong agent (a specific person: Steven Spielberg, Ralph Lauren), we can use either the active or the passive voice. The active voice puts more emphasis on the person who performs the action. The passive voice puts more emphasis on the action or the result. In general, the active voice is more common than the passive voice when an agent is mentioned.
Active: *The first Oscar ceremony* took place in 1929. **Passive:** *It* **was attended** by 250 people. **Active:** *The Oscar ceremony* is popular all over the world. **Passive:** *It* **is seen** by millions of viewers each year.	Sometimes the passive voice is used to continue with the same subject of the preceding sentence.
Active: Steven Spielberg **directed** *Star Wars*, didn't he? **Passive:** No. *Star Wars* **was directed** by George Lucas.	We can use the passive voice to shift the emphasis to the object of the preceding sentence.
Passive: The dress **was designed** by Vera Wang. **Passive:** The music **was composed** by Bob Dylan. **Passive:** The movie projector **was invented** by Thomas Edison.	We often use the passive voice when the agent *made, discovered, invented, designed, built, wrote, painted,* or *composed* something.
The song **was written** *by Randy Newman*. It **was performed** *by him* too.	When the agent is included, use *by* + noun or object pronoun.

EXERCISE 5 Fill in the blanks with the passive voice of the verb in parentheses ( ). Use the past tense.

1. Mickey Mouse _____ by Walt Disney.
   (create)

2. The movie projector _____ by Thomas Edison.
   (invent)

3. *Romeo and Juliet* _____ by William Shakespeare in 1595.
   (write)

4. *Romeo and Juliet* _____ into a movie in 1968.
   (make)

5. *My Heart Will Go On* _____ by Celine Dion.
   (sing)

6. *Star Wars* _____ by George Lucas.
   (direct)

EXERCISE 6 Fill in the blanks with the active or passive voice of the verb in parentheses ( ). Use the tense indicated.

EXAMPLES   I _____**saw**_____ an old movie on TV last night.
                        (past: see)

The movie _____**was filmed**_____ in black and white.
                        (past: film)

It _____**will be shown**_____ again on TV tonight.
                        (future: show)

1. Many movies _____ in Hollywood.
   (present: make)

2. Steven Spielberg _____ many movies.
   (present perfect: make)

3. We _____ a DVD this weekend.
   (future: rent)

4. Vera Wang _____ beautiful dresses.
   (present: design)

5. The actress _____ a dress that _____
   (past continuous: wear)   *(past: design)*

   by Ralph Lauren.

6. Who _____ the music for the movie? The music
   (past: write)

   _____ by Randy Newman.
   (past: write)

7. The first Academy Awards presentation _____
   (past: have)

   250 guests.

8. I _____ *Star Wars*.
   (present perfect: never/see)

9. Computer animation _____ in many movies.
   (present: use)

10. Movie reviewers _____ predictions weeks before
    (present: make)
    the Oscar presentation.

11. Oscar winners _____ the people who helped them.
    (present: always/thank)

2.6 Verbs with Two Objects

Some verbs have two objects: a direct object (D.O.) and an indirect object (I.O.).

EXAMPLES	EXPLANATION
I.O. **D.O.** **Active:** They gave Spielberg an award. **Passive 1:** Spielberg was given an award. **Passive 2:** An award was given to Spielberg.	When an active sentence has two objects, the passive sentence can begin with either object. Notice that if the direct object (*an award*) becomes the subject of the passive sentence, *to* is used before the indirect object.

Language Note: Some verbs that use two objects are:				
bring	lend	pay	serve	teach
give	offer	sell	show	tell
hand	owe	send	take	write

EXERCISE 7 **Change the following sentences to passive voice in two ways. Omit the agent.**

EXAMPLE They gave the actress an award.

**The actress was given an award.**

**An award was given to the actress.**

1. They handed the actress an Oscar.

   _____

   _____

2. Someone served the guests dinner.

   _____

   _____

(continued)

3. Someone told the students the answers.

_____

_____

4. Someone will send you an invitation.

_____

_____

5. They have shown us the movie.

_____

_____

6. They will give the winners flowers.

_____

_____

7. Someone has given you the key.

_____

_____

The History of Animation

**Before
You Read**

1. Do you know how cartoons are created?

2. Are cartoons just for children? Do adults enjoy cartoons too?

Gertie the Dinosaur
Created by Winsor McCay

🔊 **Read the following textbook article. Pay special attention to active and passive verbs.**

Animated movies **have changed** a lot over the last 100 years. Winsor McCay **is considered** the father of animation. In the early 1900s, McCay **animated** his films by himself. He **drew** every picture separately and had them photographed, one at a time. Hundreds of photographs **were needed** to make a one-minute film. Sometimes it would take him more than a year to make a five-minute cartoon.

Walt Disney

In 1914, the development of celluloid (a transparent material) made animation easier. Instead of drawing each picture separately, the animator could make a drawing of the background, which **remained** motionless, while only the characters **moved.**

Walt Disney **took** animation to a new level. He **created** Mickey Mouse, **added** sound and music to his movies, and **produced** the first full-length animated film, *Snow White and the Seven Dwarfs.* Many people think he was a great cartoonist, but he wasn't. Instead, he was a great story editor and clever businessman who had other artists do most of the drawings.

Today most animated films **are** not **drawn** by hand. The animation **is done** by computer software. Also special effects for movies, such as *Star Wars*, **are done** by computer animation. To create the illusion of movement, an image **is put** on the computer and then quickly **replaced** by a similar image with a small change. While this technique is similar to hand-drawn animation, the work **can be done** much faster by computer. In fact, anyone with a home computer and special software **can create** a simple animation.

(continued)

1901 Walt Disney was born.

1914 Winsor McCay **created** the first animation on film, *Gertie the Dinosaur*.

1918 Walt Disney **opened** a cartoon studio in Kansas City, Missouri.

1923 Disney **moved** his studio to Hollywood.

1928 The first Mickey Mouse cartoon **was introduced**. It was the first talking cartoon.

1937 Disney **produced** *Snow White and the Seven Dwarfs*, the first full-length animated cartoon.

1995 *Toy Story* **became** the first full-length film animated entirely on computers.

2009 *WALL-E* **won** the Academy Award for best animated film.

2.7 Transitive and Intransitive Verbs

EXAMPLES	EXPLANATION
Compare: verb object **Active:** McCay **created** the first animated film. **Passive:** The first animated film **was created** in 1914. verb object **Active:** Walt Disney **didn't draw** his cartoons. **Passive:** His cartoons **were drawn** by studio artists.	Most active verbs are followed by an object. They can be used in the active and passive voice. These verbs are called *transitive* verbs.
Active Only: Disney **lived** in Hollywood most of his life. He **became** famous when he created Mickey Mouse. He **worked** with many artists. What **happened** to the first Mickey Mouse cartoon? I'd like to see it.	Some verbs have no object. We cannot use the passive voice with these verbs: agree die look seem arrive fall occur sleep be go rain stay become happen recover walk come live remain work These are called *intransitive* verbs.
Compare: a. Disney **left** Kansas City in 1923. b. The DVD **was left** in the DVD player.	*Leave* can be intransitive or transitive, depending on its meaning. In sentence (a), *leave* means "go away from." It is an intransitive verb. It has no passive form. In sentence (b), leave means "not taken." It is a transitive verb. It has a passive form.
Compare: a. Cartoons **have changed** a lot over the years. b. The light bulb **was changed** by the janitor. a. In a cartoon, it looks like the characters **are moving**, but they are not. b. The chairs **were moved** to another room.	*Change* and *move* can be intransitive or transitive. When a change happens through a natural process (a), it is intransitive. When someone specific causes the change (b), it is transitive.
Compare: Walt Disney **was born** in 1901. He **died** in 1966.	Notice that we use *was/were* with *born*, but we don't use the passive voice with *die*. *Born* is not a verb. It is a past participle used as an adjective.

EXERCISE 8 **Which of the following sentences can be changed to passive voice? Change those sentences. If no change is possible, write *no change*.**

EXAMPLES
Today they create most animation with computer software.
<u>Today most animation is created with computer software.</u>

Walt Disney moved to Hollywood in 1923.
<u>No change.</u>

1. What happened at the end of the movie?

2. Someone left a box of popcorn on the seat.

3. Many movie stars live in California.

4. Paul Newman was a famous actor. He died in 2008.

5. I slept during the movie.

6. You can rent *Finding Nemo* on DVD.

7. They will show a movie at 9:30 in the auditorium.

8. They have sold all the tickets.

EXERCISE 9 **Fill in the blanks with the active or passive form of the verb in parentheses ( ). Use the tense indicated.**

EXAMPLES
Walt Disney ___<u>was</u>___ a clever businessman.
(past: be)

His cartoons ___<u>are seen</u>___ all over the world.
(present: see)

1. Walt Disney _____ famous when he
(past: become)
_____ Mickey Mouse.
(past: create)

2. Walt Disney _____ most of his cartoon characters.
(past: not/draw)

3. Most of his cartoons _____ by studio artists.
(past: draw)

4. Walt Disney _____ 26 Oscars.
(past: give)

5. Walt Disney _____ his studio to Hollywood.
(past: move)

6. Walt Disney _____ in Hollywood most of his life.
(past: live)

7. Disney _____ in 1966.
(past: die)

8. Today's animations _____ using computers.
(present: create)

9. Cartoon characters look like they _____.
(present continuous: move)

10. Even today, Disney's old cartoons _____ beautiful.
(present: look)

EXERCISE 10 Fill in the blanks with the active or passive form of the verb in parentheses ( ). Use the past tense.

CD 1, TR 10

Ronald Reagan ____**was elected**____ president of the
(example: elect)
United States in 1980. Before he ____**became**____
(example: become)
president, he was governor of California. Even before
that, he _____ as a Hollywood actor.
(1 work)
He _____ in 53 Hollywood movies between
(2 appear)
1937 and 1964. He _____ a great actor, and
(3 not/consider)
he never _____ an Oscar.
(4 win)
On March 20, 1981, the day the Oscar ceremony
_____ to take place, something terrible
(5 schedule)
_____. Reagan _____ in an
(6 happen) *(7 shoot)*
assassination attempt. Fortunately, he _____
(8 past: not/die)
from his wounds. One of his aides, who was with him at the time,
_____. Out of respect for the president, the Academy
(9 also/wound)
Awards ceremony _____ for one day. Reagan
(10 postpone)
_____ and continued to serve as president until he
(11 recover)
_____ his second term in 1989. He _____
(12 finish) *(13 die)*
in 2004 at the age of 93.

EXERCISE 11   Find the mistakes with the underlined verbs in the sentences below and correct them. Not every sentence has a mistake. If the sentence is correct, write *C*.

EXAMPLES   Before the 1950s, most movies <u>filmed</u> in black and white. *were*

I <u>like</u> old movies.   *C*

1. We <u>went</u> to see a movie.

2. I don't like scary movies. I <u>can't be slept</u> afterwards.

3. <u>Did</u> the movie <u>directed</u> by Steven Spielberg?

4. People in the audience <u>are eaten</u> popcorn.

5. The popcorn is fresh. It <u>is been popped</u> right now.

6. Popcorn <u>sells</u> in the lobby of the theater.

7. Before the movie, coming attractions <u>are show</u>.

8. At the end of the movie, we <u>were left</u> the theater and went home.

9. A lot of popcorn containers and candy wrappers <u>was left</u> on the floor of the theater.

10. Some movies <u>can be enjoy</u> by the whole family.

11. Tickets <u>can bought</u> online ahead of time.

12. What <u>was happened</u>? I can't find my ticket.

13. The theater is big. Fourteen movies <u>are shown</u> at the same time.

14. The movie is for adults. Children <u>don't permitted</u> to enter.

15. I <u>enjoyed</u> the movie. Did you?

16. Parking is free at the theater, but the parking pass <u>must be validated</u> in the theater.

17. Some movies should not <u>seen</u> by children.

18. Senior citizens <u>can get</u> a discount on tickets.

19. At the Oscar ceremony, the actors <u>are arrived</u> in limousines.

20. The actresses <u>wear</u> beautiful dresses.

2.8 The Passive Voice with *Get*

EXAMPLES	EXPLANATION
Hollywood actors **get paid** a lot of money. I don't like violent movies. A lot of people **get shot** and **killed.**	In conversation, we sometimes use *get* instead of *be* with the passive. *get paid = be paid* *get shot = be shot* *get killed = be killed* We usually omit the agent after *get*. Compare: He **was shot** by a cowboy. He **got shot** three times.
How much **do** actors **get paid** for a movie? She **didn't get paid** last Friday.	When *get* is used with the passive voice, questions and negatives are formed with *do, does, did,* and other auxiliaries. *Be* is not used with *get*. *Wrong:* She *wasn't get paid* last Friday.
She **got hired** for the job. He **got laid off** last month.	*Get* is frequently used with: *shot, killed, injured, wounded, paid, hired, fired, laid off, picked, caught, done, sent, stolen.*

EXERCISE **12** **Fill in the blanks with *get* + the past participle of the verb in parentheses ( ). Choose an appropriate tense.**

EXAMPLE Who _____got chosen_____ for the part in the movie?
          (choose)

1. Reagan _____ on the day of the Oscars.
   (shoot)

2. No one _____.
   (kill)

3. Did you _____ for the movie role?
   (hire)

4. Famous actors _____ millions of dollars for a film.
   (pay)

5. His car _____ from in front of his house.
   (steal)

6. The little boy told a lie, and he _____.
   (punish)

7. Everything will _____ little by little.
   (do)

8. The test scores _____ to the wrong person.
   (send)

9. One student _____ cheating on the exam.
   (catch)

10. If you leave your car there, it might _____.
    (tow)

2.9 Participles Used as Adjectives

A present participle is verb + -ing. A past participle is the third form of the verb (usually -ed or -en). Both present participles and past participles can be used as adjectives.

EXAMPLES	EXPLANATION
We saw an **entertaining** movie. *Star Wars* is an **exciting** movie. *The Matrix* has **amazing** visual effects.	In these examples, a *present participle* is used as an adjective.
What's in the **sealed** envelope? I wasn't **bored** during the movie. Are you **interested** in action movies? Do you like **animated** films?	In these examples, a *past participle* is used as an adjective.

Charlie Chaplin

Before You Read

1. Have you ever heard of Charlie Chaplin?

2. Have you ever seen a silent movie? Do you think a silent movie can be interesting today?

CD 1, TR 11

Read the following magazine article. Pay special attention to participles used as adjectives.

Charlie Chaplin was one of the greatest actors in the world. His **entertaining** silent movies are still popular today. His **amusing** character "Little Tramp" is well **known** to people throughout the world. Chaplin had an **amazing** life. His idea for this poor character in **worn**-out shoes, round hat, and cane probably came from his childhood experiences.

Born in poverty in London in 1889, Chaplin was abandoned by his father and left in an orphanage by his mother. He became **interested** in acting at the age of five. At ten, he left school to travel with a British acting company. In 1910, he made his first trip to America. He was **talented**, athletic, and **hardworking**, and by 1916 he was earning $10,000

Charlie Chaplin, 1889–1977

a week.[2] He was the highest-**paid** person in the world at that time. He produced, directed, and wrote the movies he starred in.

Even though "talkies" came out in 1927, he didn't make a movie with sound until 1940, when he played a comic version of the **terrifying** dictator, Adolf Hitler.

As Chaplin got older, he faced **declining** popularity as a result of his politics and personal relationships. After he left the U.S. in 1952, Chaplin was not allowed to re-enter because of his political views. He didn't return to the U.S. until 1972, when he was given a special Oscar for his lifetime of **outstanding** work.

2.10 Participles Used as Adjectives to Show Feelings

The participles of a verb can be used as adjectives.

Chaplin's movies <u>interest</u> us.
(verb)

Chaplin's movies are <u>interesting</u>.
(present participle)

We are <u>interested</u> in his movies.
(past participle)

EXAMPLES	EXPLANATION
The movie *bored* us. (*bored* = verb)	In some cases, both the present participle (a) and the past participle (b) of the same verb can be used as adjectives.
a. The movie was **boring**. I left the **boring** movie before it was over.	The present participle (a) gives an active meaning. The movie *actively* caused a feeling of boredom.
b. Some people were **bored**. The **bored** people got up and left.	The past participle (b) gives a passive meaning. It describes the receiver of a feeling. The people were bored by the movie.
Chaplin had an **interesting** life. He was poor and then became very rich. I am **interested** in Chaplin. I would like to know more about him. The main character in *Friday the 13th* is a **frightening** man. I was **frightened** and couldn't sleep after seeing the movie.	A person can cause a feeling in others or he can receive a feeling. Therefore, a person can be both *interesting* and *interested*, *frightening* and *frightened*, etc.
The book is **interesting**. The movie is **entertaining**.	An object (like a book or a movie) doesn't have feelings, so a past participle, such as *interested* or *entertained*, cannot be used to describe an object.

[2]In today's dollars, that amount would be close to $200,000 a week.

(continued)

Language Notes:

1. The following pictures show the difference between (a) a *frightening* man and (b) a *frightened* man.

a. The man is frightening the children. = He's a *frightening man.*

b. The man is frightened by the robber. = He's a *frightened man.*

2. Common paired participles are:

amazing	amazed	exhausting	exhausted
amusing	amused	frightening	frightened
annoying	annoyed	frustrating	frustrated
boring	bored	interesting	interested
confusing	confused	puzzling	puzzled
convincing	convinced	satisfying	satisfied
disappointing	disappointed	surprising	surprised
embarrassing	embarrassed	terrifying	terrified
exciting	excited	tiring	tired

EXERCISE 13 **Use the verb in each sentence to make two new sentences. In one sentence, use the present participle. In the other, use the past participle.**

EXAMPLE The game entertains the children.

The game is entertaining.

The children are entertained.

1. The movie frightened the children.

_____

_____

2. The book interests the children.

_____

_____

3. The children are amusing the adults.

_____

_____

4. The trip tired the children.

_____

_____

5. The game excited the children.

_____

_____

6. The vacation exhausted the adults.

_____

_____

7. The movie bored the adults.

_____

_____

8. Chaplin interests me.

_____

_____

EXERCISE 14 Fill in the blanks with the correct participle, present or past, of the verb in parentheses ( ).

CD 1, TR 12

Last night my friend and I went to see a new movie. We thought it

was ___boring___. It had a lot of stupid car chases, which
  (example: bore)

were not _____ at all. And I didn't like the characters.
           (1 excite)

They weren't very _____.
                  (2 convince)

We were pretty _____ because the reviewers said it was a
               (3 disappoint)

good movie. They said it had _____ visual effects. But for
                             (4 amaze)

me, it wasn't _____ at all. I was _____ that I
              (5 interest)   (6 annoy)

wasted $10 and a whole evening for such a _____ movie.
                                          (7 disappoint)

The only thing that was _____ was the popcorn.
                        (8 satisfy)

EXERCISE 15 **ABOUT YOU** Fill in the blanks and discuss your answers.

EXAMPLE I'm interested in ___sports___.

1. I'm interested in _____ movies.

2. Now I'm worried about _____.

3. In the past, I was worried about _____.

4. In my opinion, _____ is an amazing (choose one)
      actor / athlete / politician.

5. I'm not interested in _____.

6. I'm annoyed when people _____.

7. _____ is a boring subject for me.

8. I feel frustrated when _____.

9. I am amazed that _____ in the U.S.

10. It's not surprising that _____ in the U.S.

11. Sometimes I feel embarrassed when I _____

_____

12. I was very excited when _____.

13. When I came to this school, I was surprised that _____

_____.

2.11 Other Past Participles Used as Adjectives

Some sentences look passive (*be* + past participle), but there is no action in the sentence. The past participles below are used as adjectives.

EXAMPLES	EXPLANATION
a. No one knows the winners' names because the envelope is **sealed**. b. Is this seat **taken**? c. Chaplin was **born** in England.	In some cases, we are looking at the result of a previous action. We no longer care about the agent, and the action itself is not important.[3] a. **Previous Action:** Someone *sealed* the envelope. b. **Previous Action:** Someone *took (occupied)* the seat. c. **Previous Action:** His mother *bore* a child.
d. The dress is **made** of silk. e. The door is **locked** now. f. He bought a **used** car.	d. **Previous Action:** The dress *was made* by someone. e. **Previous Action:** The door *was locked* by the janitor. f. **Previous Action:** The car *was used* by another owner.

[3]These forms are sometimes called "stative passives."

EXAMPLES	EXPLANATION
Many people are **involved** in making a movie. Hollywood is **located** in California. Is Geraldine Chaplin **related** to Charlie Chaplin? We are **done** with the video. When you are **finished** with the video, return it to the store. Is the theater **air-conditioned**? The theater was very **crowded**.	In some cases, we use a past participle as an adjective even though there is no previous action. The sentences to the left have no equivalent active form.
a. The glass is **broken**. b. Don't touch the **broken** glass. a. The child is **lost** in the park. b. Let's take the **lost** child to the park office. a. The child seems **tired**. b. Let's put the **tired** child to bed.	Past participles can be used: a. after *be* and other linking verbs (*seem, look, feel, sound,* etc.). <center>OR</center> b. before a noun.
Chaplin was a ***well*-known** actor. He was a ***highly* paid** actor.	To emphasize and further describe the adjectives used as past participles, an adverb can be added.

Language Notes:
1. Some phrases that contain an adverb + past participle are:

   a well-liked teacher   a highly skilled worker
   a well-educated person   a closely watched experiment
   a well-behaved child   a slightly used book
   a well-dressed woman   closely related languages
   a well-fed dog   an extremely crowded room

2. The following are some common combinations of **be** + past participle:

be air-conditioned	be filled (with)	be married (to)
be accustomed (to)	be finished (with)	be permitted (to)
be allowed (to)	be gone	be pleased (to) (with) (by)
be born	be injured	be prepared (to) (for)
be broken	be insured	be related (to)
be closed	be interested (in)	be taken (*occupied*)
be concerned (about)	be involved (in)	be used
be crowded	be known (for) (as)	be used to
be divorced (from)	be located	be worried (about)
be done	be locked	be wounded
be dressed	be lost	
be educated	be made (of, in)	

EXERCISE 16 **Underline the past participle in the following sentences.**

EXAMPLE   Movie theaters are <u>crowded</u> on Saturday night.

1. The movie theater is closed in the morning.
2. Where is the movie theater located?
3. How many people were involved in making *WALL-E*?
4. Children are not allowed to see some movies.
5. Many movies are made in Hollywood.
6. Ronald Reagan was involved in movies before he became a politician.
7. Chaplin was born in England.
8. He was not an educated man.
9. Chaplin was a well paid actor.
10. He was well known all over the world.
11. Charlie Chaplin was married several times.

EXERCISE 17 **Find the mistakes and correct them. Not every sentence has a mistake. If the sentence is correct, write C.**

EXAMPLES   The theater located near my house.
                                 is

Are you interested in action movies?   *C*

1. Is Halle Berry marry?

2. I'm concerned about the violence in movies.

3. Almost every seat in the theater is fill.

4. Is this seat taken?

5. How many people are involved in making a movie?

6. Walt Disney born in 1901.

7. When you're finish with the DVD, please return it to the video store.

8. Is the Oscar make of gold?

Being Famous

Before
You Read

1. In the U.S., movie stars get divorced a lot. Is this true in other countries?

2. Do you think being famous would be fun?

CD 1, TR 13

Read the following Web article. Pay special attention to *be* and *get* before past participles and adjectives.

http://www.hollywood*lives.com

Becoming a Hollywood star is a dream for many. Glamour, money, beauty, and even power make the occupation very attractive. However, the life of a Hollywood star can **be difficult** and **challenging**, both personally and professionally.

Hollywood stars **are known** for their short and frequent marriages—and divorces. Elizabeth Taylor

Elizabeth Taylor and Richard Burton

got married eight times. In fact, she married the same man (Richard Burton) twice—and divorced him twice. Britney Spears **got married** one day and **got divorced** the next day. But, of course, there are exceptions. Paul Newman and Joanne Woodward **were married** for 50 years, until Newman died. And Meryl Streep **has been married** to the same man for over 30 years.

Why is **being famous** so difficult? Some actors **get rich** overnight and don't handle their sudden wealth and fame easily. Life can **be difficult** in the public eye, when reporters record an actor's every moment. Also, Hollywood stars need to look great to stay on top. They do not like to **get old**. Many Hollywood stars use cosmetic surgery to look young. Many work out with a personal trainer because they don't want to **get fat** or out of shape.

(continued)

Some Hollywood actors go into politics when they **get tired** of acting. They use their popularity as actors to win elections. Ronald Reagan and Arnold Schwarzenegger both went from being actors to becoming governor of California. Ronald Reagan went on to become president of the U.S.[4] A famous wrestler, Jessie Ventura, even got to be governor of Minnesota. Life in the public eye seems wonderful, but it can **be difficult** at times.

Schwarzenegger as actor

Schwarzenegger as governor

2.12 Past Participles and Other Adjectives with *Get*[5]

EXAMPLES	EXPLANATION
a. *Is* Julia Roberts **married**? b. When did she *get* **married**?	a. *Be* + past participle describes the status of a noun over a period of time.
a. The actress *is* **divorced**. b. She *got* **divorced** soon after she *got* **married**.	b. *Get* + past participle means *become*. There is no reference to the continuation of this status.
a. You're yawning. I see you *are* **tired**. b. When Arnold Schwarzenegger *got* **tired** of acting, he went into politics.	
a. Movie stars *are* **rich**. b. A lot of people would like to **get rich** quickly.	a. *Be* + adjective describes the status of a noun over a period of time.
a. My grandfather *is* **old**. b. Most stars don't want to **get old**. They want to look young forever.	b. *Get* + adjective means *become*.

Usage Note: Notice the difference between *to be married, to marry, to get married.*
Meryl Streep **is married**. She **has been married** to the same man for many years. (*Be married* describes one's status.)
She **married** Don Gummer in 1978. (The verb *marry* is followed by an object.)
Meryl and Don **got married** in 1978. (*Get married* is not followed by an object.)

[4]Schwarzenegger can't become president because he was not born in the U.S.
[5]For a list of expressions with *get*, see Appendix C.

Past Participles with *get*		Adjectives with *get*	
get accustomed to	get hurt	get angry	get old
get acquainted	get lost	get dark	get rich
get bored	get married	get fat	get sleepy
get confused	get scared	get hungry	get upset
get divorced	get tired	get nervous	get well
get dressed	get used to		
get worried			

EXERCISE 18 **Circle the correct words to complete this conversation between a young man and a young woman.**

CD 1, TR 14

A: Angelina Jolie is my favorite actress. When she (*was* / (got)) married,
(example)

I felt so sad. But then she (*was* / *got*) divorced just two years later,
(1)

I was so happy. But then, she started dating Brad Pitt.

B: Happy? Sad? Do you think Angelina (*is* / *gets*)
(2)

interested in you? She doesn't even know you!

A: I keep sending her letters. I would like to (*be* / *get*)
(3)

acquainted with her.

B: She's not going to answer your letters. She

(*is* / *gets*) too rich and famous to pay attention to you.
(4)

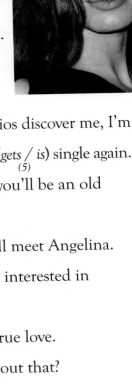

A: Well, I'm an actor too, you know.

B: Mostly you're just a waiter.

A: I'm not always going to be a waiter. When acting studios discover me, I'm

going to be famous, and Angelina will notice me if she (*gets* / *is*) single again.
(5)

B: Well, it's possible that she'll (*get* / *be*) divorced. But you'll be an old
(6)

man when, and if, you are famous.

A: That doesn't matter. Someday it will happen, and I'll meet Angelina.

B: By that time, she will (*be* / *get*) old and you won't be interested in
(7)

her anymore.

A: I'll always (*get* / *be*) interested in her. She's my one true love.
(8)

B: Oh, really? What does your girlfriend have to say about that?

A: I never talk to her about Angelina. One time I told her how much

I like Angelina, and she (*was* / *got*) angry.
(9)

B: I don't think your girlfriend has anything to worry about.

Summary of Lesson 2

1. Passive Voice

Passive Voice = *Be* + Past Participle	Use
With an agent: Mickey Mouse **was created** by Walt Disney. *Star Wars* **was directed** by George Lucas.	The passive voice can be used with an agent, especially if we want to emphasize the result of the action.
Without an agent: a. Hollywood **was built** at the beginning of the twentieth century. b. Children **are** not **allowed** to see some movies. c. The Oscar ceremony **is seen** all over the world. d. I **was told** that you didn't like the movie.	The passive voice is usually used without an agent: a. when it is not important to mention who performed the action b. when the agent is obvious c. when the agent is not a specific person but people in general d. to hide the identity of the agent **Note:** Do not mention the agent if it is not a specific person. *Wrong:* Spanish is spoken *by people* in Mexico.

Reagan **got shot** in 1981.
No one **got killed**. Some people **got wounded**.
	Get can be used instead of *be* in certain conversational expressions. Do not use *get* when the agent is mentioned.
	    Wrong: Reagan got shot *by John Hinckley.*
	    Right: Reagan **was** shot *by John Hinckley.*

2. Participles Used as Adjectives

Examples	Explanation
a. Silent movies are very **interesting**. b. The students are **interested** in the life of Charlie Chaplin.	Use the present participle (a) to show that the noun (silent movies) produced a feeling. Use the past participle (b) to show that the noun (the students) received a feeling.
The movie theater will be **closed** at midnight. Is this seat **taken**?	Use the past participle to show the result of a previous action. **Previous Actions:** Someone *will close* the theater. Someone *took* the seat.
The child is **lost**. The bus is **crowded**. Where is Hollywood **located**?	Some past participles are not related to a previous action.
She **got confused** when the teacher explained participles. I **got lost** on my way to your house. She **got upset** when she couldn't find her keys.	Use *get* with past participles and other adjectives to mean *become*.

Editing Advice

1. Use *be*, not *do / does / did* to make negatives and questions with the passive voice.

   wasn't
   My watch ~~didn't~~ made in Japan.

   was
   When ~~did~~ the movie filmed?

2. Don't use the passive voice with intransitive verbs.

   The accident ~~was~~ happened at 10:30 p.m.

   Her grandfather ~~was~~ died three years ago.

3. Don't confuse the *-ing* form with the past participle.

   eaten
   The popcorn was ~~eating~~ by the child.

4. Don't forget the *-ed* ending for a regular past participle.

   ed
   The floor was wash ʌ by the janitor.

   d
   I'm very tire ʌ now. I have to go to sleep.

5. Don't forget to use a form of *be* in a passive sentence.

   was
   The movie ʌ seen by everyone in my family.

6. Use *by* to show the agent of the action.

   by
   Tom Sawyer was written ~~for~~ Mark Twain.

7. Use an object pronoun after *by*.

   her
   My mother prepared the soup. The salad was prepared by ~~she~~ too.

8. In questions and negatives, use *do*, *does*, or *did* when you use *get* with the passive voice.

   Did
   ~~Were~~ you get fired from your job?

9. Don't forget to include a verb (usually *be*) before a participle used as an adjective.

      is
My college ˄ located on the corner of Broadway and Wilson Avenues.

     was
The movie ˄ boring, so we left.

10. Use *be*, not *do*, with past participles used as adjectives.

     isn't
My sister ~~doesn't~~ married.

  Are
~~Do~~ you bored in your math class?

Editing Quiz

Some of the shaded words and phrases have mistakes. Find the mistakes and correct them. If the shaded words are correct, write *C*.

    C
A: Did you ever see the movie *Titanic*? It was the most successful
  (example)   **made**
  film ever ~~make~~.
    (example)

B: I saw part of it. It was shown on my flight to the U.S. But I never
       (1)

  finished watching it because I fell asleep. It was a long and tiring
                (2)

  flight. I was too exhaust to keep my eyes open.
      (3)

A: You were probably bore because you saw it on a tiny screen. It
        (4)   *(5)*

  should seen on a large screen or at a theater. It's such an interested
  (6)   *(7)*

  movie. It was direct for James Cameron.
     (8) *(9)*

B: I've never heard of James Cameron. What else was he directed?
                 (10)

A: The *Terminator* movies. And *Avatar* was directed by he too. *Avatar* is
             (11)   *(12)*

  a 3-D movie.

B: What's that? I've never heard of 3-D.

A: It's a movie with a lot of special effects. Special glasses are worn during
(13)

the movie, which make everything appear three-dimensional.

B: Wow! I'd like to see a movie like that.

A: I saw it in 3-D at a theater. I was eaten popcorn when the movie
(14)

was started and then, suddenly, I couldn't believe what I was seeing.
(15)

B: When did Avatar made?
(16)

A: In 2009.

B: Is it still in the movie theaters?

A: No, but the DVD can rented.
(17)

B: Can it be seeing in 3-D on DVD?
(18)

A: I don't know.

B: So, tell me. What was happened at the end of Titanic? Was the main
(19)   (20)

character died? Or did the man and woman get marry?
(21)   (22)   (23)

A: I'm not going to tell you the ending and spoil it for you. I have the

DVD. I've been watched it three times. Do you want to borrow it?
(24)

B: Thanks. I'd love to.

Lesson 2 Test/Review

PART 1 **Fill in the blanks with the passive or active form of the verb in parentheses ( ). Use the tense indicated.**

EXAMPLES   The movie _____will be filmed_____ in New York.
(future: film)

The movie director _____has won_____ many awards.
(present perfect: win)

1. Which actor _____ next year?
(future: choose)

(continued)

2. Meryl Streep _____ in many movies.
(present perfect: see)

3. My sister _____ popcorn during movies.
(simple present: not/eat)

4. A new movie _____ about World War II.
(present continuous: make)

5. I _____ the Oscar ceremony last year.
(past: not/see)

6. The audience _____ the movie.
(past: enjoy)

7. We _____ our tickets tomorrow.
(future: buy)

8. Her parents _____ her to watch R-rated movies.
(present: not/permit)

9. While the movie _____, one of the actors
(past continuous: make)

_____.
(past: hurt)

10. *Star Wars* is a great movie. It _____ on a large
(should/see)

screen, not on a TV screen.

11. Today's animation _____ on a computer. It
(simple present: do)

_____ by hand.
(simple present: not/draw)

12. Charlie Chaplin _____ interested in acting at
(past: become)

the age of five.

13. Chaplin _____ the U.S. in 1952 and
(past: leave)

_____ in 1972.
(past: return)

14. President Lincoln _____ while he
(past: shoot)

_____ a play. He _____ a few
(past continuous: watch)   (past: die)

days later. The killer _____.
(past: catch)

PART 2 The following sentences would be better in the passive voice. Change to the passive voice using the same tense as the underlined verbs. Do not mention the agent.

EXAMPLE   They <u>considered</u> Charlie Chaplin a great actor.
Charlie Chaplin was considered a great actor.

1. They <u>use</u> subtitles for foreign movies.

   _____

2. They <u>don't permit</u> children to see this movie.

   _____

3. When <u>did</u> they <u>build</u> this theater?

   _____

4. Someone <u>is cleaning</u> the theater now.

   _____

5. Someone <u>has left</u> a popcorn box on the floor.

   _____

6. Someone <u>will make</u> a movie about Chaplin's life.

   _____

7. When <u>is</u> someone <u>going to close</u> the theater?

   _____

PART 3 The following sentences would be better in the active voice. Change to the active voice using the same tense as the underlined verbs.

EXAMPLE   The movie <u>has been seen</u> by my whole family.
My whole family has seen the movie.

1. I <u>will be driven</u> to the theater by my sister.

   _____

2. The movie <u>wasn't seen</u> by me.

   _____

3. The movie <u>is being filmed</u> by George Lucas.

   _____

4. A decision <u>should be made</u> by the director.

   _____

5. A new costume <u>is needed</u> by the actor.

   _____

(continued)

6. <u>Were</u> you <u>met</u> at the theater by your friend?

_____

7. When <u>was</u> the DVD <u>broken</u> by the child?

_____

PART 4 **Fill in the blanks with the present participle or the past participle of the verb in parentheses ( ).**

EXAMPLES   The movie was very good. It wasn't ___**boring**___ at all.

(bore)

I liked the ending of the movie. I felt very __**satisfied**__ with the ending.

(satisfy)

1. We read an _____ story about Charlie Chaplin.

(interest)

2. He became _____ in acting when he was a child.

(interest)

3. He was well _____ all over the world.

(know)

4. When he left the U.S. in 1952, he was not _____ to re-enter.

(allow)

5. Chaplin was _____ four times.

(marry)

6. He was an _____ actor.

(entertain)

7. I am never _____ during one of his movies.

(bore)

8. There's an _____ new movie at the Fine Arts Theater.

(excite)

9. Are you _____ in seeing it with me?

(interest)

10. The movie theater is _____ on Saturday night.

(crowd)

11. I was _____ when I saw _Friday the 13th_.

(frighten)

12. It was a very _____ movie.

(frighten)

13. I didn't like the movie I saw last week. I was very _____ in it.

(disappoint)

14. My friend liked the movie. He thought it was a very

_____ movie.

(excite)

Expansion

Classroom Activities

1 Tell if these statements are true in your native country. Form a small group and discuss your answers in your group.

1. Popcorn is sold in movie theaters.
2. Movie tickets can be bought on the Internet.
3. Most people have a DVD player and watch movies at home.
4. Musicals are popular.
5. Many movies are shown in the same theater at the same time.
6. Movie tickets are expensive.
7. Senior citizens pay less money to enter a movie theater.
8. Children are not allowed to see some movies.
9. Actors are well-paid.
10. Many famous actors get divorced.
11. Actors are given awards for great performances.
12. Animated films are popular.

2 Make a list of the movies you've seen recently. Compare your list with another student's list.

Talk About It

1 Is it important to give awards to actors and actresses? Why or why not?

2 Have you ever seen an Academy Awards ceremony? What did you think of it?

3 How are American films different from films made in other countries?

4 Who are your favorite actors and actresses?

5 What American movies have been popular in your native country?

About It

1 Write about an entertainment event that you have recently attended (such as a movie in a theater, a concert, an art fair, or a museum exhibit). Did you enjoy it? Why or why not? Was there anything surprising or unusual about it?

2 Write a short summary of a movie you saw recently.

3 Write about a famous person you admire. Give a short biography of this person and tell why you admire him or her.

EXAMPLE

A Person I Admire

I really admire actress Angelina Jolie. She's not only an amazing and talented actress, she's also a humanitarian. When she was filming in Cambodia, she was shocked by the conditions she saw there . . .

 For more practice using grammar in context, please visit our Web site.

Grammar

The Past Continuous[1]

The Past Perfect

The Past Perfect Continuous[2]

Comparison of Past Tenses

Context

Disasters and Tragedies

[1]The past continuous is sometimes called the *past progressive*.
[2]The past perfect continuous is sometimes called the *past perfect progressive*.

3.1 Overview of Past Tenses

In this lesson, we will be looking at all the past tenses.

TENSE	EXAMPLES
Simple Past Tense	She **drove** to her sister's house last night.
Past Continuous	She **was driving** when the accident happened.
Present Perfect	She **has driven** there many times.
Present Perfect Continuous	She **has been driving** since she was 18 years old.
Past Perfect	She knew the road well because she **had driven** it many times.
Past Perfect Continuous	She **had been driving** for three hours when the accident happened.

The *Columbia* Tragedy

Before You Read

1. What well-known accidents do you remember from history?

2. Do you remember what you were doing when a famous event occurred?

CD 1, TR 15

Read the following textbook article. Pay special attention to the past continuous and the simple past tense verbs.

Did You Know?

The Columbia *was the first reusable space vehicle. Before the* Columbia, *manned space flight had been limited to rockets, which could only be used once, making the space program much more expensive.*

On January 16, 2003, the space shuttle *Columbia* **left** on a science mission orbiting the Earth, with seven crew members aboard. It **stayed** in space for 16 days. On February 1, 2003, it **was traveling** back to Earth after completing its mission. NASA (the National Aeronautics and Space Administration) **received** its last communication from the *Columbia* on February 1, 2003, at 9:00 A.M. While the *Columbia* **was flying** over east Texas just 16 minutes from its landing in Florida, it **disintegrated**.[3] Families who **were** happily **waiting** for the return of their relatives at the Kennedy Space Center in Florida **received** the tragic news. People all over the world **were** shocked and saddened by this tragic loss of lives.

NASA **studied** the causes of this disaster. The investigation **concluded** that a piece of the left wing **fell** off as the *Columbia* **was lifting off**. This **created** a hole in the wing, and super-hot gases **entered** the wing's interior. As the *Columbia* **was approaching** its final destination, its left wing **burned**.

[3]*To disintegrate* means to break into small pieces.

The *Columbia* **was** the United States' second major disaster in space. The first one **was** in January 1986, when the space shuttle *Challenger* **exploded** 73 seconds after liftoff, killing all seven crew members.

NASA **was going to send** another manned rocket into space in March 2003, but this mission **was** postponed. Safety issues **needed** to be studied before another mission could take place. The next manned mission **didn't take place** until 2005.

1957	The USSR[4] puts the first satellite in space to orbit the Earth.
1961	The USSR puts the first man into space.
1966	The USSR lands a spacecraft on the moon.
1969	The first astronauts walk on the moon (Americans).
1970s and 1980s	The USSR and the U.S. explore Venus, Mars, Jupiter, and Saturn in fly-bys.
1986	The USSR launches the space station *Mir*.
1986	The U.S. spacecraft *Challenger* explodes shortly after liftoff. All seven crew members die.
1995	U.S. astronauts meet Russian cosmonauts at space station *Mir*.
2003	Seven U.S. astronauts are killed in the *Columbia* shuttle disaster.
2004	The U.S. lands a spacecraft on Mars.
2005	The U.S. sends seven astronauts into space in the spacecraft *Discovery*.

[4]The USSR no longer exists as a country. In 1991, it broke up into 15 countries, the largest of which is Russia.

3.2 The Past Continuous Tense—Forms

Statements

Subject	Was/Were	Present Participle	Complement	Explanation
I She He It The rocket	was	traveling	fast.	To form the past continuous tense, use *was* or *were* + present participle (verb + *-ing*).
We You They The astronauts	were			

Language Notes:
1. To make the negative, put *not* between *was/were* and the present participle.
   I **was** *not* **living** in the U.S. in January 2003.
   Americans **were** *not* **expecting** this tragedy.
2. The contraction for *were not* is *weren't*. The contraction for *was not* is *wasn't*.
3. An adverb can be placed between *was/were* and the present participle.
   You **were** *probably* **watching** the news.

Questions and Short Answers

Question Word	Was/Wasn't Were/Weren't	Subject	Present Participle	Complement	Short Answer
	Was	the rocket	traveling	fast?	Yes, it was.
How fast	was	it	traveling?		
	Weren't	they	flying	over Florida?	No, they weren't.
Where	were	they	flying?		
	Were	you	watching	it on TV?	No, I wasn't.
Why	weren't	you	watching	it on TV?	
Who	was		watching	it on TV?	

Passive

Subject	Was/Were	Being	Past Participle	Complement
The landing	was	being	filmed.	
Experiments	were	being	done	in space.

EXERCISE 1 Fill in the blanks with the correct form of the verb in parentheses ( ). Use the past continuous tense.

EXAMPLE The *Columbia* ___was approaching___ Florida.
(approach)

1. Family members _____.
(wait)

2. The *Columbia* _____ over Texas.
(travel)

3. It _____ over Florida.
(not/travel)

4. It _____ to Earth after a successful mission.
(return)

5. The astronauts _____ forward to seeing their families.
(look)

6. Reporters _____ to interview the astronauts.
(prepare)

7. How many people _____?
(wait)

8. Where _____?
(they/wait)

3.3 The Past Continuous Tense—Uses

EXAMPLES	EXPLANATION

What **were** you **doing** at 9:00 A.M. on February 1, 2003?
    I **was watching** TV.
    My brother **was sleeping**.
	The past continuous tense is used to show that an action was in progress at a specific past time. It didn't begin at that time.

The *Columbia* **disintegrated** while it **was traveling** back to the Earth. Family members **were waiting** in Florida when the *Columbia* accident **happened**. The *Columbia* **was approaching** the Earth when it **lost** communication with NASA.	We use the past continuous tense together with the simple past tense to show the relationship of a longer past action to a shorter past action.
While the astronauts **were orbiting** the Earth, they **were doing** scientific studies. While the *Columbia* **was approaching** its Florida destination, family members **were waiting** for the astronauts.	The past continuous can be used in both clauses to show that two past actions were in progress at the same time.

(continued)

EXAMPLES	EXPLANATION
Compare *when* and *while*. a. **While** the *Columbia* **was flying** over Texas, it disintegrated. b. The *Columbia* was flying over Texas **when** it **disintegrated**.	The meaning of sentences (a) and (b) is basically the same. a. *While* is used with a past continuous verb (*was flying*). In conversation, many people use *when* in place of *while*. b. *When* is used with the simple past tense (*disintegrated*).
As the *Columbia* was approaching its final destination, its left wing burned. **While** the *Columbia* was approaching its final destination, its left wing burned.	*As* and *while* have the same meaning.
The astronauts **were going to** return with scientific data. Family members **were going to** celebrate with the astronauts. NASA **was going to** send astronauts into space in March 2003, but this mission was postponed.	*Was/were going to* means that a past plan was not carried out.

Punctuation Note:
If the time clause precedes the main clause, separate the two clauses with a comma.
    The *Columbia* was flying over Texas when it disintegrated. (No comma)
    When the *Columbia* disintegrated, it was flying over Texas. (Comma)

EXERCISE 2   **ABOUT YOU** Ask and answer. Ask the student next to you what he or she was doing at this particular time.

EXAMPLE   at 4 A.M.

    A: What were you doing at 4 A.M.?
    B: I was sleeping, of course.

1. at ten o'clock last night
2. at seven o'clock this morning
3. at two o'clock last night
4. when the teacher entered the classroom today
5. at _____ (*your choice of time*)
6. while the teacher was explaining the past continuous

EXERCISE 3 **Fill in the blanks with the simple past or the past continuous form of the verb in parentheses ( ).**

EXAMPLE   We _____*were watching*_____ cartoons on TV when we
                          (watch)

_____*heard*_____ the bad news.
            (hear)

1. While the *Columbia* _____ to Earth, it
                                (return)

_____.
   (disintegrate)

2. My sister _____ when I _____ her
                  (sleep)   (wake)

up to tell her about the accident.

3. When my father _____ about the accident,
                          (hear)

he _____ to work.
      (drive)

4. My brother _____ a TV program when the disaster
                    (watch)

_____.
   (happen)

5. While the *Columbia* _____ to Earth, family
                                (return)

members _____ in Florida.
            (wait)

6. What _____ when the accident
            (you/do)

_____?
   (happen)

7. The *Challenger* _____ off when it
                          (lift)

_____ in 1986.
   (explode)

8. Many people _____ the *Challenger* liftoff when the
                      (watch)

accident _____.
              (occur)

The Past Continuous; The Past Perfect; The Past Perfect Continuous; Comparison of Past Tenses   **103**

3.4 The Past Continuous or the Simple Past

EXAMPLES	EXPLANATION

Compare:
a. What **were** you **doing** when you heard the news?
   I **was watching** TV.
b. What **did** you **do** when you heard the news?
   I **called** my sister.
 	
a. She **was driving** to work when she had an accident.
b. She **called** the police when she had an accident.
	a. Use the past continuous to show what was in progress *at* the time a specific action occurred.
	
	b. Use the simple past to show what happened *after* a specific action occurred.

a. On February 1, 2003, relatives **were waiting** in Florida for the astronauts. They **were getting** ready to celebrate. Camera crews **were preparing** to take pictures of the landing. Suddenly, at 9:00 A.M., just minutes before the landing, NASA lost communication with the *Columbia*. b. A NASA official **announced** the tragedy to the public. The president **went** on TV to express his sadness. NASA **began** an investigation of the accident. Investigators **went** to Texas to talk with witnesses.	a. Use the past continuous to show the events *leading up to* the main event of the story (the accident). b. Use the simple past tense to tell what happened *after* the main event of the story (the accident).

EXERCISE 4 Fill in the blanks to complete these conversations.

CD 1, TR 16

1. *A reporter is interviewing a family in Texas after the* Columbia *disaster.*

A: What _____were you doing_____ at 9 A.M. on February 1, 2003?

                        (example: you/do)

B: I _____. A loud noise _____

          (1 sleep)   *(2 wake)*

me up. I _____ out of bed and

               (3 jump)

_____ outside. I saw my husband outside.

    (4 run)

He _____ our car. We thought it was an earthquake.

       (5 fix)

Then we _____ pieces of metal on our property.

              (6 see)

I _____ to pick up a piece, but my husband told me

    (7 go)

not to. Instead we _____ the police. They told us not

                        (8 call)

to touch anything.

2. A reporter is interviewing a member of NASA after the Columbia disaster.

A: How fast _____ when the accident
               (9 the Columbia/travel)

_____?
(10 happen)

B: It _____ at 12,500 m.p.h. We
    (11 travel)

_____ with the *Columbia* when, suddenly,
(12 communicate)

communication _____.
              (13 stop)

A: What _____ when you _____
       (14 you/do)   (15 realize)

that the crew members were lost?

B: We _____ the family members and the press.
    (16 notify)

Many of the family members _____ at the Kennedy
                  (17 wait)

Space Center in Florida when the accident _____.
                  (18 happen)

A: What _____ after that?
    (19 happen)

B: An investigation _____. We
              (20 begin)

_____ to look for the pieces of the shuttle and
(21 start)

_____ to understand the reason for the accident.
(22 try)

A: _____ all the pieces?
  (23 you/find)

B: No, of course not. Many of the people of East Texas

_____ to tell us about finding pieces on their land.
(24 call)

Hunters _____ to tell us that while they
       (25 call)

_____ in forests, they _____
(26 hunt)   (27 find)

pieces of metal. We _____ enough pieces to come to
       (28 find)

a conclusion about the cause of the accident.

EXERCISE 5   **Fill in the blanks with the simple past or the past continuous tense of the verb in parentheses ( ).**

EXAMPLES   I _____was walking_____ to school when I _____saw_____ a car
             (walk)   (see)

accident. The police _____came_____ and _____gave_____
                       (come)   (give)

a ticket to one of the drivers.

1. I _____ ready for bed when someone
       (get)

_____ to my door. I _____ the door
   (come)   (open)

and saw my neighbor. He _____ in front of me with a
                     (stand)

DVD in his hand. He said, "I just rented a movie. Would you like to

watch it with me?" I didn't want to be impolite, so I said yes. While we

_____ the movie, I _____ asleep.
   (watch)   (fall)

2. While the baby _____, the babysitter
       (sleep)

_____ TV. Suddenly the baby _____
   (watch)   (start)

to cry, and the babysitter _____ into the room to see
                (run)

what had happened. She _____ up the baby and
                (pick)

started to rock her. Then she _____ her back to bed.
                (put)

3. When I _____ home, my sister and brothers
       (get)

_____ TV. I said, "I'm hungry. Let's eat." But they
   (watch)

_____ off the TV. I _____ to cook
   (not/turn)   (start)

dinner. They all _____ into the kitchen to see what I
                (come)

_____.
   (cook)

4. She _____ to the radio while she
       (listen)

_____ on the computer. Suddenly she
   (work)

_____ the news of a terrible accident. She
   (hear)

_____ to the TV to find out more information.
   (go)

5. While Sam _____, his cell phone
      (drive)

_____. He _____ on his phone
  (ring)   (talk)

when he _____ a car accident. He
      (have)

_____ a light post. Fortunately, he
  (hit)

_____ his seatbelt, so he wasn't hurt.
  (wear)

6. When the storm _____ last night, we
      (begin)

_____ a scary movie. The lights went out, so we
  (watch)

_____ to use candles. While I _____
  (have)   (look)

for matches and candles, my little brother suddenly

_____ the room with a flashlight and a scary mask.
  (enter)

He really _____ me.
     (scare)

7. While I _____ for my gloves in a drawer, I
     (look)

_____ an old photograph of myself. In this photo, I
  (find)

_____ a silly looking bathing suit. I can't even
  (wear)

remember who _____ the picture.
      (take)

8. I _____ my composition on the computer when
  (type)

suddenly we _____ electrical power. When the power
      (lose)

_____ back on, I _____ on the
  (come)   (turn)

computer, but all my work was gone. I know how important it is to

save my work. I _____ to save it on my flash drive,
      (go)

but I couldn't find it. So I _____ everything and
      (lose)

_____ to start all over.
  (have)

The *Titanic*

1. Have you ever traveled by ship? Where did you go? What was the trip like?

2. Did you see the 1997 movie *Titanic*? If so, did you enjoy it? Why or why not?

CD 1, TR 17

Read the following textbook article. Pay special attention to the past perfect tense.

Did You Know?

Only four female passengers in first class died. (These women chose to stay with their husbands.) Almost half of the female passengers in third class died.

The year was 1912. The radio **had** already **been invented** in 1901. The Wright brothers **had** already **made** their first successful flight in 1903. The *Titanic*—the ship of dreams—**had** just **been built** and was ready to make its first voyage from England to America with its 2,200 passengers.

The *Titanic* was the most magnificent ship that **had** ever **been built**. It had luxuries that ships **had** never **had** before: electric light and heat, electric elevators, a swimming pool, a Turkish bath, libraries, and much more. It was built to give its first-class passengers all the comforts of the best hotels.

But rich passengers were not the only ones traveling on the *Titanic*. Most of the passengers in third class were emigrants who **had left** behind a complete way of life and were coming to America with hopes of a better life.

The *Titanic* began to cross the Atlantic Ocean on April 10. The winter of 1912 **had been** unusually mild, and large blocks of ice **had broken** away from the Arctic region. By the fifth day at sea, the captain **had received** several warnings about ice, but he was not very worried; he didn't realize how much danger the ship was in. On April 14, at 11:40 P.M., an iceberg was spotted⁵ straight ahead. The captain tried to reverse the direction of his ship, but he couldn't because the *Titanic* was traveling too fast and it was too big. It hit the iceberg and started to sink.

The *Titanic* **had** originally **had** 32 lifeboats, but 12 of them **had been removed** to make the ship look better. While the ship was sinking, rich people were put on lifeboats. Women and children were put on the lifeboats before men. By the time the third-class passengers were allowed to come up from their cabins, most of the lifeboats **had** already **left**.

Several hours later, another ship arrived to help, but the *Titanic* **had** already **gone** down. Only one-third of the passengers survived.

---

⁵To *spot* means *to see suddenly.*

3.5 The Past Perfect Tense—Forms

Statements

Subject	*Had*	*Not /* Adverb	Past Participle	Complement	Explanation
The captain	**had**		**received**	several warnings.	To form the past perfect, use *had* + past participle.
He	**had**	not	**paid**	attention.	
The winter	**had**		**been**	unusually mild.	
The ship	**had**	originally	**had**	32 lifeboats.	
Some passengers	**had**	never	**been**	on a ship before.	

Language Notes:
1. The pronouns (except *it*) can be contracted with *had*: *I'd, you'd, she'd, he'd, we'd, they'd.*
   He'd received several warnings.
2. Apostrophe + **d** can be a contraction for both *had* or *would*. The verb form following the contraction will tell you what the contraction means.
   He'd spoken. = He *had* spoken.
   He'd speak. = He *would* speak.
3. For a negative contraction, use *hadn't*.
   He **hadn't** paid attention.
4. For an alphabetical list of irregular past tenses and past participles, see Appendix M.

Questions and Short Answers

Question Word	*Had*	Subject	Past Participle	Complement	Short Answer
	Had	the *Titanic*	**crossed**	the ocean before?	No, it **hadn't**.
How much experience	had	the captain	**had**?		
Who	had		**heard**	of the *Titanic* before?	

(continued)

Passive

Subject	*Had*	Adverb	*Been*	Past Participle
Lifeboats	had		been	removed.
Many passengers	had	never	been	found.
The airplane	had	already	been	invented.

EXERCISE **6**   **Fill in the blanks with the past perfect tense of the verb in parentheses ( ) plus any other included words.**

EXAMPLE   When we read about the *Titanic*, the story was not new to me because I

_____**had seen**_____ the movie.
(see)

1. The captain of the *Titanic* _____
(make)

a serious mistake when he didn't listen to the warnings.

2. When the *Titanic* disaster occurred, how much experience

_____?
(the captain/have)

3. I didn't realize that airplanes _____
(passive: *invent*)

by the time of the *Titanic*.

4. In 1912, World War I _____.
(not/yet/begin)

5. The story about the *Titanic* was new to me because I

_____ an article about it before.
(never/read)

6. _____ this story
(you/already/hear)

before we read about it in class?

7. How many lifeboats _____?
(have/the Titanic/originally)

8. Why_____?
(they/passive: *remove*)

3.6 The Past Perfect Tense—Use

The past perfect tense is used with the simple past tense to show the relationship of two past events.

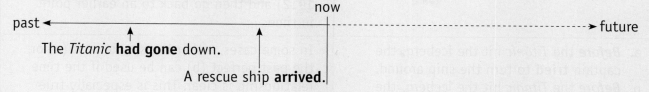

EXAMPLES	EXPLANATION
By the time the rescue ship *arrived*, the *Titanic* **had** already **gone** down. By *1912*, the Wright brothers **had** already **invented** the airplane.	The past perfect is used to show that something happened before a specific date, time, or action.
When people *got* on the lifeboats, the rescue ship **hadn't arrived** *yet*. *When* the rescue ship *arrived*, many passengers **had** *already* **died**.	The past perfect is used to show that something happened or didn't happen before the verb in the *when* clause. *Yet* and *already* help show the time relationship.
There was a lot of ice in the water *because* the previous winter **had been** unusually mild. I knew about the *Titanic* *because* I **had seen** a movie about it.	The past perfect can be used after *because* to show a prior reason.
The captain *didn't realize* how close his ship **had come** to the iceberg. I *didn't know* that you **had seen** a movie about the *Titanic*.	The past perfect can be used in a noun clause[6] when the main verb is past.
The passengers in third class were emigrants *who* **had left** behind their old way of life. The *Titanic* was the most magnificent ship *that* **had** *ever* **been built**.	The past perfect can be used in a *who/that/which* clause to show a prior action. The past perfect is sometimes used with *ever* after a superlative form.
When they *began* their trip to America, many emigrants on the *Titanic* **had** *never* **left** their homelands *before*.	The past perfect can be used with *never . . . before* in relation to a past event (in this case, *they began their trip*).
The ship **had been** at sea *for five days* when it hit an iceberg.	The past perfect can be used with *for* + a time period to show the duration of an earlier past action.

[6]For more about noun clauses, see Lesson 9.

(continued)

EXAMPLES	EXPLANATION
The year of the *Titanic* disaster **was** *1912*. The airplane **had** already **been invented**.	The simple past and the past perfect do not have to occur in the same sentence. We can start at some point in time (in this case, 1912) and then go back to an earlier point in time.
a. **Before** the *Titanic* hit the iceberg, the captain **tried** to turn the ship around. b. **Before** the *Titanic* hit the iceberg, the captain **had tried** to turn the ship around. a. The captain *realized* that he **made** a mistake. b. The captain *realized* that he **had made** a mistake.	In some cases, either the simple past (a) or the past perfect (b) can be used if the time relationship is clear. This is especially true with *before, after, because,* and in a noun clause (after *knew, realized, understood,* etc.).

EXERCISE 7 Fill in the blanks with the simple past or the past perfect tense of the verb in parentheses ( ).

EXAMPLE The *Titanic* had luxuries that ships _____had never had_____ before.
(never/have)

1. By 1912, the radio _____.
   (passive: already/invent)

2. The *Titanic* was the biggest ship that _____.
   (passive: ever/build)

3. The *Titanic* _____ 32 lifeboats.
   (originally/have)

4. When the *Titanic* _____ England, many of the
   (leave)

   lifeboats _____.
   (passive: remove)

5. By April 1912, pieces of ice _____ away from
   (break)

   the Arctic region.

6. The captain of the *Titanic* _____ attention
   (not/pay)

   to the warnings he _____.
   (receive)

7. When the *Titanic* _____ an iceberg, it
   (hit)

   _____ at sea for five days.
   (be)

8. By the time the poor emigrants _____ allowed to come
   (be)

   up from their cabins, most of the lifeboats _____.
   (already/leave)

9. By the time the rescue ship _____,
(arrive)

the *Titanic* _____.
(already/sink)

EXERCISE **8** **ABOUT YOU** **Tell if the following had already happened or hadn't happened yet by the time you got to class.**

EXAMPLE the teacher / collect the homework
By the time I got to class, the teacher had already collected the homework.

OR

When I got to class, the teacher hadn't collected the homework yet.

1. the teacher / arrive

2. most of the students / arrive

3. the class / begin

4. the teacher / take attendance

5. I / do the homework

6. the teacher / hand back the last homework

7. the teacher / explain the past perfect

EXERCISE **9** **Fill in the blanks with the simple past or the past perfect tense of the verb in parentheses ( ).**

EXAMPLE By the time the U.S. _____**sent**_____ a man into space (1962),
(send)

the Russians ____**had already put**____ a man in space (1961).
(already/put)

1. When an American astronaut _____ on the moon in
(step)

1969, no person _____ on the moon before.
(ever/walk)

2. By 2003, NASA _____ hundreds of successful
(complete)

space flights.

3. When the *Columbia* mission took off in 2003, NASA

_____ only two serious accidents in its space program.
(have)

4. By the time the 16 days were up, the *Columbia* crew

_____ all its scientific experiments.
(do)

(continued)

5. Until 9 A.M. on February 1, 2003, NASA _____ good
(have)

communication with the *Columbia*.

6. At first, NASA couldn't understand what _____.
(happen)

7. When they lost communication with the *Columbia*, they were

afraid that all of the astronauts _____.
(die)

8. The original date for the *Columbia* mission was July 2002. The date

was postponed until 2003 because cracks in the fuel line

_____.
(passive: find)

9. NASA _____ that the *Columbia*
(know)

_____ a piece of its wing on liftoff, but they didn't
(lose)

think it would be a problem.

10. They _____ that this problem
(not/realize)

_____ a hole in the wing.
(create)

11. By the time the investigation _____ in April 2003,
(end)

NASA _____ 40 percent of the pieces of the *Columbia*.
(collect)

12. By the time the U.S. _____ a mission to Mars, the
(send)

reasons for the *Columbia* accident _____.
(already/passive: discover)

3.7 *When* with the Simple Past or the Past Perfect

Sometimes *when* means *after*. Sometimes *when* means *before*.

EXAMPLES	EXPLANATION
a. **When** the captain saw the iceberg, he **tried** to turn the ship around. b. **When** the captain saw the iceberg, the ship **had been** at sea for five days.	If you use the simple past in the main clause (a), *when* means **after**.
a. **When** the *Columbia* lifted off, it **lost** a piece of its wing. b. **When** the *Columbia* lifted off in January 2003, it **had had** 27 successful missions.	If you use the past perfect in the main clause (b), *when* means **before**.

EXERCISE 10 **Write numbers to show which action happened first.**

EXAMPLES

 1   2
When she got home, she took an aspirin.

 2   1
When she got home, she had already taken an aspirin.

1. When they came into the room, their son left.

2. When they came into the room, their son had just left.

3. When I got home from school, I did my homework.

4. When I got home from school, I had already done my homework.

5. When she got to my house, she had eaten dinner.

6. When she got to my house, she ate dinner.

7. The teacher gave a test when Linda arrived.

8. The teacher had already given a test when Linda arrived.

EXERCISE 11 **Fill in the blanks with the verb in parentheses ( ). Use the simple past to show that *when* means *after*. Use the past perfect to show that *when* means *before*.**

EXAMPLES

When I saw the movie *Titanic*, I _____ **told** _____ my friends about it.
                                            (tell)

When I saw the movie *Titanic*, I __ **had never heard** __ of this ship before.
                                            (never/hear)

1. When people saw the *Titanic* for the first time, they

   _____ such a magnificent ship before.
          (never/see)

2. When the ship was built, people _____ amazed at how
                                              (be)

   beautiful it was.

3. When the ship left England, 12 lifeboats _____.
                                                   (passive: remove)

4. When the Arctic ice started to melt, pieces of ice

   _____ away.
          (break)

5. When the ship hit an iceberg, the captain _____
                                                    (receive)

   several warnings.

(continued)

The Past Continuous; The Past Perfect; The Past Perfect Continuous; Comparison of Past Tenses   115

6. When the passengers heard a loud noise, they _____
(run)

to get on the lifeboats.

7. When the *Titanic* sank, a rescue ship _____ to pick
(come)

up the survivors.

8. When the rescue ship arrived, many passengers

_____ .
(already/die)

9. When the *Columbia* accident happened, the astronauts

_____ in space for 16 days.
_(be)_

10. When people in East Texas heard a loud sound, they

_____ it was an earthquake.
(think)

11. When the *Columbia* accident happened, people

_____ shocked.
_(be)_

12. When relatives of the astronauts heard the news, they

_____ to cry.
(start)

13. When they were in their fields, farmers in East Texas found pieces

of the *Columbia* that _____ on their land.
(fall)

14. When the investigation into the cause of the accident was finished,

NASA _____ to send astronauts into space again.
(begin)

Wildfires in Southern California

1. Do you know about any fires that burned for a long time?

2. Do you know anyone who has lost a home because of a natural disaster?

CD 1, TR 18

Read the following magazine article. Pay special attention to the past perfect and the past perfect continuous tenses.

Did You
Know?

California has had many wildfires. Some of the California fires started from natural causes, such as lightning. But it is believed that the 2009 fires, which destroyed 64 homes and killed two firefighters, were started by arson.

In October 2003, wildfires in San Diego County burned out of control. Many residents had to leave their homes as they were warned of the approaching fire. They watched and waited as firefighters battled the fire.

One of the fires was started accidentally by a lost hunter in a forest, who **had been trying** to signal his location. Strong winds spread the fire quickly. The San Diego area **had had** very little rain or humidity, and there were millions of dry dead trees that caught fire quickly.

The fire **had been burning** for a week by the time firefighters got it under control. Many residents returned only to find that they **had lost** their homes and all their possessions. "We **had been living** in the same house for the past 26 years when we lost our home," said a San Diego woman, whose family went to stay with relatives nearby. "Now we have nothing, not even a photograph of our former lives."

Many of the firefighters were exhausted because they **had been working** around the clock to get the fire under control. Firefighters from other areas in the U.S. came to help contain the fire. By the time the fire was brought under control, over 2,400 homes and businesses **had been destroyed** and 16 people **had died**.

3.8 The Past Perfect Continuous Tense—Forms

Statements

Subject	*Had*	*Not /* Adverb	*Been*	Present Participle	Complement	Explanation
We	had		been	living	in the same house.	To form the past perfect continuous tense, use: *had + been + verb –ing.*
Firefighters	had		been	working	around the clock.	
California	had	not	been	getting	much rain.	
A hunter	had	probably	been	trying	to send a signal.	

Questions and Short Answers

Question Word	*Had*	Subject	*Been*	Present Participle	Complement	Short Answer
	Had	it	been	raining?		No, it **hadn't.**
How long	had	the fire	been	burning?		
	Had	you	been	living	in that house?	Yes, we **had.**
Who	had		been	living	in that house?	

EXERCISE **12** **Fill in the blanks with the past perfect continuous tense.**

EXAMPLE Firefighters ___had been working___ around the clock to control the fire.
(work)

1. The fire _____ for two days by the time firefighters
(burn)

   put it out.

2. We _____ in the same house for 30 years when
(live)

   the fires started.

3. A hunter _____ to send a signal.
(try)

4. The families of the astronauts _____ for several hours
(wait)

   when they heard the news.

5. The *Titanic* _____ for five days when it sank.
(travel)

3.9 The Past Perfect Continuous Tense—Uses

The past perfect continuous tense is used with the simple past tense to show the relationship of two past events.

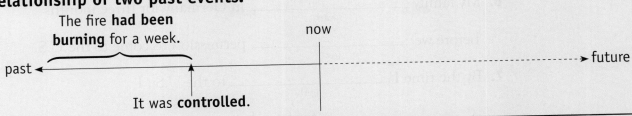

EXAMPLES	EXPLANATION
The fire **had been burning** *for a week* by the time it was controlled. We **had been living** in the same house *for 26 years* when we lost our home.	The past perfect continuous tense is used with a continuous action that was completed before another past action. The duration of the continuous action is expressed with *for*.
a. When the fire started, Southern California **had had** very little rain. b. When residents returned, they found out that their homes **had been destroyed**. c. By the time the fire ended, 16 people **had died**.	We use the past perfect, not the past perfect continuous, with: a. nonaction verbs b. an action of little or no duration c. multiple or repeated actions

EXERCISE **13** Fill in the blanks with the simple past tense or the past perfect continuous tense of the verb in parentheses ( ).

EXAMPLE When I ____came____ to the U.S., I ___had been studying___
                (come)   (study)

     English for three years.

1. I _____ for two years when I _____
        (wait)   (get)

     a chance to leave my country.

2. I _____ in the same house all my life when I
        (live)

     _____ my city.
        (leave)

3. I _____ very sad when I left my job because I
        (feel)

     _____ with the same people for ten years.
        (work)

4. I _____ to be a nurse for six months when a
        (study)

   war _____ in my country.
        (break out)

(continued)

5. When I _____ my country, the war
         (leave)

_____ for three years.
(go on)

6. My family _____ in Germany for three months
                      (wait)

before we _____ permission to come to the U.S.
                  (get)

7. By the time I _____ to the U.S., I
                          (get)

_____ for four days.
(travel)

EXERCISE **14**

CD 1, TR 19

Fill in the blanks with the past perfect continuous tense for a continuous action. Fill in the blanks with the past perfect tense for a one-time action, multiple or repeated actions, or a nonaction verb.

In the year 1800, the population of Chicago was only 5,000. But the population __had been growing__ steadily since the beginning of the
                          (example: grow)
century. In 1871, Chicago __had recently passed__ St. Louis to become
                                  (example: recently/pass)
the fourth largest city in the U.S. Chicago _____ a place
                                                      (1 reach)
of importance when the Great Chicago Fire began on October 8, 1871.

That October was especially dry because there _____
                                                          (2 be)
very little rain. At the time, most of the streets, sidewalks, bridges, and
buildings were made of wood. On Sunday night, a fire broke out in a barn. The
firefighters were exhausted that night because they _____
                                                              (3 fight)
a fire since the day before. Strong winds from the south quickly spread the
fire to the center of the city. When the firefighters finally arrived at the

fire, the fire _____ out of control. It wasn't until two days
(4 spread)

later, when rain began to fall, that the fire finally died out. By this time,

almost 300 people _____ and more than one hundred
(5 die)

thousand Chicagoans _____ their homes. Millionaires,
(6 lose)

who _____ in mansions, as well as poor laborers, found
(7 live)

themselves homeless. Chicagoans, rich and poor, who

_____ contact with each other, gathered in parks and
(8 have/never)

wondered how they would rebuild their lives.

Because of its great location for industry, Chicago remained strong

after the fire. By 1873, the city _____, this time with brick
(9 passive: rebuild)

instead of wood. Chicago continued to grow as a commercial center, and,

by 1890, its population _____ more than one million.
(10 reach)

Today Chicago is the third largest city in the U.S.

3.10 The Past Perfect (Continuous) Tense or the Present Perfect (Continuous) Tense

The past perfect (continuous) tense and the present perfect (continuous) tense cannot be used interchangeably.

EXAMPLES	EXPLANATION
Have you ever **seen** a movie about the *Titanic*? I **have** never **been** on a ship. How many disasters **have** we **read** about so far?	The present perfect is used when we look back from the present time.
When the *Titanic* was built, people **had** never **seen** such a magnificent ship before. By the time the fires ended in California, many people **had lost** their homes.	The past perfect is used when we look back from a past time.

(continued)

EXAMPLES	EXPLANATION
The U.S **has been exploring** space since the 1950s. Lately, we **have been reading** stories about disasters.	The present perfect continuous is used when we look back from the present time to a continuous action. 1950s now past ◄———————┼ - - - - - - ► future has been exploring
When the *Columbia* accident happened, it **had been orbiting** the Earth for sixteen days. When the *Titanic* sank, it **had been traveling** for five days.	The past perfect continuous is used when we look back from a past time to a prior continuous action. 2003 now past ◄———————┼ - - - - - - ► future had been orbiting

EXERCISE 15 Fill in the blanks with the present perfect, the present perfect continuous, the past perfect, or the past perfect continuous tense of the verb in parentheses ( ). In some cases, answers may vary.

A: I'm really interested in space exploration.

CD 1, TR 20

B: How long _____ <u>have you been</u> _____ interested in it?
(example: you/be)

A: Ever since I was a child. By the time I was 10 years old, I

_____ to the space museum in Washington, D.C.
(1 be)

about five times.

B: Who took you?

A: My parents took me most of the time. But one time my fifth grade

class _____ all semester about space, and
(2 study)

our teacher took the class. Since that time, I _____
(3 always/dream)

about becoming an astronaut. I saw a film about the first moon

landing in 1969. It was so exciting to think that no man

_____ on the moon before.
(4 ever/walk)

B: Do you think it's possible for you to become an astronaut?

A: Sure. Why not? I _____ my bachelor's degree in
(5 already/get)

engineering. Lately I _____ a lot about the training that
(6 read)

astronauts go through. I _____ to NASA asking them
(7 already/write)

to send me more information on how to get into the space program.

And next semester I'm going to enter a master's program in physics.

B: Don't you have to be a pilot first?

A: Yes. I _____ 500 hours of flying lessons.
(8 already/take)

B: Aren't you worried about the risks of going into space? NASA

_____ several major disasters so far.
(9 have)

A: Of course there are risks. But the space program needs to continue.

By the time of the *Columbia* disaster, it _____ 27
(10 already/have)

successful missions. And in general, there _____
(11 be)

more successes than failures up to now. Since the *Columbia* tragedy,

NASA _____ ways to improve the safety of its astronauts.
(12 study)

Hurricane Katrina

Before You Read

1. Has your native country ever experienced a natural disaster, such as a hurricane or tornado?

2. How did the country and the people recover from this natural disaster?

The Past Continuous; The Past Perfect; The Past Perfect Continuous; Comparison of Past Tenses **123**

Read the following magazine article. Pay special attention to past tense verbs (simple past, past continuous, past perfect, past perfect continuous, present perfect, and present perfect continuous).

New Orleans **has been** a favorite tourist attraction for Americans. It is known for its great music, fun nightlife, interesting food, historic buildings, and pleasant climate. For many years, tourists **have been going** to New Orleans to experience the fun of Mardi Gras[7] in February or March. But all of this **changed** in August 2005.

New Orleans, which is several feet below sea level, **has** always **depended** on levees[8] to protect it from surrounding water. In August 2005, a hurricane **was traveling** over the Gulf of Mexico, causing damage from Florida to Texas. As the hurricane **was approaching** and **gaining** strength, the mayor of New Orleans **ordered** the residents to leave. By the time the storm **hit** land on August 29, most people **had left**. But there **were** many people who **were** too poor or sick to leave. Others **stayed** because they **didn't want** to leave pets behind. Some **believed** that they **had survived** smaller flooding in the past and that they would survive this one too. But the impact of the hurricane **caused** the levees to fail, and within a short time, 80 percent of the city **was** underwater. As the water **was rushing** into their houses, residents **ran** to the roofs of their houses to wait for rescue teams. Some **had been waiting** for three days by the time they **were rescued**.

Little by little, families **were evacuated** from the roofs of their houses. By the time the rescue effort **was** over, at least 1,800 people **had died** by drowning or from lack of food, water, and medical attention. Many of the rescued **were taken** to shelters. When they **were** finally able to return to their homes, they **realized** that they **had lost** everything.

To this day, New Orleans **has** not **been** able to recover from the devastation of Katrina. Since the disaster **struck**, the city **has been rebuilding**, hoping to bring New Orleans back to its place as one of the most interesting cities in the U.S. And the survivors of this disaster **have been trying** to rebuild their lives too. Some **have started** lives in new locations, too sad or afraid to go back to the places where they **had experienced** so much loss. Many **have had** to replace everything they **had lost** in the disaster.

Hurricane Katrina **has been** the worst natural disaster in U.S. history to date.

[7]*Mardi Gras* is a carnival. It occurs the last day before Lent begins. Lent, which ends with Easter, is a serious period for Christians.
[8]A *levee* is a wall built to hold back water.

3.11 Comparison of Past Tenses

EXAMPLES	EXPLANATION
a. The mayor **ordered** the residents to leave. b. My grandmother **lived** in New Orleans for 30 years. c. The hurricane **hit** land on August 29, 2005. d. We **visited** New Orleans five times.	The **simple past tense** shows an action that started and ended in the past. It does not show the relationship to another past action. It can be used for a short action (a) or a long action (b). It can be used for a single action (c) or a repeated action (d).
On August 29, the hurricane **was approaching** quickly. As the water **was rushing** into the houses, residents ran to the roofs.	The **past continuous tense** shows that something was in progress at a specific time in the past.
a. When the storm **hit**, most people **had left**. b. By the time the rescue effort **was over**, 1,800 people **had died**.	The **past perfect tense** shows the relationship of an earlier past action to a later past action. a. earlier = *had left*; later = *hit* b. earlier = *had died*; later = *was over*
Some people **had been waiting** *for three days* by the time they **were rescued**. The *Titanic* **had been traveling** *for five days* when it **sank**.	The **past perfect continuous tense** is used with a continuous action of duration that happened before another past action. *For* is used to show the duration of the previous action.
New Orleans **has** always **been** a tourist attraction. California **has had** many fires.	The **present perfect tense** uses the present time as the starting point and looks back.
Since 2005, New Orleans residents **have been trying** to put their lives back together. NASA **has been exploring** space since the 1950s.	The **present perfect continuous tense** uses the present time as the starting point and looks back at a continuous action that is still happening.
a. *When* the hurricane **hit**, people went to the roofs of their houses. b. *When* the hurricane **hit**, some people **were sleeping**. c. *When* the hurricane **hit**, many people **had** already **left** their homes.	Be especially careful with *when*. In sentence (a), they went to the roofs *after* the hurricane hit. In sentence (b), they were sleeping *at the same time* the hurricane hit. In sentence (c), they left their homes *before* the hurricane hit.

Language Notes:
1. Sometimes the past continuous and the past perfect continuous can be used in the same case. The past perfect continuous is more common with a *for* phrase.
   - People **were waiting** on their roofs when they were rescued.
   - People **had been waiting** on their roofs *for three days* when they were rescued.
2. Sometimes the simple past or the past perfect can be used in the same case.
   - Some people **had taken** a few things before they left.
   - Some people **took** a few things before they left.

EXERCISE **16** **Fill in the blanks with the correct past tense. Use the passive voice where indicated. In some cases, more than one answer is possible.**

EXAMPLE Hurricane Katrina _____**struck**_____ New Orleans on August 29, 2005.
$\hspace{8.5cm}$ (strike)

1. Many hurricanes _____ New Orleans over the years.
$\hspace{4cm}$ (strike)

2. _____ New Orleans?
$\hspace{0.5cm}$ (you/ever/visit)

3. By the time rescuers came, many people _____.
$\hspace{9cm}$ (already/die)

4. When I came to the U.S., I _____ of New Orleans
$\hspace{5.5cm}$ (never/hear)
before.

5. How many disaster stories _____ so far?
$\hspace{6cm}$ (we/read)

6. What _____ when you _____ the
$\hspace{2cm}$ (you/do) $\hspace{4cm}$ (hear)
news about Katrina?

7. I _____ TV when I _____ the news.
$\hspace{1.2cm}$ (watch) $\hspace{5.5cm}$ (hear)

8. I have a friend who left his home in New Orleans in 2005. He
_____ in Chicago since 2005. He has never returned
$\hspace{1.5cm}$ (live)
to New Orleans.

9. The *Titanic* _____ in Ireland.
$\hspace{3.5cm}$ (passive: build)

10. The *Titanic* _____ fast when it
$\hspace{3.5cm}$ (travel)
_____ an iceberg.
$\hspace{1cm}$ (hit)

11. Many people _____ when they
$\hspace{3.5cm}$ (sleep)
_____ a loud noise.
$\hspace{0.8cm}$ (hear)

12. When third-class passengers _____ to the top deck,
$\hspace{6.5cm}$ (go)
most of the lifeboats _____.
$\hspace{3.5cm}$ (already/leave)

13. A few hours later, another ship _____, but the *Titanic*
$\hspace{6cm}$ (arrive)
_____.
$\hspace{0.5cm}$ (already/sink)

14. In 1985, the ship _____ in the North Atlantic.
(passive: find)

15. In 1912, the sinking of the *Titanic* was the worst tragedy that

_____.
(ever/occur)

16. People are still interested in the *Titanic*. People _____
(be)

interested in it for almost a hundred years.

EXERCISE 17 **A teacher and a student are talking about heroes in the Hurricane Katrina disaster. Fill in the blanks with the correct past tense to complete this conversation. In some cases, more than one answer is possible.**

CD 1, TR 22

S: Yesterday we _____ **read** _____ the story about
(example: read)

Hurricane Katrina. _____ New Orleans?
(1 you/ever/visit)

T: I _____ New Orleans many times. It's one of my
(2 visit)

favorite cities in the U.S. I think I'll go back someday because

I love the food and the music there. Even though the city

_____ completely, tourists _____
(3 not/be/rebuild)   (4 start)

to go back. _____ in the U.S. in August 2005,
(5 you/live)

at the time of Hurricane Katrina?

S: No, I _____. I _____ in Mexico
(6)   (7 live)

at that time. But we _____ about the hurricane on
(8 hear)

the news. We heard many interesting rescue stories.

T: I'm always interested in rescue stories. Which one interested you the most?

S: In 2005, I _____ an interesting program about the
(9 see)

heroes of Hurricane Katrina, and one of them was a six-year-old boy.

T: What _____?
(10 he/do)

(continued)

S: After the hurricane, volunteer workers _____ (11 find) a six-year old boy with six other small children. He was the oldest in the group, and he _____ (12 carry) a five-month-old baby. There were five other small children with him. By the time rescue workers found them, they _____ (13 walk) around the streets for several hours. The oldest boy, Deamonte Love, told the volunteers that a helicopter _____ (14 take) them from their parents and that his mother _____ (15 cry) when they _____ (16 leave).

T: What _____ (17 happen) next? _____ (18 they/find) his mother?

S: Yes. A few days later, his mother _____ (19 passive: find) in a shelter.

T: How did she get separated from her children?

S: While the family and neighbors _____ (20 wait) to be rescued, their building filled with water. They went to the roof and waited. A helicopter _____ (21 arrive) and picked up the kids. They said that they would come back in 25 minutes for the adults. But the helicopter _____ (22 not/come) back. By the time the adults were rescued a few days later, they _____ (23 live) without electricity or food for four days.

T: I didn't realize that so many children _____ (24 become) separated from their parents. Were all the children brothers and sisters?

S: No. The baby was Deamonte's brother and the others were cousins and neighbors.

T: Deamonte _____ (25 be) a real hero.

Summary of Lesson 3

1. Showing the relationship between two past actions:

The Past Perfect

The reference point is past.	Another action preceded it.
When the rescue ship **arrived**,	many people **had died**.
In **1912**,	the airplane **had** already **been invented**.

The Past Perfect Continuous

The reference point is past.	A continuous action preceded it.
The captain **couldn't turn** the ship around	because it **had been traveling** so fast.
When the family **was rescued**,	they **had been waiting** on the roof for three days.

The Past Continuous

An action was in progress . . .	. . . at a specific time or when a shorter action occurred.
They **were sleeping**	at 11:40 P.M.
We **were watching** TV	when we heard about the *Columbia* accident.

2. Relating the past to the present:

The Present Perfect	The Present Perfect Continuous
Have you ever **seen** the movie *Titanic*? I **have** never **seen** it, but I'd like to. I **have seen** two movies so far this month. I've always **been** interested in space exploration.	She is watching the movie now. She **has been watching** it for 45 minutes. I've **been reading** a book about space exploration.

3. Describing the past without relating it to another past time:

The Simple Past Tense
The mayor **ordered** the residents of New Orleans to leave. The hurricane **struck** on August 29, 2005. Some people **stayed**. They **didn't want** to leave their pets. Some families **lost** everything.

Editing Advice

1. The simple past tense does not use an auxiliary.

   came
   He ~~was come~~ home at six o'clock last night.

2. Don't forget *be* in a past continuous sentence.

   was
   I ‸ walking on the icy sidewalk when I fell and broke my arm.

3. Do not use a present tense for an action that began in the past. Use the present perfect (continuous) tense.

   have been
   I ~~am~~ married for ten years.

   has been
   She ~~is~~ working at her present job for seven months.

4. Don't forget *have* with perfect tenses.

   have
   I ‸ been living in the U.S. for six months.

5. Don't confuse the present perfect and the past perfect tenses. The past perfect tense relates to a past event. The present perfect tense relates to the present.

   had
   When I started college, I ~~have~~ never owned a laptop before.

   has
   She's a teacher now. She ~~had~~ been a teacher for 15 years.

6. Use the simple past tense with *ago*.

   came
   He ~~was coming~~ to the U.S. four years ago.

7. Use *when*, not *while*, for an action that has no continuation.

   when
   I was washing the dishes ~~while~~ I dropped a plate.

8. Use the simple past tense, not the present perfect tense, in a *since* clause.

   came
   She has had her car ever since she ~~has come~~ to the U.S.

9. Don't use the continuous form for a repeated action.

   drunk
   By the time I got to work, I had ~~been drinking~~ four cups of coffee.

10. Don't confuse the *-ing* form with the past participle.

   seen
   When he moved to Chicago, he had never ~~seeing~~ a skyscraper before.

11. Be careful to choose the correct past tense in a sentence with *when*.

   came
   When I left my hometown, I ~~had come~~ to New York.

   had begun
   When I arrived in class, the test ~~began~~ already.

12. Don't confuse active and passive.

   found
   In 1985, the *Titanic* was ~~finding~~.

Editing Quiz

Some of the shaded words and phrases have mistakes. Find the mistakes and correct them. If the shaded words are correct, write C.

saw
Last night I ~~seen~~ a program on TV about the survivors of the *Titanic*.
(example)

C
Even though I had already seen the movie *Titanic*, I was still interested in
(example)

this program because it told the stories of real people.

The last American survivor, Lillian Asplund, was died in 2006. She was
(1)

just five years old when she traveling on the ship with her parents and
(2)

brothers. They were returning to the U.S. from Sweden, where they have spent
(3)   (4)

several years.

She and her mother got on a lifeboat with one of her brothers, but her
(5)

father and other three brothers have waited. Her father promised that he
(6)   (7)

would get on the next lifeboat. When Lillian and her mother saw him for

the last time, her father was smile. She never saw her father and brothers
(8)   (9)

again. Her mother lived until the age of 91, but she had never gotten over
(10)   (11)

the tragedy of losing her husband and three sons.   (*continued*)

The last survivor was an English woman, Millvina Dean. At two months old, she has been (12) the youngest passenger on the *Titanic*. She and her family were immigrate (13) to the U.S. from England when the tragedy occurred (14). She and her mother and brother were rescuing (15), but her father went down with the ship. With her husband gone, Millvina's mother decided (16) to take the children back to England. Because Millvina was just a baby at the time, she had no memories of the tragedy and didn't even know that she had being (17) on the *Titanic* until she was eight years old. At that time, her mother told (18) her the story of what had happened (19). Until 1997, she has lived (20) quietly in England when, suddenly, journalists became (21) interested in her. She was invited (22) to travel by ship to the U.S. and she accepted (23). This was the second time in her life that she traveled by ship.

Ms. Dean died (24) in 2009 at the age of 97. Her brother died on April 14, 1992, the anniversary of the *Titanic* disaster! He was 80 years old.

It's amazing that people are still fascinated with the story of the *Titanic*. People are (25) interested in this story for 100 years! And I am (26) interested since I saw the movie *Titanic*.

PART 1 **Read a survivor's account of the night of the *Titanic* disaster.[9] Fill in the blanks with the simple past, the past perfect, or the past continuous tense of the verb in parentheses. In some cases, more than one answer is possible.**

We _____**had just fallen**_____ asleep when my wife
(example: just/fall)

_____ a noise. She _____ me up and
(1 hear)　　　　　　　　　　　　(2 wake)

_____ that something _____ to the
(3 say)　　　　　　　　　　　(4 happen)

ship. We _____ up on deck and everything
　　　　　(5 go)

_____ normal at first. The orchestra
(6 seem)

_____ .
(7 still/play)

At first the officers _____ that the *Titanic* could not
　　　　　　　　　　　(8 insist)

sink in less than ten hours. We were told that the *Titanic*

_____ with other nearby ships and that help would reach
(9 communicate)

us in an hour or two.

The crew _____ to lower the lifeboats. They
　　　　　(10 start)

_____ us that there _____ no danger,
(11 assure)　　　　　　　　　　　(12 be)

that they were just taking precautions.

After about six or seven lifeboats were lowered, people

_____ to realize that they _____ in great
(13 start)　　　　　　　　　　　(14 be)

danger. I saw an officer shoot two passengers who _____
　　　　　　　　　　　　　　　　　　　　　　(15 fight)

to get on a lifeboat.

The thirteenth boat _____ with about 25 children
　　　　　　　　　　(16 passive: fill)

and a few women. While the boat _____ , all of them
　　　　　　　　　　　　　(17 passive: lower)

_____ .
(18 scream)

I _____ one of the officers on the *Titanic* because
　(19 know)

I _____ with him before on another ship. He
　(20 travel)

_____ me into the thirteenth boat and
(21 push)

_____ me to take care of the children.
(22 order)

[9]This account is adapted from *The Bulletin*, San Francisco, April 19, 1912.

(continued)

The Past Continuous; The Past Perfect; The Past Perfect Continuous; Comparison of Past Tenses **133**

As our boat _____ (23 leave), we _____ (24 hear) the orchestra playing a religious song.

I will never forget the terrible scene as our boat _____ (25 move) away. Husbands and fathers _____ (26 wave) and _____ (27 throw) kisses to their wives and children.

The ship _____ (28 sink) only three hours after it _____ (29 hit) the iceberg.

PART 2 **Fill in the blanks with one of the past tenses: simple past, past continuous, present perfect (continuous), or past perfect (continuous). In some cases, more than one answer is possible.**

A: What ___**happened**___ (happen) to your car?

B: I _____ (1 have) an accident yesterday.

A: How _____ (2 it/happen)?

B: I _____ (3 drive) to work when a dog _____ (4 run) in front of my car. I _____ (5 stop) my car suddenly, and the car behind me _____ (6 hit) my car because the driver _____ (7 follow) me too closely.

A: _____ (8 you/get) a ticket?

B: No, but the driver who hit me did.

A: Who will pay to have your car fixed?

B: The other driver. When he _____ (9 hit) me, he _____ (10 get) out of his car and _____ (11 give) me his insurance card. He's a new driver. He _____ (12 only/have) his driver's license for two months.

A: You're a new driver too, aren't you?

B: Oh, no. I _____ (13 drive) for 20 years.

A: I thought you _____ (14 get) your driver's license a few months ago.

134   Lesson 3

B: In this state, I have a new license. But I _____ (15 have) a driver's license for many years before I _____ (16 move) here.

A: _____ you ever _____ (17 get) a ticket?

B: One time. I _____ (18 drive) about 65 miles an hour on the highway when a police officer _____ (19 stop) me. She said that the speed limit was only 55. She _____ (20 give) me a ticket for speeding. She also gave me a ticket because I _____ (21 not/wear) my seat belt.

Expansion

Classroom Activities

❶ **In a small group or with the entire class, turn to the person next to you and say a year. The person next to you has to tell a short story about his/her life at or before that time.**

EXAMPLES
2005
I had just graduated from high school. I was living with my parents. I hadn't thought about coming to the U.S. at that time.

1983
I hadn't been born yet.

2004
I had just had my second child. We were living with my wife's parents.

❷ **On an index card, write the following sentence, filling in the blank to make a true statement about yourself. The teacher will collect the cards and read the sentences. Try to guess who wrote the sentences.**

When I came to this school, I had never _____ before.

EXAMPLE   When I came to this school, I had never called a teacher by his first name before.

❸ **On an index card, write the following sentence, filling in the blank to make a true statement about yourself. The teacher will collect the cards and read the sentences. Try to guess who wrote the sentences.**

I've never _____, but I'd like to.

EXAMPLE   I have never gone fishing, but I'd like to.

Talk
About It

❶ Why do you think that women and children were put on lifeboats before men?

❷ Do you think the space program should continue?

Write
About It

❶ Choose one of the following topics and write a short composition.

- an accident or unusual experience that happened to you
- an important event in the history of your native country
- a famous person who died in an accident, assassination, or another unusual way

❷ Write about a tragedy in recent history. Tell what you *were doing* when you heard the news. Tell what you *did* when you heard the news.

EXAMPLE

> ### A Great Tragedy
>
> I was living in Peru when I heard about the
> September 11 tragedy in the U.S. I had just arrived at
> school, where I saw a lot of people talking and looking
> very sad. I asked my classmates what had happened...

 For more practice using grammar in context, please visit our Web site.

Grammar
Modals—Present and Future

Related Expressions

Context
Consumer Warnings

4.1 Overview of Modals and Related Expressions

The modal verbs are *can, could, shall, should, will, would, may, might,* and *must*.

EXAMPLES	EXPLANATION
She **should** leave. (advice) She **must** leave. (necessity) She **might** leave. (possibility)	Modals add meaning to the verbs that follow them.

He **can help** you.
They **should eat** now.
You **must pay** your rent.
	The base form follows a modal.
	    Wrong: He can *helps* you.
	    Wrong: They should *eating* now.
	    Wrong: You must *to* pay your rent.
	The modal never has an *-s* ending.
	    Wrong: He *cans* help you.

You **should not** leave now. He **cannot** speak English.	To form the negative, put *not* after the modal. *Cannot* is written as one word.
A pen **should be used** for the test. The movie **can be seen** next week.	A modal can be used in passive voice: modal + *be* + past participle
He **must** go to court. = He **has to** go to court. You **must not** park your car there. = You **are not supposed to** park your car there. He **can** speak English well. = He **is able to** speak English well.	The following expressions are like modals in meaning: *have to, have got to, be able to, be supposed to, be allowed to, be permitted to, had better.*
British: We **shall** study modals. **American:** We **will** study modals.	For the future tense, *shall* is more common in British English than in American English. Americans sometimes use *shall* in a question to make a suggestion or invitation. *Shall* we dance?

Language Note: Observe statements and questions with modals:
> **Affirmative:** He *can* speak German.
> **Negative:** He *can't* speak French.
> ***Yes/No* Question:** *Can* he speak English?
> **Short Answers:** Yes, he *can.*/No, he *can't.*
> ***Wh-* Question:** What languages *can* he speak?
> **Negative Question:** Why *can't* he speak French?
> **Subject Question:** Who *can* speak French?

Sweepstakes or Scam?

Before
You Read

1. Do you get a lot of junk mail?

2. What do you do with these pieces of mail?

CD 2, TR 01

Read the following magazine article. Pay special attention to modals.

Did you ever get a letter with your name printed on it telling you that you have won a prize or a large amount of money? Most people in the U.S. get these letters.

We often get mail from sweepstakes companies. A sweepstakes is like a lottery. To enter a sweepstakes, you usually **have to** mail a postcard. Even though the chances of winning are very small, many people enter because they have nothing to lose and **might** even win something.

Are these offers of prizes real? Some of them are. Why would someone give you a prize for doing nothing? A sweepstakes is a chance for a company to promote its products, such as magazines. But some of these offers **might** be deceptive,[1] and you **should** read the offer carefully. The government estimates that Americans lose more than one billion dollars every year through "scams," or tricks to take your money. You **should** be careful of letters, e-mails, and phone calls that tell you:

- You **must** act now or the offer will expire.
- You **may** already be a winner. To claim your gift, you only **have to** pay postage and handling.
- You've won! You **must** call a 900 number to claim your prize.
- You've won a free vacation. All you **have to** do is pay a service fee.

You **shouldn't** give out your credit card number or Social Security number if you are not sure who is contacting you about the sweepstakes.

Senior citizens **should** be especially careful of scams. Eighty percent of the victims of scams are 65 or older. They often think that they **have to** buy something in order to win a prize and often spend thousands of dollars on useless items. Or they think that their chances of winning **might** increase if they buy the company's product. But in a legitimate sweepstakes, you **don't have to** buy anything or send any money. The law states that "no purchase necessary" **must** appear in big letters. In addition, the company **is supposed to** tell you your chances of winning.

How **can** you avoid becoming the victim of a scam? If you receive a letter saying you are a guaranteed winner, you **ought to** read it carefully. Most people just throw this mail in the garbage.

---

[1]Something that is *deceptive* tries to make you believe something that is not true.

4.2 Possibilities—*May, Might, Could*

EXAMPLES	EXPLANATION
You **may** already be a winner. You **might** win a prize. This **could** be your lucky day!	Use *may, might, could* to show possibilities about the present or future.
She **may not** know that she is a winner. Some people **might not** understand the conditions of a sweepstakes.	For negative possibility, use *may not* or *might not*. Don't use *could not*. It means *was/were not able to*. Do not make a contraction with *may not* or *might not*.
Do you think I might win? **Do you think I could** get lucky?	To make questions about possibility with *may, might, could*, say, "Do you think . . . may, might, could . . .?" The clause after *Do you think* uses statement word order.
Compare: a. **Maybe** you are right. b. You **may be** right. a. **Maybe** he is a winner. b. He **may be** a winner.	*Maybe*, written as one word (a), is an adverb. It is usually put before the subject. *May be*, written as two words (b), is a modal + verb. The meaning of (a) and (b) are the same, but notice that the word order is different. *Wrong:* He *maybe* is a winner.

EXERCISE 1 Fill in the blanks with appropriate verbs to complete this conversation. Answers may vary.

A: What are you going to do this summer?

B: I haven't decided yet. I might _____**go**_____ back to Peru, or I may
(example)

_____ here and look for a summer job. What about you?
(1)

A: I'm not sure either. My brother might _____ here. If he
(2)

does, we might _____ some interesting places in the U.S. I
(3)

received a letter a few days ago telling me that if I mail in a postcard,

I could _____ a trip for two to Hawaii.
(4)

B: I don't believe those letters. When I get those kinds of letters, I just

throw them away.

A: How can you just throw them away? You could _____ a winner.
(5)

B: Who's going to give us a free trip to Hawaii for doing nothing?

A: Well, I suppose you're right. But someone has to win those prizes. It could _____ me. And if I buy a lot of magazines from this
(6)
company, my chances of winning might _____.
(7)

B: That's not true. Those letters always say, "No Purchase Necessary."

A: I really want to go to Hawaii with my brother.

B: Then I suggest you work hard and save your money.

A: I might _____ 90 years old by the time I have enough money.
(8)

EXERCISE 2 Answer these questions by using the word in parentheses ( ).

EXAMPLE   Is the company legitimate? (*might*)
It might be legitimate.

1. Does the company give out prizes? (*may*)
2. Are the prizes cheap? (*could*)
3. Will I be chosen as a winner? (*might*)
4. Will this company take my money and give me nothing? (*might*)
5. Will I win a trip? (*could*)

EXERCISE 3 **ABOUT YOU** Fill in the blanks with possible results for the following situations.

EXAMPLE   If I pass this course, _I might take a computer course next semester._

1. If I work hard, _____
2. If I save a lot of money, _____
3. If I drink a lot of coffee tonight, _____
4. If I eat a lot of sugar, _____
5. If I don't get enough sleep, _____
6. If I exercise regularly, _____
7. If I increase my computer skills, _____
8. If I win a lot of money, _____
9. If I come late to class, _____
10. If I don't do my homework, _____

4.3 Necessity and Urgency with *Must, Have To, Have Got To*

MODAL	EXPLANATION
Individuals and companies **must** (or **have to**) obey the law. Sweepstakes companies **must** (or **have to**) tell you the truth. "No Purchase Necessary" **must** (or **has to**) appear in big letters.	For legal obligation, use *must* and *have to*. *Must* has a very official tone. It is often used in court, in legal contracts (such as rental agreements), and in rule books (such as a book of driving rules and laws).

You **must** act now! Don't wait or you will lose this fabulous offer!
 	
You'**ve got to** act now!
 	
You **have to** act now!
	Must, have to, and *have got to* express a sense of urgency. All three sentences to the left have the same meaning.
	
	Have got to is usually contracted:
	   I have got to = I've got to
	   He has got to = He's got to

I'**ve got to** help my sister on Saturday. She **has to** move.	Avoid using *must* for personal obligations. It sounds very official or urgent and is too strong for most situations. Use *have to* or *have got to*.

Pronunciation Note: In relaxed, informal speech,
- *have to* is often pronounced "hafta."
- *has to* is pronounced "hasta."
- *have got to* is often pronounced "gotta." (*Have* is often not pronounced before "gotta.")

EXERCISE 4 **Fill in the blanks with an appropriate verb to talk about sweepstakes rules. Answers may vary.**

EXAMPLE   Sweepstakes companies must ____obey____ the law.

1. Sweepstakes companies must _____ "No Purchase Necessary" in big letters in the information they send to you.

2. Sweepstakes companies sometimes tell people that they must _____ a 900 number to win a prize.

3. Sweepstakes companies often tell people, "You must _____ now. Don't wait."

4. Companies must _____ the truth about the conditions of the contest.

5. If a sweepstakes company tells you that you must _____ something, it is not a legitimate sweepstakes.

EXERCISE **5** **Fill in the blanks with an appropriate verb (phrase) to talk about driving rules. Answers may vary.**

EXAMPLE   Drivers must ___stop___ at a red light.

1. A driver must _____ a license.
2. In a car, you must _____ a baby in a special car seat.
3. You must _____ when you hear a fire truck siren.
4. In many cities, drivers must _____ a parking sticker on their windshields.
5. A car must _____ a license plate.
6. In some cities, you must not _____ a cell phone while driving.

EXERCISE **6**   **ABOUT YOU**   **Fill in the blanks with words that describe personal obligations.**

EXAMPLE   I have to ___call my parents___ once a week.

1. After class, I've got to _____.
2. This weekend, I have to _____.
3. Before the next class, we've got to _____.
4. Every day I have to _____.
5. Once a month, I've got to _____.
6. When I'm not sure of the spelling of a word, I have to _____ _____.
7. Before I go to sleep at night, I have to _____.
8. A few times a year, I've got to _____.
9. My English isn't perfect. I have to _____.
10. Before I take a test, I've got to _____.

EXERCISE **7**   **ABOUT YOU**   **Make a list of personal obligations you have to do on the weekends.**

EXAMPLE   On Saturdays, I have to take my sister to ballet lessons.

_____
_____
_____

EXERCISE **8** **ABOUT YOU** Make a list of obligations you have at your job, at your school, or in your house.

EXAMPLE   At work, I've got to answer the phone and fill out orders.

_____

_____

_____

_____

_____

_____

4.4 Obligation with *Must* or *Be Supposed To*

EXAMPLES	EXPLANATION
"No Purchase Necessary" **must** appear in big letters. This is the law. The sweepstakes company **must** tell you your chances of winning. People who win money **must** pay taxes on their winnings.	*Must* has an official tone.
Compare: a. Police officer to driver: "You **must** wear your seat belt." b. Driver to passenger: "You**'re supposed to** wear your seat belt." a. Teacher to student: "You **must** write your composition with a pen." b. Student to student: "You**'re supposed to** write your composition with a pen."	a. A person in a position of authority (such as a police officer, parent, or teacher) can use *must*. The tone is very official. b. Avoid using *must* if you are not in a position of authority. Use *be supposed to* to remind someone of a rule.
Companies **are supposed to** follow the law, but some of them don't. Drivers **are supposed to** use a seat belt, but they sometimes don't. Students **are supposed to** be quiet in the library, but some talk.	*Be supposed to*, not *must*, is used when reporting on a law or rule that has been broken.

Pronunciation Note:
The ***d*** in *supposed to* is not usually pronounced.

EXERCISE **9** A teenager is talking about rules his parents gave him and his sister. Fill in the blanks with *be supposed to* + an appropriate verb. Answers may vary.

EXAMPLE   I <u>'m supposed to babysit</u> for my little sister when my parents aren't home.

1. I _____ my homework before I watch TV.
2. I (not) _____ on the phone with my friends for more than 30 minutes.
3. I _____ my room once a week. My mother gets mad when I leave it dirty.
4. If I go to a friend's house, I _____ my parents where I am so they won't worry.
5. I have a part-time job. I _____ some of my money in the bank. I (not) _____ my money on foolish things.
6. I _____ my parents with jobs around the house. For example, I _____ the dishes once a week. I _____ the garbage every day.
7. My sister _____ her toys away when she's finished playing.
8. She (not) _____ the stove.
9. She (not) _____ TV after 8 P.M.
10. She _____ to bed at 8:30 P.M.
11. We _____ our homework before dinner.

EXERCISE **10**   **ABOUT YOU** Report some rules in one of the following places: in your apartment, in court, in traffic, in a library, in class, on an airplane, or in the airport.

EXAMPLES   In my apartment, the landlord is supposed to provide heat in the winter.

On an airplane, we're not supposed to use a cell phone.

_____

_____

_____

_____

_____

_____

EXAMPLES   My sister is supposed to finish her homework before watching TV, but she usually watches TV as soon as she gets home from school.

I'm supposed to wash the dishes in my house, but I often leave them in the sink for the next day.

_____

_____

_____

_____

_____

_____

4.5 Advice with *Should, Ought To,* and *Had Better*

EXAMPLES	EXPLANATION
Senior citizens **should** be careful of scams. You **should** read the offer carefully to see what the conditions are.	*Should* shows advisability. It is used to say that something is a good idea.
You **shouldn't** give your credit card number to people you don't know. You **shouldn't** believe every offer that comes in the mail.	*Shouldn't* means that something is a bad idea. The action is not advisable.
If you receive a letter saying you are a winner, you **ought to** throw it away. You **ought to** work hard and save your money. Don't expect to get rich from a sweepstakes. You **ought to** be careful when someone offers you something for nothing.	*Ought to* has the same meaning as *should*. **Note:** *Ought* is the only modal followed by *to*. We don't usually use *ought to* for negatives and questions. Use *should*. *Ought to* is pronounced /ɔtə/.
I'm expecting an important phone call. I'**d better** leave my cell phone on so I won't miss it. You'**d better not** give your credit card number to strange callers, or they might use it to make purchases in your name.	*Had better (not)* is used in conversation to show caution or give a warning. A negative consequence may result. Use *'d* to contract *had* with a pronoun. In some fast speech, *'d* is omitted completely.
Compare: a. Companies and individuals **must** obey the law. b. You **should** read the letter carefully.	a. Use *must* for rules, laws, and urgent situations. b. Use *should* for advice.

EXERCISE **12** **Give advice to people who are saying the following. Answers will vary.**

EXAMPLES   I'm lonely. I don't have any friends.
You should get a dog or a cat for companionship.

I'm so tired. I've been working hard all day.
You ought to get some rest.

1. I've had a headache all day.

   _____

2. The teacher wrote something on my paper, but I can't read it.

   _____

3. Every time I write a composition and the teacher finds mistakes, I
   have to write it all over again.

   _____

4. I got a letter telling me that I won a million dollars.

   _____

5. My old TV doesn't work well anymore. It's too expensive to repair.

   _____

6. I received an offer for a new job. It pays double what I get now.

   _____

7. My car is making a strange noise. I wonder what it is.

   _____

8. I sit at a desk all day. I don't get enough exercise. I'm gaining weight.

   _____

9. Whenever I tell my personal problems to my coworker, he tells other
   people.

   _____

10. I have to write a résumé, but I don't have any experience with this.

    _____

EXERCISE 13 **ABOUT YOU** Give advice about what people should do or say in the following social situations in your native culture. Share your answers with the class.

EXAMPLE   If you are invited to someone's house for dinner, ___you should bring a small gift___.

1. If you invite a friend to eat in a restaurant, _____

2. If you bump into someone, _____

3. If you don't hear or understand what someone says, _____

4. If someone asks, "How are you?" _____

5. If you want to leave the dinner table while others are still eating, _____

6. If a woman with a small child gets on a crowded bus, _____

7. If you're invited to someone's house for dinner, _____

8. If you meet someone for the first time, _____

EXERCISE 14 Give a warning by using *you'd better (not)* in the following conversations. Answers may vary.

EXAMPLE   A: Someone's at the door. I'll go and open it.
           B: You ___'d better not open it___ if you don't know who it is.

1. A: The caller wants my Social Security number.
   B: Do you know who the caller is?
   A: No.
   B: You _____ him your Social Security number then.

2. **A:** I got a letter about a sweepstakes. Do you think I should enter?

   B: You've probably got nothing to lose. But you _____ the letter carefully to make sure that it's legitimate.

3. **A:** This offer says the deadline for applying is Friday.

   B: You _____. You don't have much time.

4. (*phone conversation*)

   A: Hello?

   B: Hello. I'd like to speak with Mrs. Green.

   A: Speaking.

   B: You are a winner! You _____ or you might lose this offer. You don't have much time.

   A: You keep calling me and telling me the same thing. You _____, or I'll report you.

5. **A:** You are the only person in the office who wears jeans.

   B: What's wrong with that?

   A: You _____ appropriately, or you might lose your job.

6. **A:** I don't like my supervisor's attitude. I'm going to tell her about it.

   B: You _____. She might not like it.

7. **A:** I typed my composition on the computer, but I forgot to bring a flash drive to save it. I'll just print it.

   B: Here. Use my flash drive. You _____ in case you have to revise it.

8. (*a driver and a passenger in a car*)

   A: I'm getting sleepy. Can you drive for a while?

   B: I can't. I don't have my driver's license yet. You _____ for a while.

Telemarketing

Before You Read

1. Do you ever get calls from people who are trying to sell you something? How do you respond to these calls?

2. Do you have Caller ID on your home phone?

CD 2, TR 03

Read the following Web article. Pay special attention to *may, can, be permitted to, be allowed to*, and other modals.

http://www.telemarketing*info.com

You have just sat down to dinner when suddenly the phone rings. Someone is trying to sell you a magazine, a phone service, or a vacation. Has this ever happened to you?

Millions of these calls are placed each year. Consumers became so annoyed with "robocalls" (calls with recorded messages) that the government passed a law in 2009 prohibiting companies from using them without your written permission. Companies that continue to use robocalls **may** face a penalty of $16,000 per call. But calls made by humans continue. If you find these calls annoying, as most people do, there is something you can do to take action.

In 2003, the U.S. government[2] created a "Do Not Call" registry. You **can** register your phone number online or by phone. If you do so, most telemarketers **are not permitted to** call you. However, some telemarketers **can** still call you: political organizations and charities. Also, companies with which you do business, such as your bank, **may** call you to offer you a new product or service. However, when they call, you **can** ask them not to call you again. If you make this request, they **are not allowed to** call you again.

It **may take** up to 31 days for your registration to take effect, and it lasts for as long as you keep your phone. You **can** register all of your phone numbers. In the meantime, here are some suggestions for dealing with telemarketers:

- You **could** get Caller ID to see who is calling.
- You **could** ask your phone company if they have a "privacy manager," a service that screens unidentified phone calls. The phone will not even ring in your house unless the caller identifies himself.

[2]The Federal Trade Commission (FTC) is the government department that created this registry.

- If you are not interested in the offer, you **can** try to end the phone call quickly. But you **shouldn't** get angry at the caller. He or she is just trying to make a living.
- If you do decide to buy a product or service, remember, you **should** never give out your credit card number if you are not sure who the caller is.

4.6 Permission and Prohibition

EXAMPLES	EXPLANATION
Political organizations **may** call you. (They **are permitted to** call you.) Charities **can** call you. (They **are allowed to** call you.)	Use *may* or *can* to show that something is permitted. Alternate forms are *be allowed to* and *be permitted to*.
If you put your phone number on a "Do Not Call" registry, companies **may not** call you. If you ask a company to stop calling you, this company **cannot** call you again.	Use *may not* or *cannot (can't)* to show that something is prohibited. *May not* has no contracted form.
You **can** wear jeans to class. **Can** you call your teacher by her first name?	In addition to legal permission, *can* also has the meaning of social acceptability.

Language Note: The meaning of *cannot* or *may not* (not permitted) is very similar to the meaning of *must not* (prohibited).

Compare:
a. You *can't* talk during a test.
b. You *may not* talk during a test.
c. You *must not* talk during a test.

a. You *can't* bring food into the computer lab.
b. You *may not* bring food into the computer lab.
c. You *must not* bring food into the computer lab.

EXERCISE 15 Fill in the blanks to talk about what is and isn't permitted. Answers will vary.

EXAMPLE We can _____talk_____ in the hall, but we can't _____talk_____ in the library.

1. If you put your name on a "Do Not Call" registry, companies may not _____.

2. In the library, you may not _____.

3. During a test, we can _____ but we cannot _____.

4. Books, CDs, and DVDs are protected by law. We are not permitted to _____.

5. In this building, we may not _____.

EXERCISE 16 **ABOUT YOU** Fill in the blanks with an appropriate permission word to talk about what is or isn't permitted in your native country.

EXAMPLES High school students ___are permitted to___ leave the school building for lunch.

Students _____can't_____ use a cell phone in class.

1. Teenagers _____ drive.

2. People under 18 _____ get married.

3. Children _____ work.

4. Children _____ see any movie they want.

5. A married woman _____ get a passport without her husband's permission.

6. Teachers _____ talk about religion in public schools.

7. Drivers _____ talk on a cell phone while driving.

8. Students _____ write in their textbooks.

9. People _____ travel freely.

10. People _____ live anywhere they want.

EXERCISE 17 Write about what is or isn't permitted in these places. Use *can, may, be allowed to,* or *be permitted to.*

EXAMPLES In the U.S., _teenagers can get a job._

In a theater, _you can't yell "fire."_

1. In the U.S., _____
2. In the computer lab, _____
3. In this classroom, _____
4. In a courtroom, _____
5. In my house/apartment building, _____
6. In an airplane, _____
7. In an airport, _____
8. In this city, _____

EXERCISE 18 **ABOUT YOU** Tell if these things are socially acceptable in your country or native culture.

EXAMPLE Students can call their teachers by their first names.
In my country, students can't call their teachers by their first names. It's very impolite.

1. Parents can take small children to a party for adults.
2. If you are invited to a party, you can invite your friends.
3. Students can wear jeans to class.
4. Students can use a cell phone in class.
5. Students can remain seated when the teacher enters the room.
6. Students can call their teachers by their first names.
7. Students can talk to each other during a test.
8. Students can argue with a teacher about a grade.
9. Teenagers can date.
10. Men and women can hold hands in public.

Identity Theft

Before You Read

CD 2, TR 04

1. What do you do with your important mail, such as bills or bank statements?

2. Do you have a password for different things, such as e-mail or an ATM? Do you memorize all your passwords?

Read the following conversation. Pay special attention to negative modals and related expressions.

A: I hate to have so much paper. Every time I get a credit card or bank statement, I just throw it in the garbage.

B: You **shouldn't** do that. Someone can steal your identity.

A: What do you mean?

B: There are identity thieves who go through the garbage looking for personal information, like bank account numbers or Social Security numbers. I read an article that said that about 9 million Americans have their identities stolen each year.

A: What do the thieves do with these numbers? They **can't** use my number without my credit card.

B: They can and they do. They can make a purchase by phone and charge it to your credit card. You **may not** realize that your identity has been stolen until you review your statement a month later.

A: So what should I do?

B: You **shouldn't** just throw away papers with personal information. You should shred them. I bought a shredder at an office supply store and shred all papers with my personal information. I've also started to do my banking online. That way I don't get so much paper in the mail.

A: How does that work?

B: For most of my bills, like electricity and telephone, the money goes directly to these companies from my checking account. I **don't** even **have to** write checks. And I **don't have to** pay for a stamp. And I **don't have to** worry about identity theft.

A: Can you help me sign up for online banking?

B: Sure. Let's go to your computer and find your bank's Web site. Now you have to choose a password.

A: I think I'll use my birth date.

B: You **shouldn't** use your birth date or any other obvious number.

A: OK. I chose another password, but it's rejected. I used my mother's maiden name.

B: You **can't** use all letters. Your bank says you have to choose a combination of letters and numbers.

A: OK. I've got one now. I'm going to write down the password in my checkbook.

B: You'd **better not**. What if someone steals your checkbook? You'd better memorize your password.

A: Now they're asking me all these questions: "What's your pet's name? Who was your favorite teacher? What's the name of your elementary school?" Why are they asking me all these questions?

B: Those are security questions. Only you know the answers to those questions. The bank wants to make sure it's you and not someone else going into your account.

A: Thanks for telling me about this.

4.7 Comparing Negative Modals

EXAMPLES	EXPLANATION
Students **must not** talk during the test. You **must not** park at a bus stop.	*Must not* shows that something is prohibited. There is no choice in the matter. *Must not* has an official tone.
Sweepstakes companies **are not supposed to** ask you for your Social Security number. I told the telemarketers not to call me anymore, but they did. They**'re not supposed to** do that.	*Be supposed to* is used as a reminder of a rule. It has an unofficial tone. Often the rule has already been broken.
You **can't** use all letters for your password. Telemarketers **may not** call you if you ask them to take you off their list.	*Cannot* and *may not* show that something is not permitted. The meaning is similar to *must not* but is less formal.
You **shouldn't** use your birth date as your password. You **shouldn't** give strange callers your credit card number.	*Should not* shows that something is a bad idea.
A: I'm going to write my password in my checkbook. **B:** You**'d better not**. What if someone steals your checkbook? **A:** I'm going to throw my credit card statement in the garbage. **B:** You**'d better not** do that. Someone might steal your identity.	*Had better not* gives a warning. A negative consequence is stated or implied.
The advantages of banking online are: • You **don't have to** use a stamp. • You **don't have to** remember to pay your bills. They are paid automatically. • There are no paper statements, so you **don't have to** worry so much about identity theft.	*Not have to* shows that something is not necessary or required.

Language Notes:

1. Even though *must* and *have to* are similar in meaning in affirmative statements, they are completely different in meaning in negative statements.

    Companies *must* obey the law. = Companies *have to* obey the law.

    You *must not* talk during the test. = This is prohibited.

    You *don't have to* use a pen for the test. = It is not necessary. You have a choice. You can use a pencil.

2. Don't confuse *should not* and *don't have to*.

    You *shouldn't* put important papers in the garbage. (It's not a good idea.)

    To enter a sweepstakes, you *don't have to* buy anything. (It's not necessary to buy anything.)

EXERCISE 19 **ABOUT YOU** Tell if students at this school or another school you have attended have to or don't have to do the following.

EXAMPLES wear a uniform
Students in my country don't have to wear a uniform.

take final exams
Students at this school have to take final exams.

1. stand up to answer a question
2. go to the board to answer a question
3. call the teacher by his or her title (for example, "Professor")
4. buy their own textbooks
5. pay tuition
6. attend classes every day
7. have a written excuse for an absence
8. get permission to leave the classroom
9. study a foreign language
10. attend graduation

EXERCISE 20 **ABOUT YOU** Tell if you have to or don't have to do the following.

EXAMPLES work on Saturdays
I have to work on Saturdays.

dress formally for school
I don't have to dress formally for school.

1. throw out the garbage every day
2. study English
3. get up early on Sundays
4. cook every day
5. come to school on Saturdays

EXERCISE 21 Fill in the blanks with *don't have to* or *must not*.

EXAMPLE If you receive a sweepstakes postcard, you ___don't have to___ send it back.

1. You _____ buy anything to win. No purchase is necessary.
2. Sweepstakes companies _____ break the law.
3. In a legitimate sweepstakes, you _____ call a 900 number to win a prize.

(continued)

Modals—Present and Future; Related Expressions **157**

4. I use automatic bill payment. I save money because I
_____ use a stamp to pay my bills.

5. You _____ steal. It's against the law.

6. If you register on the "Do Not Call" list, telemarketers
_____ call you.

7. You _____ register with the "Do Not Call" list. It's
your choice.

EXERCISE **22** **Fill in the blanks with *don't have to* or *should not* to describe situations in a public library.**

EXAMPLES   You _____shouldn't_____ make noise in the library.

You _____don't have to_____ know the name of the author to find a book.
You can find the book by the title.

1. You _____ wait until the due date to return a book.
You can return it earlier.

2. You _____ take out more books than you need. Other
people might want them.

3. You _____ disturb other people.

4. You _____ return your books to the circulation desk.
You can leave them in the book drop.

5. You _____ study in the library. You can study at home.

6. You _____ return books late if you don't want to pay
a fine.

EXERCISE **23**   **ABOUT YOU** **Work with a partner. Use *be (not) supposed to* to write a list of rules the teacher has for this class. Use affirmative and negative statements.**

EXAMPLES   We're not supposed to use our books during a test.

We're supposed to write five compositions this semester.

_____

_____

_____

_____

_____

EXERCISE 24 Write a list of driving rules. Use *must not* or *can't*. (Use *you* in the impersonal sense.)

EXAMPLE You must not pass a car when you're going up a hill.

_____

_____

_____

_____

_____

EXERCISE 25 Circle the correct words to complete these sentences.

EXAMPLES We (**shouldn't**/ don't have to) talk loudly in the library.

We (shouldn't /**don't have to**) bring our dictionaries to class.

1. The teacher says we (can't / don't have to) use our books during a test.

2. The teacher says we (shouldn't / don't have to) sit in a specific seat in class. We can sit wherever we want.

3. We (can't / don't have to) talk to each other during a test. It's not permitted.

4. We (must not / don't have to) type our compositions. We can write them by hand.

5. We (shouldn't / can't) speak our native language in class. It's not a good idea.

6. We (don't have to / aren't supposed to) come back after the final exam, but we can in order to pick up our tests.

7. Parents often tell children, "You (shouldn't / don't have to) talk to strangers."

8. Parents (aren't supposed to / don't have to) send their kids to public schools. They can send them to private schools.

9. Teachers (aren't supposed to / don't have to) teach summer school if they don't want to.

10. English teachers (shouldn't / don't have to) talk fast to foreign students.

11. A driver who is involved in an accident must report it to the police. He (must not / doesn't have to) leave the scene of the accident.

(continued)

12. I'm warning you. You (*don't have to* / *'d better not*) spend so much time watching TV. You won't have time to study.

13. Drivers (*don't have to* / *must not*) go through red lights.

14. You (*shouldn't* / *don't have to*) make noise and disturb your neighbors.

15. Most American students (*don't have to* / *had better not*) study a foreign language in college. They have a choice.

16. I have a test tomorrow morning. I (*'d better not* / *must not*) stay out late tonight, or I won't be alert in the morning.

17. Some students (*shouldn't* / *don't have to*) pay tuition because they have a scholarship.

18. You (*may not* / *don't have to*) bring food into the computer lab. It's against the rules.

19. You (*shouldn't* / *may not*) eat while driving. Even though it's permitted, it's not a good idea.

20. You (*don't have to* / *shouldn't*) leave your cell phone on in class. It might disturb the class.

21. Those students are talking in the library. They should be quiet. They (*must not* / *are not supposed to*) talk in the library.

EXERCISE 26 **Fill in the blanks to make true statements.**

EXAMPLE I don't have to ___make an appointment to see the teacher___.

1. In this class, we aren't supposed to _____.

2. In this class, we don't have to _____.

3. The teacher doesn't have to _____, but he/she does it anyway.

4. In this building, we must not _____.

5. You'd better not _____, or the teacher will get angry.

6. We're going to have a test next week, so you'd better not _____ the night before.

7. When another student doesn't know the answer, you shouldn't _____. You should let him try to find it himself.

8. You can't _____ in the computer lab. It's not permitted.

9. Teachers should be patient. They shouldn't _____ when students don't understand.

10. You don't have to _____ to win a sweepstakes prize.

EXERCISE **27**
In your opinion, what laws should be changed? What new laws should be created? Fill in the blanks to complete these statements, using *must/must not, have to/don't have to, can/can't, should/shouldn't.* **You may work with a partner or in small groups.**

EXAMPLE There ought to be a law that says *that people who want to have a baby must take a course in parenting.*

1. There ought to be a law that says _____

_____

2. There ought to be a law that says _____

_____

3. There ought to be a law that says _____

_____

4.8 Making Suggestions

EXAMPLES	EXPLANATION
How **can** I protect myself from identity theft? You **could** shred all your important papers. You **can** get your bank statements online rather than by mail.	*Can* and *could* are used to offer suggestions. More than one choice is acceptable. *Can* and *could* have the same meaning in offering suggestions. *Could* does not have a past meaning in offering suggestions.
Compare *can/could* **and** *should*: a. I'm having a problem with annoying telemarketing calls. You **could** get Caller ID. Or you **can** just hang up. Or you **can** put your phone number on a "Do Not Call" registry. b. A caller asked for my credit card number. You **should** be careful. You **shouldn't** give out your credit card number to strangers.	a. Use *could* or *can* to offer one or more of several possibilities. b. Use *should* or *shouldn't* when you feel that there is only one right way.

EXERCISE 28 **Offer at least two suggestions to a person who says each of the following statements. You may work with a partner.**

EXAMPLE I need to find a book about American history.
You could go to a bookstore. You can get one at the public library.
You could try an online bookstore.

1. I'm leaving for vacation tomorrow, and I need to find out about the weather in the city where I'm going.

2. I type very slowly. I need to learn to type faster.

3. My landlord is raising my rent by $50, and I can't afford the increase.

4. I'd like to learn English faster.

5. I want to know the price of an airline ticket to my country.

6. I need to buy a new computer, and I want to compare prices.

7. I'm going to a party. The hostess asked each guest to bring something to eat.

8. I need to lose ten pounds.

Infomercials

Before You Read

1. Do you think TV commercials are interesting?
2. Do you believe what you see in commercials?

CD 2, TR 05

Read the following magazine article. Pay special attention to *be supposed to.*

We sometimes see "programs" on TV for products that **are supposed to make our lives better.** These look like real, informative TV shows, but they are not. They are called "infomercials" (*information* + *commercial*).

You**'re supposed to** think that you are watching an informative TV show and getting advice or information from experts and celebrities. These "shows" usually last 30 minutes, like regular TV shows. And they have commercial breaks, like regular TV shows, to

make you believe they are real shows. These "shows" tell you that their products **are supposed to** make you thin, young, rich, or beautiful. For example, you may see smiling people with great bodies using exercise equipment. You**'re supposed to** believe that it's easy and fun to lose weight if you buy this equipment. But weight loss takes hard work and a lot of time.

Be careful when buying products from infomercials, because the results may not be what you see on TV.

4.9 Expectations with *Be Supposed To*

Be supposed to is used to show that we have an expectation about something based on information we received.

EXAMPLES	EXPLANATION
This diet pill **is supposed to** make you thinner in 30 days.	In the examples on the left, we have an expectation about something because we received information from a friend, TV, radio, a newspaper, the Internet, etc. The information we receive is not necessarily correct.
This cream **is supposed to** grow hair in 30 days.	
Let's rent *The Matrix* this weekend. It**'s supposed to** be a good movie.	
Let's go to Mabel's Restaurant. The food there **is supposed to** be very good.	
I was just listening to the radio. It**'s supposed to** rain this weekend, but tomorrow **is supposed to** be a nice day.	
The movie **is supposed to** begin at 8 P.M. The plane **is supposed to** arrive at 7:25.	In these examples, we have an expectation because of a schedule.

Be supposed to is used to show that something is expected of the subject of the sentence because of a rule, requirement, custom, or commitment (promise).

EXAMPLES	EXPLANATION
Sweepstakes companies **are supposed to** tell you your chances of winning.	A person is expected to do something because of a law or rule. (See section 4.4.)
Drivers **are supposed to** wear seat belts.	
We**'re not supposed to** talk during the test.	
You**'re not supposed to** talk in the library, but some students do anyway.	
I**'m supposed to** write a paper for my class.	A person is expected to meet a requirement (in these cases, by the teacher).
I**'m supposed to** write about my favorite TV commercial.	
In many cultures, you**'re supposed to** take off your shoes before you enter a house.	A person is expected to behave in a certain way because of a custom.
In the U.S., you**'re supposed to** leave a 15% to 20% tip in a restaurant if you're happy with the service.	
I can't come to class tomorrow. I**'m supposed to** take my mom to the doctor.	A person is expected to do something because he or she has made a promise or commitment.
My friends are moving on Saturday. I**'m supposed to** help them.	

EXERCISE **29** **Write a sentence telling what this new product is supposed to do.**

EXAMPLE Are you starting to look old? Try Youth Cream.
It's supposed to make you look younger.
_____

1. Are you bald? Use Hair Today, a new cream.
_____

2. Do you look weak? Use Muscle Power, a new cream.
_____

3. Do you forget things? Try Memory Builder, a new pill.
_____

4. Is English hard for you? Try *QuickEnglish*, a new video.
_____

5. Do you have stained teeth? Try WhiteBright toothpaste.
_____

6. Do you want to make money in 30 days? Buy *Fast Money*, a new book.
_____

7. Are you overweight? Try SlimTrim, a new diet drink.
_____

8. Do you want to make your work in the kitchen easier? Buy Quick-Chop, a new device for chopping vegetables.
_____

EXERCISE **30** **Fill in the blanks with the correct form of *be + supposed to* and an appropriate verb in this conversation between a wife (W) and a husband (H).**

CD 2, TR 06

W: What's that tube of cream I saw in the bathroom?

H: It's HairFast. It __'s supposed to grow__ a lot of hair on my head quickly.
          (example)

W: How often _____ it?
               (1)

H: I _____ it three times a day.
    (2)

W: How much does it cost?

H: It's about $20 for each tube.

W: Twenty dollars? How long does a tube last?

H: One tube _____ for a week.
             (3)

(continued)

W: Just a week? How long will it take you to grow hair?

H: It _____ about six months before I start to see results.
(4)

W: Do you know how much money that's going to cost us?

H: I know it's expensive, but just imagine how much better I'll look with hair.

W: You know we want to buy a new house. We _____
(5)
our extra money into our house fund. But you're wasting it on a
product that may—or may not—bring results.

H: What about all the money you spend on skin products? All those silly
creams that _____ you look younger?
(6)

W: Well, I want to look young and beautiful.

H: Do you really think those products work?

W: This expensive cream I bought _____
(7)
the wrinkles around my eyes.

H: You'll always be
beautiful to me. I have
an idea. Why don't you
forget about the creams
and I'll forget about the
hair product. We can
save our money, buy a
house, and just get old
together—in our new
home.

EXERCISE 31 **ABOUT YOU** Work with a partner. Write a list of three things the
teacher or this school expects from the students. Begin with *we*.

EXAMPLE   <u>We're supposed to come to class every day.</u>

1. _____

2. _____

3. _____

EXERCISE **32** **ABOUT YOU** Work with a partner. Write a list of three things that you expect from the teacher in this class. Begin with *he* or *she*.

EXAMPLE   *She's supposed to correct us when we make a mistake.*

1. _____

2. _____

3. _____

My Elderly Neighbor

Before
You Read

1. Why do you think elderly people enter so many sweepstakes?

2. Do you think elderly people are lonelier than younger people?

CD 2, TR 07

Read the following conversation. Pay special attention to *must*.

A: I'm worried about my elderly neighbor.

B: How old is she?

A: She **must be** about 80.

B: Why are you worried? Is her health bad?

A: No, she's fine. But she's all alone. Her children live far away. They don't call her very often.

B: She **must be** lonely.

A: I think she is. She enters sweepstakes and buys useless things all the time. She **must think** that if she buys things, she'll increase her chances of winning. I was in her garage yesterday, and she **must have** more than 50 boxes of things she doesn't use.

B: Doesn't she read the offers that are sent to her? Can't she see that her chances of winning are very small and that she doesn't have to buy anything to win?

(continued)

A: She **must not read** those letters very carefully. In addition to these letters, she told me she gets about five or six calls from telemarketers every day. Her name **must be** on hundreds of lists.

B: Our family **must get** a lot of those calls too, but we're at work all day so we don't even know about them. Telemarketers don't usually leave a message.

A: Do you think I should warn my neighbor? I read an article that says that these companies take advantage of elderly people.

B: Why don't you talk to her about it? You can tell her to use Caller ID to see who's calling, or to put her name on a "Do Not Call" list.

A: I think I should.

4.10 Logical Conclusions

Must has two completely different uses. In Sections 4.3 and 4.4, we studied *must* as an expression of necessity. In the preceding reading and in the examples below, *must* shows a conclusion.

EXAMPLES	EXPLANATION
My elderly neighbor lives alone. Her children are far away. She **must be** lonely. She **must think** that if she buys things, her chances of winning will increase.	We make a conclusion based on information we have or observations we make.
How old is she? She **must be** about 80. How many boxes does she have? She **must have** more than 50 boxes.	We can use *must* to make an estimate.
She **must not read** the letters carefully. She **must not understand** the conditions of the contest.	For a negative conclusion, use *must not*. Do not use a contraction.
Language Note: *Must*, in the above cases, talks about the present only, not the future.	

EXERCISE `33`   In each of the conversations below, fill in the blanks with an appropriate verb to make a logical conclusion.

EXAMPLE   **A:** Have you ever visited Japan?

B: I lived there when I was a child.

A: Then you must ___know how to speak___ Japanese.

B: I used to, but I've forgotten it.

1.   *This is a conversation between two female students.*

   A: Would you introduce me to Lee?

   B: Who's Lee?

   A: You must _____ who I'm talking about. He's in your speech class. He sits next to you.

   B: You mean Mr. Song?

   A: Yes, Lee Song. The tall, handsome guy with glasses. He doesn't wear a wedding ring. He must _____ single.

   B: I'm not so sure about that. Not all married men wear a wedding ring.

2.   *This is a conversation between a married woman (M) and a single woman (S).*

   M: My husband spends all his free time with our children.

   S: He must _____ kids very much.

   M: He does.

   S: How many kids do you have?

   M: We have four.

   S: Raising kids must _____ the hardest job in the world.

   M: It is, but it's also the most rewarding.

(continued)

3. This is a conversation between a teacher (T) and a student (S).

   T: Take out the paper I gave you last Monday.

   S: I don't have it. Could you give me one, please?

   T: Were you in class last Monday?

   S: Yes, I was.

   T: Then you must _____ it.

   S: Oh, yes. You're right. Here it is.

4. This is a conversation between an American (A) and an immigrant (I).

   A: It must _____ hard to start your life in a new country.

   I: Yes, it is.

   A: You must _____ lonely at times.

   I: Yes. You must _____ how it feels. You went to live in Japan for a few years, didn't you?

   A: Yes, I did. It took me a long time to get used to it.

5. This is a conversation between two friends.

   A: I saw some experts on TV talking about a cure for baldness. They must _____ what they're talking about because they're experts.

   B: You must _____ that if you see it on TV it's true. But don't believe everything you see.

6. This is a conversation between two friends.

   A: I saw your uncle yesterday at the gym. How old is he?

   B: I'm not sure. My mother is 69 and he's her older brother. So he must _____ in his seventies. He goes to the gym four days a week to work out.

   A: He must _____ in great health.

   B: He is.

7. *This is a conversation between two students in the school cafeteria.*

A: I see you're not eating your apple. In fact, you never eat fruit. You

must not _____ fruit very much.

B: You're right. I don't like fruit. Do you want my apple?

A: Thanks. You're always eating potato chips. They're so fattening.

They must _____ a million calories in them.

B: Probably, but I never think about it.

A: You should.

B: You're always talking about calories. You must

_____ about getting fat.

A: I don't worry about it. I just try to eat well.

8. *This is a conversation between two co-workers.*

A: Do you want to see a picture of my new baby?

B: Yes.

A: Here she is. She's about two months old now.

B: She's so beautiful. You and your wife must _____

very happy.

A: We are. But we don't get much sleep these days. You have a small

baby. You must _____ what I'm talking about.

B: I sure do.

9. *This is a conversation between a young couple.*

A: Do you see that beautiful ring in the window? I really love it.

Don't you?

B: Yes, it's very beautiful. (*Thinking to himself:* This is an expensive

jewelry shop. The ring must _____ over $5,000.

She must _____ that I'm rich.)

(continued)

10. *This is a conversation between two strangers on the street.*

A: I see you're looking at a map. You must _____ a

tourist. Are you lost?

B: Please repeat.

A: Are you lost?

B: Speak slowly, please.

A: ARE YOU LOST? (*To herself:* He must not _____

any English.)

B: (*To himself:* I asked her to speak more slowly and she's shouting

instead. She must _____ that I'm deaf.)

4.11 Possibility vs. Probability in the Present

May/might and *must* can show degrees of certainty.

DEGREES OF CERTAINTY	EXPLANATION
Who's calling? a. I have Caller ID. I see it's my sister. b. I don't know. I don't have Caller ID. It **might be** my sister. Or it **may be** my mother or it **could be** a telemarketer. c. It **must be** my mother. It's 3:00 P.M. and she calls me every day at three o'clock. a. My neighbor **has** a box near her door. b. She **might have** more boxes inside. I really don't know. c. I've seen her garage. She **must have** at least 50 boxes in there.	In sentences (a), we are certain that the information is true. In sentences (b), we have little or no evidence or information. There are many possibilities. In sentences (c), we conclude that something is probable based on information we have or an estimate we make.

EXERCISE 34 **Decide if the situation is probable or possible. Fill in the blanks with *must* for probability or *may/might/could* for possibility.**

EXAMPLES **A:** Where is Linda Ramirez from?

B: Ramirez is a Spanish name. She ___ *might* ___ be from Mexico. She
___ *may* ___ be from Colombia. There are so many countries where
Spanish is spoken that it's hard to know for sure.

A: She ___could___ be from the Philippines. Filipinos have Spanish names too.

B: Where is Tran Nguyen from?

A: I know that's a Vietnamese name. He ___must___ be from Vietnam.

1. **A:** What time is it?

   B: I don't have a watch. The sun is directly overhead, so it _____ be about noon.

2. **A:** Where's the teacher today?

   B: No one knows. She _____ be sick.

3. **A:** Does Yoko speak Japanese?

   B: She _____ speak Japanese. She's from Japan.

4. **A:** Where's Washington Avenue?

   B: I don't know. We're lost. There's a woman over there. Let's ask her. She _____ know.

5. **A:** Why is that student sneezing so much?

   B: I don't know. She _____ have a cold, or it _____ be an allergy.

6. **A:** Is Susan married?

   B: She _____ be married. She's wearing a wedding ring.

7. **A:** Why didn't Joe come to the party?

   B: Who knows? He _____ not like parties.

8. **A:** I need to make some copies, but don't have change for the copy machine.

   B: I _____ have some change. Let me look in my pocket.

9. **A:** I've never lived far from my parents before.

   B: You _____ miss them very much.

   A: I do.

10. **A:** Look at that young couple. They're always holding hands, smiling at each other, and kissing.

    B: They _____ be in love. *(continued)*

11. **A:** Linda never answers any questions in class.

    B: She _____ be shy or she _____ not know the answers to the questions.

12. **A:** I have a question about grammar.

    B: Let's ask the teacher. She _____ know the answer.

13. **A:** I have a question about American history.

    B: Why don't you ask our grammar teacher? He _____ know the answer.

4.12 Modals with Continuous Verbs

EXAMPLES	EXPLANATION
A: What's that noise? **B:** That's my husband using the shredder. He **must be shredding** our important papers. **A:** What are you watching on TV? **B:** It's a program about how to get muscles. **A:** You**'re supposed to be doing** your homework now. **A:** My friend isn't answering his cell phone. I know he always has it with him. **B:** He **might be taking** a shower now. I'm sure he doesn't take his phone into the shower!	Use modal + *be* + verb *–ing* for a present continuous meaning.

EXERCISE **35** **Fill in the blanks to complete each statement.**

EXAMPLE I know I should _____be studying_____ for my test and not watching TV now. But there's a great program on now.

1. My sister said she might go to a movie today. She's not answering her cell phone. She must _____ watching a movie now.

2. Why are you reading now? It's midnight. You're supposed _____ sleeping.

3. It's late. Everyone is yawning. They _____ be getting tired.

4. You're sitting too close to the TV. Move back. You shouldn't be _____ so close to the TV.

5. My daughter's been using the Internet all day. She _____ be _____ her homework or she _____ chatting with her friends.

6. Please be quiet. This is a library. You're not supposed to be _____ so loudly.

7. There's so much noise coming from my neighbor's apartment. She might _____ a party.

8. You _____ be _____ on your cell phone while driving. It could be dangerous.

EXERCISE **36** **Read this conversation. Choose the correct words in parentheses ( ) to complete the conversation. Sometimes both choices have the same meaning, so both answers are correct.**

CD 2, TR 08

A: I received a letter about a sweepstakes. I think I (may /(am supposed to)) (example) buy magazines in order to enter the contest.

B: You're wrong. You (must not /(don't have to)) buy anything.
(example)

A: But if I buy something, that (might / may) (1) increase my chances of winning.

B: That's not true. I've read several articles on the Internet about sweepstakes and scams recently.

A: Then you (must / could) know a lot (2) about this topic.

B: I think I do. But you (shouldn't / don't have to) believe everything you (3) read on the Internet either.

A: How do I know what to believe?

B: You (may / should) use common sense. If an ad tells you that you are (4) already a winner, you (shouldn't / must not) believe it.
(5)

A: But if a letter tells me I've won a million dollars, I'd be crazy not to look into it further.

B: You'd be crazy if you did. Do you think someone is going to give you a million dollars for nothing?

(continued)

A: No, but . . .

B: If you want to get rich, you (*might / should*) work hard and save your
(6)
money.

A: But it (*could / might*) take years to get rich that way.
(7)

B: That's the only way. Yes, you (*could / can*) enter sweepstakes,
(8)
but you probably won't win.

A: I get offers by e-mail too. There are offers for products that

(*must / are supposed to*) make me lose weight. I'm a bit overweight
(9)

and I (*have to / have got to*) lose 20 pounds.
(10)

B: If you want to lose weight, you (*might / ought to*) eat a healthy diet
(11)
and exercise every day.

A: But that takes time. It (*could / might*) take months before I see a
(12)
difference.

B: That's right. But it's the only way. All those ads tell you that problems

(*can / must*) be fixed with easy solutions. But life isn't like that.
(13)

A: You (*must / should*) think I'm stupid for believing all these things I
(14)
see and hear.

B: I don't think you're stupid. Some companies are very clever about

getting your interest. For example, infomercials often have celebrities

talking about a product. You (*are expected to / are supposed to*)
(15)

trust the celebrity and believe what he or she says is true.

A: The government (*should / might*) do something to stop these
(16)

ads from appearing in our e-mail, in our postal mailboxes, and on TV.

B: I agree. There are already laws telling companies what they

(*are allowed to / are permitted to*) do or not. But some companies don't
(17)

do what they (*are supposed to / could*) do. It's up to you to be
(18)

informed, use your common sense, and protect yourself.

A: Well, thanks for your advice.

Summary of Lesson 4

EXAMPLES	EXPLANATION
You **must** take a test to get a driver's license. You **must not** drive without a license.	Law or rule (official tone) Negative: Prohibition
You**'re supposed to** wear your seat belt. He's **not supposed to** park here, but he did.	Law or rule (unofficial tone) Negative: Prohibition, rule often broken
I **have to** mail a letter. I**'ve got to** mail a letter. I **don't have to** go to the post office. I can put it in the mailbox.	Personal obligation Negative: Lack of necessity, other options possible
You**'d better** study tonight, or you might fail the test. You**'d better not** stay up late tonight, or you won't be alert in the morning.	Warning; negative consequences stated or implied
You **should** exercise every day. You **ought to** exercise every day. You **shouldn't** eat so much ice cream.	Advice Negative: It's not advisable.
You **may/can** write the test with a pencil. You **cannot/may not** talk during a test.	Permission Negative: Prohibition, less formal than *must* not
Students in the U.S. **can** wear jeans to class.	Social acceptability
I get annoying telemarketing calls. What **can** I do? You **could** listen politely, or you **can** say you're not interested and hang up.	Suggestions
You **may** win a prize if you enter the contest. You **might** win a prize if you enter the contest. You **could** win a prize if you enter the contest.	Possibility about the future
It**'s supposed to** rain tomorrow. This face cream **is supposed to** make you look younger. My brother **is supposed to** call me this weekend. We**'re supposed to** write five compositions. You**'re supposed to** take your hat off in church. The movie **is supposed to** begin at 8 P.M.	Expectation because of information we receive or because of a promise, requirement, custom, or schedule
She won a lot of money. She **must** be happy. She's eating very little. She **must not** be very hungry.	Deduction or logical conclusion about the present
I can't find my keys. They **might be** in your pocket. Did you look there? They **could be** on the table. Or they **may be** in your car. She looks confused. She **may not** know the answer. She **might not** understand the question.	Possibility about the present

Editing Advice

1. Don't use *to* after a modal. (Exception: *ought to*)

   You should ~~to~~ buy a new car.

2. Use the base form after a modal.

   She can't ~~goes~~ with you.
   go

   You should ~~studying~~ every day.
   study

3. Don't forget **d** in *supposed to*, *permitted to*, and *allowed to*.

   He's not suppose˄ to drive. He's too young.
   d

   You're not allow˄ to talk during the test.
   ed

4. Don't forget **'d** to express *had better*.

   You˄ better take the bus to work. Your car isn't working well.
   'd

5. Use *have/has* before *got to* in writing.

   We˄ got to leave now.
   've

6. Don't put two modals together.

   You must ~~can~~ drive well before you can get your license.
   be able to

7. Don't forget *be* or *to* in these expressions: *be supposed to*, *be able to*, *be permitted to*, *be allowed to*.

   They˄ supposed to leave at 6 A.M.
   are

   I'm able˄ work on Saturday.
   to

8. Use the correct word order in a question with a modal.

   What ~~I should~~ do?
   should I

Editing Quiz

Some of the shaded words and phrases **have mistakes. Find the mistakes and correct them. If the shaded words are correct, write *C*. *Do not change the modal itself. Only look for mistakes in grammar.***

$$\overset{\text{must I}}{} \qquad\qquad \overset{C}{}$$

A: I'm going to enter a sweepstakes. What ~~I must~~ do to enter? Can you help
(example)   (example)

me?

B: You're suppose to mail in this postcard.
(1)

A: Must I buy something too?
(2)

B: That's not necessary. You can to enter the sweepstakes without buying
(3)

anything.

A: I think that if I buy something, I'll be able to increase my chances of
(4)

winning.

B: You ought to read this information carefully. It says here "No Purchase
(5)

Necessary."

A: Oh, I see.

B: I always throw those things away.

A: But you might winning a lot of money. Anyway, what you can lose?
(6)   (7)

It's so simple. You got to put a stamp on the postcard and fill in some
(8)

information. That's all. You should do it too. You might be able win a
(9)   (10)

million dollars.

B: I think entering a sweepstakes is a waste of time. Anyway, I'm not allowed
(11)

enter that sweepstakes.

A: Why not?

B: Because I work for that company. Employees not permitted to
(12)

participate. It says so right here. You better read the small print so you
(13)

can understand this better.
(14)

Modals—Present and Future; Related Expressions   **179**

PART 1 Look at the job application. On the following pages, circle the best words to complete each sentence. The numbers on the application refer to each one of the sentences on pages 181–182.

① Fill out the following form. Print in black ink. Mail or fax the application to:

Ms. Judy Lipton
P.O. Box 32X
Chicago, IL 60640
FAX number: 312-555-4321

Applications must be submitted by November 15.

② Name _____ _____ _____
(last)   (first)   (middle initial)

Address _____

City _____ State _____ Zip code _____

③ Telephone ( ) _____

④ E-mail address (optional) _____ Sex _____ ⑤

⑥ Date of birth _____ _____ _____ (You must be at least 18.) ⑦
(month)   (day)   (year)

⑧ Social Security number _____-_____-_____

⑨ Educational background:

	Date graduated	Degree or major
High School	_____	_____
College	_____	_____
Graduate School	_____	_____

⑩ Employment history (Please start with your present or last job.)

Company	Position	Dates	Supervisor	Reason for leaving
_____	_____	_____	_____	_____
_____	_____	_____	_____	_____
_____	_____	_____	_____	_____
_____	_____	_____	_____	_____
_____	_____	_____	_____	_____

Do not write in the shaded box. For office use only.

⑪
Rec'd. by _____
Amer. cit. _____
Doc. checked _____
Transcripts received _____

⑫ The Immigration Act of 1986 requires all successful applicants to present documents to prove U.S. citizenship or permanent residence with permission to work in the U.S.

⑬ This company is an Equal Opportunity Employer. Race, religion, nationality, marital status, and physical disability will not influence our decision to hire.

⑭ I certify that these answers are true.

⑮ Signature: _____ Date: _____

EXAMPLE You (aren't supposed to / couldn't) use a red pen to fill out the application.

1. You (have to / might) submit the application to Ms. Lipton.
   Ms. Lipton (must / should) be the person in charge of hiring. She
   wants the application by November 15. Today is November 14. You
   ('d better not / mustn't) send it by regular mail. If you use regular mail,
   it (must not / might not) arrive on time. You (could / are supposed to)
   send it by overnight express mail, or you (might / can) fax it to
   Ms. Lipton's office.

2. You (could / are supposed to) write your last name before your
   first name.

3. You (are supposed to / could) include your phone number.

4. You (shouldn't / don't have to) include your e-mail address.

5. For sex, you (might / are supposed to) write M for male or F for female.

6. To write the date of your birth in the U.S., you (should / can) write
   the month before the day. You have several choices in writing the
   date. You (must / could) write June 7 or 6/7 or 6–7. If you put the day
   before the month, an American (might / should) think you mean July 6
   instead of June 7.

7. To apply for the job, you (might / must) be over 18.

8. People who work in the U.S. (may / must) have a Social Security
   number.

9. You (may / are supposed to) include the schools you attended.

10. In the employment history section, you are asked why you left your
    last job. The employer (might / should) want to know if you were fired
    or if you left on your own.

11. You (can't / aren't supposed to) write in the shaded box. "Amer. cit."
    (must / should) mean American citizen.

12. You (must not / don't have to) be an American citizen to apply for the
    job. You can be a permanent resident. You (have to / should) prove
    your citizenship or residency. If you don't have permission to work in
    the U.S., you (might not / cannot) apply for this job.

(continued)

13. The company (*might not / may not*) choose a worker based on race, religion, or nationality.

14. You (*don't have to / must not*) lie on the application form.

15. You (*may / must*) sign the application and include the date.

PART 2 **Read the pairs of sentences. If the sentences have the same meaning, write S. If the sentences have a different meaning, write D.**

EXAMPLES   You <u>have</u> to wear your seat belt. / You <u>must</u> wear your seat belt.   S

You <u>must</u> open the window. / You <u>should</u> open the window.   D

1. She <u>can</u> drive a car. / She <u>is able to</u> drive a car.

2. He <u>can't</u> speak Korean. / He <u>might not</u> speak Korean.

3. I'<u>m supposed to</u> help my sister on Friday. / I <u>might</u> help my sister on Friday.

4. You <u>don't have to</u> drive to work. / You <u>shouldn't</u> drive to work.

5. You'<u>re not supposed to</u> write the answer. / You <u>don't have to</u> write the answer.

6. You'<u>re not allowed to</u> use a pencil for the test. / You <u>may not</u> use a pencil for the test.

7. We <u>should</u> visit our mother. / We <u>ought to</u> visit our mother.

8. You <u>should</u> make a right turn here. / You <u>must</u> make a right turn here.

9. If you need more help, you <u>could</u> go to a tutor. / If you need more help, you <u>can</u> go to a tutor.

10. You <u>shouldn't</u> wear jeans. / You <u>must not</u> wear jeans.

11. You <u>must not</u> come back after the final exam. / You <u>don't have to</u> come back after the final exam.

12. I <u>have to</u> work tomorrow. / I'<u>ve got to</u> work tomorrow.

13. You <u>can't</u> eat in the computer lab. / You <u>are not allowed to</u> eat in the computer lab.

14. I <u>may</u> go to New York next week. / I <u>might</u> go to New York next week.

15. I <u>could</u> be wrong. / I <u>might</u> be wrong.

16. <u>You don't have to</u> drive. / <u>It is not necessary to</u> drive.

17. You <u>don't have to</u> fill out the application with a red pen. / You <u>aren't supposed to</u> fill out the application with a red pen.

18. You<u>'d better</u> wake up early tomorrow morning. / You <u>could</u> wake up early tomorrow morning.

Expansion

Classroom
Activities

❶ Form a small group. Take something from your purse or pocket that says something about you. Show it to your group. Your group will make deductions about you.

EXAMPLE car keys
You must have a car.

❷ On the left are some American customs. On the right, tell if there is a comparable custom in your native culture or country. Write what that custom is.

In the U.S.	In my native culture or country
When someone sneezes, you're supposed to say, "Bless you."	
If you're invited to a party, in most cases you're not supposed to take your children.	
Americans sometimes have potluck parties. Guests are supposed to bring food to the party.	
There are some foods you can eat with your hands. Fried chicken and pizza are examples.	
Students are not supposed to talk to each other during an exam.	
When you're too sick to go to work, you're supposed to call your employer and say you're not coming in that day.	

❸ Bring in two copies of an application. It can be an application for a job, driver's license, license plate, apartment rental, address change, check cashing card, rebate, etc. Work with a partner. One person will give instructions. The other person will fill the application out. Use modals to help the other person fill it out correctly.

EXAMPLE   You're not supposed to write below this line.

❹ Find a partner and write some sentences to give advice for each of the following problems.

a. I got permission to come to the U.S. I have a dog. I've had this dog for six years, since she was a puppy, but I can't take her with me. What should I do?

b. I got a D in my biology class. I think I deserve a C. What should I do?

c. I need a new car, but I don't have enough money right now. What should I do?

d. I found an envelope with $100 in it in front of my apartment building. There is no name on it. What should I do?

e. My uncle came to live with us. He never cooks, cleans, or washes the dishes. I have to do everything. I'm very unhappy with the situation. What should I do?

Talk About It

❶ Why do you think the elderly are often the victims of scams?

❷ Have you ever seen a TV infomercial? For what kind of products? Do you believe the claims about the product?

❸ How do you respond to telemarketing calls?

❹ What do you think of TV commercials?

❺ Did you ever win a prize in a contest, sweepstakes, or raffle? What did you win?

❻ Did you ever buy a product that claims to do something but doesn't do it?

Write

About It

1 Write about a TV commercial that annoys you. Describe the commercial and tell why it annoys you.

2 Write about a time someone tricked you into buying something or paying money for something you didn't get.

3 What is your experience with telemarketing calls? Write one paragraph telling how you respond to them. Write another paragraph giving advice to someone who gets these calls.

EXAMPLE

Telemarketing Calls

It seems whenever I sit down with my family to eat dinner, the phone rings. I probably shouldn't answer the phone but I do. Companies are always telling me that I should get a new service or buy a new product that I don't need...

 For more practice using grammar in context, please visit our Web site.

Grammar
Modals in the Past

Context
American Presidents

Richard M. Nixon, president 1969–1974

Abraham Lincoln, president 1861–1865

John F. Kennedy, president 1961–1963

Slavery, Lincoln, and the Civil War

Before
You Read

1. What do you know about President Lincoln?

2. Has your country ever had a civil war?

CD 2, TR 09

Read the following textbook article. Pay special attention to *should have*, *must have*, *may have*, and *could have*.

From the time of the first English colonies in America, Africans were brought to America as slaves. Most of them were taken to the South, where they worked on farms in the production of sugar, cotton, and other crops. The prosperity of the white farmers in the South **couldn't have happened** without slaves. But many northerners were against slavery. One of those was Abraham Lincoln, the president who finally brought the end of slavery in the U.S.

Today many people consider Abraham Lincoln to be one of the greatest presidents of the United States. But during his time, many had their doubts about his ability to lead the country during the growing conflict between the North and the South. Before he became president, other politicians did not take him seriously. Lincoln's parents were poor and uneducated, and Lincoln had only 18 months of schooling. But he loved to read, and he educated himself. Lincoln dressed in poorly fitting clothes and didn't look like the polished politicians of the East. One newspaper had called Lincoln "a fourth-rate lecturer, who cannot speak good grammar." Because Lincoln had so little schooling, journalists **must have thought** he was not very smart.

Much to his opponents' surprise, Lincoln won the election for president in 1860. At that time, the Southern slave owners wanted to continue slavery, but Lincoln wanted to stop the spread of slavery. What followed was the worst internal crisis in American history: the Civil War. More than half a million soldiers died on both sides of the conflict, the most of any war that the U.S. fought in. One especially terrible battle took place at Gettysburg, Pennsylvania. On November 19, 1863, President Lincoln was invited to say a few words at the battleground. Edward Everett, the main speaker, gave a speech that lasted two hours in front of a crowd of almost 20,000 people. Lincoln followed Everett with a two-minute speech. When he was finished, the audience was silent. The audience **may have been surprised** by the brevity[1] of the speech. Some people thought he **must not have been** finished. Seeing the reaction of the crowd, Lincoln

<aside>
Did You Know?

In 1860, the population of the U.S. was 31 million; almost 4 million of these people were slaves.
</aside>

---

[1]*Brevity* is the noun form for the adjective "brief."

turned to Everett and said he was afraid his speech had been a failure. He said he **should have prepared** it more carefully. Everett did not agree. He said the speech was perfect. He said the president had said more in two minutes than he, Everett, had said in two hours. This speech, known as the Gettysburg Address, is considered one of the greatest speeches in American history. In his speech, Lincoln said that the country was dedicated to freedom and that "government of the people, by the people, for the people" had to continue.

The Civil War continued until April 9, 1865, when the North finally won. Less than three weeks later, on April 26, Lincoln was assassinated.

LINCOLN'S ADDRESS AT GETTYSBURG, NOVEMBER 19, 1863
DRAWN BY A. J. KELLER

5.1 Modals in the Past

To form the past of a modal, use modal + *have* + past participle.

Active					
Subject	Modal	*Not*	*Have*	Past Participle	Complement
I	should		have	prepared	the speech more carefully.
People	may	not	have	realized	that his speech was finished.
Southern farmers	could	not	have	become	rich without slaves.
Some people	must		have	thought	(that) Lincoln was not very smart.

Pronunciation Note: In informal speech, *have* is often pronounced like *of* or /ə/.

(continued)

To form the passive of a past modal, use modal + *have* + *been* + past participle.

Passive					
Subject	**Modal**	***Not***	***Have Been***	**Past Participle**	**Complement**
The people	**might**		**have been**	**surprised**	by the speech.
Lincoln	**could**		**have been**	**elected**	again.
Slavery	**should**	**not**	**have been**	**permitted**	in the U.S.

EXERCISE 1   Fill in the blanks to complete the sentences.

A: Did you read the story about Lincoln before class?

B: No. I didn't have time.

A: You should ___**have**___ read it. Our lesson depends on it. It's

(example)
about Lincoln.

B: Who's Lincoln?

A: What do you mean, "Who's Lincoln?" Abraham Lincoln. You must
have _____ of him. He was one of the most well-known

(1)
presidents of the U.S.

B: Oh. Abraham Lincoln. Of course I've heard of him. I thought you
said "Leeko."

A: Oh. I must _____ pronounced his name wrong. Sorry. Anyway,

(2)
he gave one of the greatest speeches of any American president. But
after the speech, he said, "I should have _____ it more carefully."

(3)

B: He must have _____ it very fast.

(4)

A: No. I don't think he wrote it fast. I think he chose his words very
carefully. The people in the audience might _____ expected a

(5)
longer speech. But it was a perfect speech, and he was a great president.

B: If he was such a good president, he must _____ well-liked.

(6)

A: He was well-liked by many in the North, but most Southerners didn't
like him because they wanted slavery to continue.

5.2 Past Possibility and Probability

EXAMPLES	EXPLANATION

Lincoln thought, "I **might have bored** the audience."
 	
Why didn't the audience react after Lincoln's speech?
 	
    They **could have been** surprised.
 	
    They **may have expected** him to say more.
	To express possibility about the past, use *may have*, *might have*, or *could have* + past participle. The sentences on the left express "maybe" about the past.
	
	I might have bored the audience. = *Maybe I bored* the audience.
	
	They could have been surprised. = *Maybe they were* surprised.
	
	They may have expected him to say more. = *Maybe they expected* him to say more.

Lincoln thought, "I **may not have given** a very good speech." Lincoln thought, "I **might not have prepared** well enough."	To show negative possibility, use *may not have* and *might not have*. Don't use *could not have* because it has a different meaning. (See Section 5.8)
Because Lincoln had so little schooling, some journalists **must have thought** he was not very smart. When Lincoln finished his speech after two minutes, some people thought that he **must not have been finished**. Lincoln thought, "They **must not have liked** my speech."	We use *must have* + past participle to make a statement of logical conclusion or deduction about a past event based on observations we make or information we have. We are saying that something is probably true. *They must have thought* he wasn't smart. = *They probably thought* he wasn't smart. *He must not have been* finished. = *He probably wasn't* finished. *They must not have liked* my speech. = *They probably didn't like* my speech.

EXERCISE 2 **Change these *maybe* statements to statements with *may have*, *might have*, or *could have*. Situation: A student dropped out of a course after the first few weeks. These are some guesses about why he did it.**

EXAMPLE   Maybe he registered for the wrong section. (may)
He may have registered for the wrong section.

1. Maybe he preferred an earlier class. (could)
2. Maybe he wanted to be in his friend's class. (might)
3. Maybe the class was too hard for him. (may)
4. Maybe he got sick. (could)
5. Maybe he didn't like the teacher. (may)
6. Maybe he found a full-time job. (might)
7. Maybe he had a lot of problems at home. (could)
8. Maybe he left town. (might)

EXERCISE 3 **Fill in the blanks with an appropriate verb for past possibility. Answers may vary.**

1. **A:** I was trying to call your house last night, but you didn't answer.

    B: What time did you call?

    A: After 8 P.M.

    B: Let's see. Where was I? I might _____have been_____ at the
    (example)
    library at that time.

    A: But I tried calling your cell phone too.

    B: I may _____ it off. I usually turn it off when
    I'm at the library. Why didn't you leave a message?

    A: I did leave a message.

    B: Oh. I might _____ it by mistake.

    A: You deleted my message?

    B: Sorry.

2. **A:** Have you seen my keys?

    B: You're always losing your keys. You may _____
    them in your pocket.

    A: No, they're not there. I already looked.

B: Well, you could _____ them as you were getting out of the car.

A: When I drop keys, I can hear them hit the ground, so I'm sure that's not it.

B: Well, you might _____ them in the door when you came in last night.

A: Oh, you're right! They're in the door. Thanks.

3. **A:** I'm so upset. I left my dictionary in class yesterday. Now I'll have to buy a new one.

   B: Why don't you ask the teacher? She might _____ _____.

   A: I already did. She didn't pick it up.

   B: Why don't you go to the "lost and found"? Somebody may _____ it and returned it there.

   A: Where's the "lost and found"?

   B: In front of the cafeteria.

4. **A:** I applied for a job three weeks ago, but so far I haven't heard anything. I probably didn't do well on the interview.

   B: You don't know that. They might _____ hundreds of candidates for the job. Anyway, why don't you call and tell the company you're still interested?

   A: But they could _____ someone else already.

   B: You won't know if they hired someone else unless you ask.

5. **A:** I asked my boss for a raise last week, and she said she'd get back to me. But so far she hasn't mentioned anything.

   B: She might _____ about it. I'm sure she has a lot on her mind and can easily forget something. Why don't you ask her again?

(continued)

6. A: I sent an e-mail to an old friend and I got a message saying it was

undeliverable.

B: You might _____ the address wrong.

A: No. I checked. I wrote it correctly.

B: Your friend may _____ his old account and

opened a new one.

EXERCISE 4 **Fill in the blanks with an appropriate verb for past probability. Answers may vary.**

1. A: Kennedy's death was such a tragedy.

B: Who's Kennedy?

A: You don't know who Kennedy was? He was so famous. You must

_____**have heard**_____ of him. There's a picture of him in this book.
    (example)

B: No, I've never heard of him. Wow. He was so handsome. He must

_____ a movie star.

A: No. He was an American president. He was assassinated in 1963

when he was only 46 years old.

B: That's terrible. It must _____ a hard time for

Americans.

A: Yes, it was. I remember my parents telling me about it. They were in

high school when it happened. They must _____

about 15 or 16 years old.

2. A: I followed your directions to go downtown yesterday. I took the

number 60 bus, but it didn't take me downtown.

B: You must _____ me. I said, "16," not "60."

A: Yes. I misunderstood you. I thought you said, "60."

B: It's hard to hear the difference between 16 and 60. Even

native speakers misunderstand each other. Anyway, you must

_____ a terrible day.

A: Yes, I had an awful day. When I got off the bus, I was totally lost, so I took a taxi downtown.

B: A taxi must _____ you over $20!

A: In fact, it cost me $30. So I wasted a lot of time and money yesterday.

3. **A:** I called you yesterday, but you didn't answer the phone.

B: You must _____ a wrong number. I always keep my cell phone on. What time did you call?

A: About 8 P.M.

B: Oh. I must _____ in the shower. Why did you call?

A: I forgot already.

B: Then it must not _____ very important.

4. **A:** How did you like the party last Saturday, Terri?

B: I wasn't there.

A: What do you mean you weren't there? We talked for a few hours.

B: You must _____ with my twin sister, Sherri. We look alike.

A: She must _____ that I was crazy. I kept calling her Terri.

B: I'm sure she didn't think anything of it. She's used to it.

5. **A:** How did you do on the last test?

B: I didn't know about the test, so I didn't study. I failed it.

A: The teacher announced it last Thursday.

B: I must _____ absent that day.

A: I think Rona must _____ it too. When she got her paper, she started to cry.

B: Did you see Paula? She was so excited when she saw her exam. She must _____ an A.

(continued)

6. A: Maria's relatives just went back to Mexico. They were here for a month.

B: She must _____ a wonderful time with them.

A: Yes, but she must _____ sad when she took them to the airport. She didn't want them to leave. She took them everywhere—to museums, to restaurants, to concerts.

B: She must _____ a lot of money.

A: She knew she was going to spend a lot of money, so she saved a lot before they came.

7. A: I thought I was driving east, but now I think I'm driving north.

B: You must _____ a wrong turn somewhere. Let's take a look at the map. (*After looking in the glove compartment*) I can't find the map.

A: I must _____ it on the kitchen table. I was looking at it before we got in the car.

B: No problem. Let's just call our friends. They'll tell us how to get to their house. Let me use your cell phone.

A: Oh, no. The battery is dead. I must _____ to recharge it.

B: Not again. You always forget to recharge it. Why don't we just stop at a gas station and get directions?

A: You know I don't like to ask for directions.

8. A: I said, "How are you?" to one of my classmates, and she answered, "I'm 58 years old." What was she thinking?

B: She must _____ that you said, "How *old* are you?"

A: She gave me a strange look. She must _____ that I was impolite asking about her age.

B: That's nothing. When I didn't speak much English, I went to a restaurant and asked the waitress for "soap" instead of "soup."

A: So did she bring you soap or soup?

B: Soup, of course.

A: Then she must _____ you in spite of your mistake.

9. **A:** I haven't seen Peter this semester. Have you?

   B: He must _____.

   A: Why would he drop out? He was close to getting his degree.

   B: He said that he wouldn't come back if he didn't get financial aid. He must not _____ financial aid this semester.

   A: That's too bad.

10. **A:** You look tan. You must _____ out in the sun.

    B: I was. I was in Florida for vacation.

    A: That must _____ wonderful.

    B: Actually, it was terrible. First, we lost our money and credit cards.

    A: What did you do?

    B: The credit card company canceled our card and gave us a new one. We used the credit card to get cash.

    A: So then the rest of your trip was fine, wasn't it?

    B: Not really. We rented a car and it kept breaking down.

    A: But it must _____ nice to get away from winter here and be in the sun.

    B: We were there for two weeks. It must _____ for all but the last few days. Finally when the rain stopped, I got some sun.

The Cuban Missile Crisis

Before You Read

1. Has your native country ever been at war with another country?

2. Do you think a nuclear war is possible today?

CD 2, TR 11 **Read the following textbook article. Pay special attention to** *could have* **+ past participle.**

In October 1962, the United States and the Soviet Union[2] came close to war. The U.S. discovered that the Soviet Union was beginning to send nuclear missiles to Cuba, which is only about 90 miles from Florida. President John Kennedy saw this as a direct threat to national security; these weapons **could have been** used to destroy cities and military bases in the U.S. On October 22, President Kennedy announced on TV that any attack from Cuba would be considered an attack from the Soviet Union, and he would respond with a full attack on the Soviets. He sent out the U.S. Navy to block Soviet ships from delivering weapons to Cuba. For 13 days, the world was at the edge of a major war. Finally, the Soviets agreed to send their missiles back and promised to stop building military bases in Cuba. In exchange, the U.S. promised to remove its missiles from Turkey.

In October 2002, there was a reunion of many of the surviving players in this crisis. Cuban president Fidel Castro met with former Secretary of Defense Robert McNamara and other Americans, Cubans, and Russians involved in the decisions made 40 years earlier. Remembering their experiences, they all agreed that this was indeed a major crisis that **could have changed** the world as we know it. Discussing the viewpoints and experiences of the Americans, McNamara explained that a nuclear attack on a U.S. ship **could** easily **have grown** into a full nuclear war between the U.S. and the Soviet Union. A former CIA[3] analyst who studied spy photos told the group that at least 16 intermediate-range missiles in Cuba **could have reached** any point in the continental United States[4] except the northwest corner. He said at the conference, "October 27 is a day I'll never forget. The planet **could have been destroyed**." A former Kennedy aide added, "It **could have been** the end of the world, but here we are, 40 years later."

Fortunately, diplomacy[5] won over war. What **could have been** a tragic event is now only a chapter in history.

[2]In 1991, the country then called the *Soviet Union*, broke up into 15 different countries, the largest of which is Russia.
[3]The *CIA* is the Central Intelligence Agency. It gathers information about other countries' secrets.
[4]The *continental* United States refers to all states except Hawaii and Alaska, which are not part of the U.S. mainland.
[5]*Diplomacy* is skillful negotiation between countries to try to work out problems without fighting.

5.3 Past Direction Not Taken

We use *could have* + past participle to show that something did not happen.

EXAMPLES	EXPLANATION
The Cuban Missile Crisis **could have been** the end of the world. An attack on a U.S. ship **could have grown** into a full nuclear war. Missiles **could have reached** almost any place in the U.S.	Use *could have* + past participle to show that something came close to happening, but didn't.
Kennedy and his advisors looked at several possibilities. They **could have attacked** immediately. They **could have invaded** Cuba. But they decided to give the Soviets a chance to remove the missiles and turn the ships around.	Use *could have* + past participle to show that a past opportunity was not taken. Several options were possible; all but one were rejected.
I heard you moved last weekend. Why didn't you tell me? I **could have helped** you.	Use *could have* + past participle to show missed opportunities.
I was so hungry (that) I **could have eaten** the whole pie by myself. I was so tired (that) I **could have slept** all day. I was so happy when I got an A on the test (that) I **could have kissed** the teacher. When the missiles were removed, we **could have jumped** for joy.	Use *could have* + past participle to show an exaggeration of a result.
Driver to pedestrian: Watch out, you idiot! I **could have killed** you. Father to son: Don't play baseball so close to the house. Your ball came within inches of the window. You **could have broken** the window.	Use *could have* + past participle to show that something almost happened.

EXERCISE 5 Fill in the blanks with the correct form of the verb in parentheses ( )
to exaggerate the result.

EXAMPLE   The party was so wonderful that I could _____**have stayed**_____ all night.
(stay)

1. I was so tired that I could _____ for 12 hours yesterday.
(sleep)

2. I was so embarrassed when I made a mistake in my speech that I could

_____ of shame.
(die)

3. She was so happy when she fell in love she could _____
(walk)

on air.

4. I was so happy when my counselor told me about my scholarship that

I could _____ him.
(kiss)

5. The movie was so good I could _____ it again
(watch)

and again.

6. Your cookies were so good that I could _____ all of them.
(eat)

7. I enjoyed dancing so much last night that I could _____
(dance)

all night.

8. It was so hot yesterday that we could _____ an egg
(fry)

on the street.

EXERCISE 6 Fill in the blanks with an appropriate verb for past direction not
taken. Answers may vary.

EXAMPLE   A: Did you read about the Cuban Missile Crisis?
B: Yes. The U.S. almost went to war with the Soviet Union.

A: Those two superpowers could _____**have destroyed**_____ the whole world!

1. A: I heard you bought a condo.

B: We did.

A: Why didn't you buy a house? Was it too expensive?

B: We could _____ a house, but we don't have enough time to take care of things. So we thought a condo would be better. There's someone to take care of the grass in the summer and the snow in the winter.

2. A: What do you do for a living?

B: I'm a waiter, but I could _____ a famous actor. Everyone says I've got a lot of talent. And my wife could _____ a career in modeling. She's so beautiful.

A: It's not too late to follow your dream.

B: We have small kids to support. So I think my acting dreams and her modeling dreams are over.

3. A: Do you want to see our new apartment? We moved last Saturday.

B: Why did you move? You had a lovely apartment. I'm surprised you didn't stay there.

A: We could _____ there. The rent wasn't too bad and the landlord was nice. But it was too far from school and work.

B: Who helped you move?

A: We did it all ourselves.

B: Why didn't you let me know? I could _____ you.

A: We didn't want to bother our friends.

B: What are friends for?

A: Anyway, you have a small car. We needed to rent a van.

B: I could _____ my sister's van. She always lets me borrow it if I have to move stuff.

A: We appreciate your kindness, but everything worked out fine.

(continued)

4. A: I can't believe you tried to fix the ceiling light without shutting off the electricity first. You could _____ yourself.

B: But I didn't. I'm still alive and the light is fixed.

A: You shouldn't take chances. And you got up on that tall ladder when you were home alone. You could _____, and no one would have been here to help you.

B: But I didn't fall. You worry too much. Everything's okay. The light is fixed, and I didn't break a leg.

5. A: I bought stocks and sold them a few months later. Now they're worth four times as much as what I sold them for. I could _____ a lot of money.

B: You never know with the stock market. You could _____ a lot of money too.

6. A: Sorry I'm so late.

B: What happened?

A: I had to take three buses to get to a job interview in the suburbs. It took me almost two hours to get there.

B: Why didn't you tell me? I could _____ you there in my car.

A: I didn't want to bother you.

B: You wasted a whole day today. You could _____ home hours ago.

A: That's not a problem. I'm home now. And I did my homework while I was on the bus on the way there. On the way home, I slept most of the way. It's a good thing the person sitting next to me woke me up. I could _____ my bus stop.

EXERCISE 7 **ABOUT YOU** Fill in the blanks to tell about a missed opportunity in your life. Share your answers in a small group or with the entire class.

EXAMPLE I could have gone to Germany instead of coming to the U.S., but it's

easier to find a job in my profession in the U.S.

I could have _____ instead of

_____, but

_____.

Election 2000: Bush vs. Gore

Before
You Read

1. What do you know about the election process in the U.S.?

2. Do you think it's important for every citizen to vote?

CD 2, TR 12

Read the following conversation. Pay special attention to *should have* **+ past participle.**

A: Did you vote in the last election?

B: I couldn't. I'm not a citizen. You're a citizen. Did you vote?

A: No. I was busy that day. Besides, one person's vote is not important.

B: That's not true. You **should have voted**. Didn't you hear about the presidential election in 2000?

A: No. I wasn't in the U.S. at that time. What happened?

B: George W. Bush was running against Al Gore.

A: So? George Bush won, didn't he?

B: Yes. But a lot of people thought Al Gore **should have won**.

A: Why?

B: The election was very close. Al Gore had more of the popular vote, but he lost.

(continued)

A: How could that happen? He **shouldn't have lost** if he had the people's vote.

B: The U.S. has a strange way of picking a president. It's very complicated, but each state has a certain number of electoral votes based on population. It's possible to win the popular vote and lose the electoral vote.

A: I don't understand.

B: It's really hard to understand. But anyway, Florida had 25 electoral votes, which is a lot. The candidate who would win Florida in 2000 would win the election.

A: So how did Florida vote?

B: At first the news reported that Gore had won. A few hours later, they said that Bush had won.

A: The news reporters **should have waited** until all the votes were counted.

B: I agree. Usually the result of an election is known the same night or early the next morning. But Gore asked that the votes be counted again, just to make sure. The Florida Supreme Court decided that Bush won the state by about 500 votes.

A: Wow! That's a close election.

B: You see? That's why you **should have voted**. Every vote counts.

5.4 Past Mistakes

EXAMPLES	EXPLANATION
You **should have voted** in the last election. The news reporters **shouldn't have announced** the winner so soon. Who **should have won** the election of 2000?	We use *should have* + past participle to comment on a mistake in the past. We are not really giving advice because it is impossible to change the past.
You **ought to have voted**.	Less frequently, we use *ought to have* + past participle. *Ought to* is not usually used for negatives.

Usage Note: When a person receives an unexpected gift, he may be a little embarrassed. This person might say, *"You shouldn't have."* This means, "You shouldn't have gone to so much trouble or expense." or "You shouldn't have given me a gift. I don't deserve it." Saying this is considered polite, and an appropriate response might be, *"But it's my pleasure."*

EXERCISE 8 **Fill in the blanks with an appropriate verb for past mistakes.**

EXAMPLES A: I didn't study for the last test, and I failed it.

B: You should ___ **have studied** ___.

A: I know, but there was a great party the night before, and I went with my friends.

B: You shouldn't ___ **have gone** ___ to a party the night before a test.

1. A: I'm so hungry. I didn't have time to eat breakfast this morning.

   B: You should _____ something before class.

   A: I know, but I was late.

   B: What time did you get up?

   A: About 45 minutes before class.

   B: You should _____ earlier. By the way, what topic did you use for your composition?

   A: Oh, my gosh! I forgot about the composition.

   B: You should _____ down the assignment.

   A: You're right. I'll get a calendar, and from now on, I'll write down all my assignments.

2. (*cell phone conversation*)

   A: Hi. I'm at the supermarket now. Did you ask me to buy cereal?

   B: Yes. Don't you remember? You should _____ the list.

   A: I know, but I thought I'd remember everything, so I didn't take the list.

   B: This is what we need: a gallon of milk, a bag of dog food, and a watermelon.

   A: Those things are heavy. How do you expect me to carry all of those things home?

   B: In the car, of course.

   A: Oh. I came here by bike. I should _____.

   B: Yes, you should have.

(continued)

3. A: How was your trip during spring break?

 B: It was great. You should _____ with us.

 A: I wanted to go with you, but I didn't have enough money.

 B: You should _____ your money instead of spending it eating out in restaurants all the time.

 A: You're right. And I shouldn't _____ so many CDs.

 B: Did you get my postcard?

 A: No. When did you send it?

 B: Over two weeks ago. I should _____ it to the post office instead of putting it in the hotel mailbox.

4. (*husband and wife*)

 H: I washed my blue pants with my new white shirt and now my shirt looks blue.

 W: You should _____ the clothes by color before putting them in the washing machine. I always separate mine.

 H: I should _____ my clothes to you to wash.

 W: I may be your wife, but I'm not your maid. So don't give me your dirty clothes.

5. (*wife and husband*)

 W: This is a terrible trip. Why did you suggest going to the mountains? We should _____ to the coast. It's too cold here. I don't like cold weather.

 H: You should _____ me that before we left.

 W: I *did* tell you that, but you didn't pay attention. We didn't take jackets. We should _____ our jackets.

 H: We can go and buy some.

W: I don't want to spend money on jackets when we've got perfectly good ones at home.

H: Maybe we should _____ home instead of taking a trip.

6. (*student and teacher*)

S: Can you tell me my midterm grade?

T: Didn't you receive it by mail?

S: No. I moved right after the semester began.

T: You should _____ a change of address in the school office when you moved.

S: I'll report it today. So can you tell me my grade?

T: It's a C.

S: Why a C? I got Bs and As on the tests.

T: But you didn't do all your homework. You should _____ all your homework.

S: But I had to work full-time.

T: You should _____ about that before you registered for four courses.

S: You're right. I didn't think much about homework when I registered.

7. A: I took a young woman from class out for dinner last week, but I didn't have enough money.

B: You should _____ enough money with you.

A: I took about $30 with me. I thought we were going to go to a fast-food place, but she chose a fancy restaurant.

B: You should _____ the restaurant.

(continued)

A: I realized that later. She ordered appetizers, then dinner, then dessert and coffee. I thought she would pay for part of the dinner. But when the bill came, she just sat there.

B: You should _____ her that you wanted to split the bill.

A: I couldn't tell her that. I was trying to impress her.

B: So what did you do?

A: I went to the bathroom and called my brother on my cell phone. He rushed over to the restaurant and brought me some money. He pretended that our meeting there was an accident.

B: You should _____ her the truth. Lying to her is no way to start a relationship.

A: I don't think I'm going to go out with her again.

8. A: What happened to your car?

B: I had an accident. Someone hit me from behind.

A: What did the police say?

B: We didn't call the police. The other driver gave me his phone number and told me he would pay for the damage. But when I called, it was a disconnected number.

A: You should _____ the police.

B: And I should _____ information from his driver's license.

A: You mean you didn't even take information from his driver's license?

B: No. He looked honest.

A: You should _____ information about his insurance too.

B: I know. It's too late to get it now.

5.5 *Be Supposed To* in the Past

EXAMPLES	EXPLANATION
We **were supposed to** get the results of the election on election night, but we didn't.	*Was/were supposed to* is used for rules or promises that have been broken or expectations that have not been met.
The teacher **was supposed to** explain the election process to us, but she didn't have time.	
We **were supposed to** have a test today, but the teacher was absent.	
I **was supposed to** call my parents last night, but I forgot.	

EXERCISE 9 **Fill in the blanks with a verb. Answers may vary.**

EXAMPLE She was supposed to ___finish___ the report by Friday, but she didn't have enough time.

1. I was supposed to _____ my homework, but my printer wasn't working. So I wrote it by hand.

2. You were supposed to _____ me this morning. I waited all morning for your call.

3. Our plane was supposed to _____ at 9:45, but it was late. We had to wait in the airport for two more hours to start our trip.

4. The teacher was supposed to _____ our compositions yesterday, but he was sick and didn't do it.

5. It was supposed to _____ last weekend, so we canceled our picnic. But it never rained.

6. I got a parking ticket yesterday. I wasn't supposed to _____ on the east side of the street, but I didn't see the signs.

7. I couldn't get into the building. I was supposed to _____ my student ID, but I left it at home.

8. The kids weren't supposed to _____ the cookies before they ate dinner, but they did.

9. The play was supposed to _____ at 8 P.M., but it didn't begin until 8:10.

10. You were supposed to _____ out the application with a black pen, but you used a red pen.

The Media and Presidential Elections

Before
You Read

1. Have you ever voted in an election?

2. Do you think we learn a lot about candidates from TV?

CD 2, TR 13

Read the following textbook article. Pay special attention to _must have_ + past participle and _had to_ + base form. Also pay attention to _couldn't have_ + past participle and _couldn't_ + base form.

Harry S. Truman, president 1945–1953

The media—newspapers, magazines, radio, television, and now the Internet—play an important part in getting out information and often shaping public opinion. The media even played a historical role in two notable presidential elections.

When President Franklin Roosevelt died in 1945, Vice President Harry S. Truman became president. But in 1948, Truman **had to campaign** for re-election. He ran against Thomas Dewey. At that time, television was still new and most people did not own one. So candidates **had to travel** from city to city by train to meet the people. Truman traveled tirelessly, but Dewey was considered the stronger candidate.

Polls[6] were so sure of a Dewey victory that they stopped asking for public opinion a week before the election. The media, especially newspapers and the radio, thought that Truman **couldn't win**. When Truman went to bed the night of the election, he thought that he would lose.

The election results were coming in slowly and newspapers **had to prepare** the news of the election. On the basis of early opinion polls, the media concluded that Dewey **must have won** the election, and many newspapers showed Dewey's victory. However, they were wrong. Truman won by 2 million votes. When the votes were all counted, the newspapers **had to admit** their mistake.

[6]A _poll_ is an analysis of public opinion on different matters compiled by special agencies. Statistics are made based on the answers to questions.

Another example of how the media can influence results took place in the 1960 presidential race between John Kennedy and Richard Nixon. For the first time in history, the two candidates debated[7] each other on TV. They **had to** answer difficult

Kennedy and Nixon debate

questions. Many people who heard the Nixon-Kennedy debate on the radio thought that Nixon was the stronger candidate. But people who saw the debate on TV thought that the young, handsome Kennedy was the stronger candidate. Also, Nixon was sweating under the hot lights, and people thought that he **must have been** nervous and uncomfortable with the questions. It was a close election, but Kennedy won. Many people think Kennedy **couldn't have won** without TV.

In the 2008 presidential election, John McCain lost to Barack Obama. Obama reached out to the Internet generation; McCain didn't even know how to use a computer. He **had to** depend on his wife to read and send e-mail. Although it may not be important for a president to be an Internet user (after all, he has staff who can do it for him), McCain wasn't in touch with the social, cultural, and economic realities of the Internet.

It is clear that political hopefuls now need the media to get their images and messages across.

5.6 *Must Have* vs. *Had To*

Must have + past participle and *had to* + base form have completely different meanings.

EXAMPLES	EXPLANATION
Truman became president in 1945 when Franklin Roosevelt died. But he **had to** campaign for re-election in 1948. Truman **had to** travel by train to meet the people. During the debate, the candidates **had to** answer difficult questions. John McCain **had to** depend on his wife to do e-mail.	To show necessity (personal or legal) in the past, we use *had to* + base form. We cannot use *must* in the past with this meaning.
Based on opinion polls, the newspapers concluded that Dewey **must have won**. Truman **must have been** surprised when he found out that he had won. TV viewers thought that Nixon **must have been** nervous and uncomfortable during the debate.	When *must* shows a conclusion or deduction in the past, use *must have* + past participle.

[7]In a *debate*, the candidates have to answer questions (on TV or radio) so that the public can judge who is the better candidate.

EXERCISE 10 Below is a conversation between two American citizens about the 2000 presidential election. Write *had to* + base form for a past necessity. Write *must have* + past participle for a past deduction or conclusion.

CD 2, TR 14

A: The 2000 election between Al Gore, the Democratic candidate, and George W. Bush, the Republican candidate, was so strange.

B: It was?

A: Don't you remember? The election was close and they <u>had to count</u> the votes again to see who won. It took them
(example: count)
five weeks to figure out who won the election.

B: Bush and Gore <u>must have been</u> nervous the whole time,
(example: be)
waiting to find out the results.

A: Yes, they probably were. And there were so many problems with the election that they _____ to the Supreme
(1 go)
Court to decide who won.

B: Did you vote in that election?

A: Of course.

B: You always vote for a Democrat, so you _____
(2 vote)
for Gore.

A: Yes, I did.

B: You _____ very disappointed when they finally
(3 be)
announced that Gore lost.

A: Yes, I was. What about you? Who did you vote for?

B: I _____ overtime that day so I didn't vote.
(4 work)

A: That's no excuse for not voting. Besides, your boss is required to give you time off to vote.

B: One person's vote doesn't matter much anyway.

A: It did in 2000. Every vote counted. The election was on November 7 and we _____ until December 13 to find out who
(5 wait)
won the election because it was such a close race.

5.7 Could + Base Form vs. Could Have + Past Participle

There are several ways to express *can* in the past, depending on the meaning you want to convey.

EXAMPLES	EXPLANATION
Now I can speak English well. A few years ago, I **could speak** only a few words of English. I **was able to communicate** in very simple English.	In affirmative statements, *could* + base form means *used to be able to*. The person had this ability over a period of time. *Was/were able to* can also be used for ability over a past period of time.
President Kennedy **was able to prevent** a war. He **was able to convince** the Soviets to send back their missiles. I looked on the Internet and **was able to find** Lincoln's Gettysburg Address.	Use *was/were able to* for success in doing a single action. Do not use *could* for a single action.
I **couldn't vote** in the last election because I wasn't a citizen. I **wasn't able to vote** in the last election because I wasn't a citizen. The newspapers **weren't able to predict** the outcome of the 1948 election. The newspapers **couldn't predict** the outcome of the 1948 election.	In negative statements, *couldn't* and *wasn't/ weren't able to* are used interchangeably.
Al Gore **could have run** for president again, but he decided to stay out of politics. The Cuban Missile Crisis **could have destroyed** the world.	Use *could have* + past participle for an action that didn't happen.
Some people thought that Kennedy **couldn't have won** the election without TV. Farmers in the South **couldn't have become** rich without slaves.	Use *couldn't have* + past participle to show that something was impossible in the past.

EXERCISE 11 **ABOUT YOU** Fill in the blanks and discuss your answers.

EXAMPLE When I didn't know much English, I couldn't <u>talk to people on the phone</u>.

1. When I was young, I could always count on _____.
2. When I was younger, I could _____ better than I can now.

(continued)

3. When I was younger, I couldn't _____ as well as
I can now.

4. One of my goals was to _____.
I was/wasn't able (*choose one*) to achieve my goal.

5. I could never understand why _____.

6. When I didn't know much English, I couldn't _____.

7. I couldn't _____ a few years ago
because _____.

8. When I first came to the U.S., I was/wasn't (*choose one*) able to

_____.

EXERCISE 12 **Fill in the blanks with *have* + a past participle.**

EXAMPLE I could _____*have driven*_____ to work, but I decided to ride
my bike instead.

1. When Lincoln gave the Gettysburg Address, he could
_____ a long speech, but he decided to give a very
short speech.

2. My sister is a citizen and she could _____ in the last
election, but she was sick that day.

3. We could _____ the election results on TV, but we
decided to listen to the news on the radio instead.

4. She could _____ English in her country, but she
decided to study French instead.

5. I could _____ my mom, but I sent her a text message
instead to tell her I'd be home late.

6. You could _____ your homework on the computer,
but I see you did it by hand.

7. Why didn't you tell me you were moving last Saturday? I'm sure you
needed help. I could _____ you.

8. I could _____ the bus today, but the weather was
nice so I decided to walk.

9. I could _____ a quick e-mail to my grandmother but
I decided to write her a long letter by hand.

10. We could _____ in a restaurant last weekend, but we
saved money and ate at home.

5.8 More on *Couldn't Have*

EXAMPLES	EXPLANATION
A: My parents voted for Kennedy in 1964. B: What? They **couldn't have voted** for him in 1964. He died in 1963. A: I think I saw your brother at the library yesterday. B: It **couldn't have been** him. He's in Europe on vacation.	*Couldn't have* + past participle is used to show disbelief or to show that someone's statement is absolutely impossible. We are saying that we can't believe this information because it is illogical.
Thanks so much for helping me paint my house. I **couldn't have done** it without you.	When we want to show gratitude or appreciation for someone's help, we often say, *"I couldn't have done it without you."*
Compare: a. I **couldn't vote** in the last election because I was out of town. b. You say you voted in the last election? You **couldn't have voted** because you weren't a citizen at that time. a. I **couldn't move** the refrigerator myself, so my brother helped me. b. You say you moved the piano by yourself? You **couldn't have moved** it by yourself. It's too heavy for one person.	In sentences (a), you know that something didn't happen in the past. In sentences (b), you are responding in disbelief to someone's statement about the past.

EXERCISE 13 **Fill in the blanks to make statements of disbelief.**

EXAMPLE   A: When I was a child, I saw President Kennedy.

B: You ___couldn't have seen him___. He died before you were born.

1. A: U.S. athletes won ten gold medals at the 1980 Olympics.

   B: They _____.

   The U.S. didn't participate in the 1980 Olympics.

2. A: We had an English test on December 25.

   B: You _____.

   The school was closed on Christmas Day.

3. A: President Kennedy ran for re-election in 1964.

   B: He _____.

   He died in 1963.

(continued)

4. A: George W. Bush ran for re-election in 2008.

B: You're wrong. He _____ because he had already been president for two terms, and that's the limit.

5. A: Look at the big fish I caught yesterday.

B: You _____ that fish. It has a price tag on it. You must have bought it at the store.

6. A: I got an A on my math test.

B: That's impossible. The teacher said that the highest grade was a B+. You _____ an A.

7. A: One student gave the teacher a perfect composition with no mistakes.

B: The teacher thinks that the student _____ it by himself. She thinks somebody must have helped him.

8. A: Somebody called me last night at midnight and didn't leave a message. Was it you?

B: It _____ me. I was sleeping at midnight.

9. Teacher: You failed the test.

Student: What? I _____ the test. I studied for hours!

10. A: I can't find my house keys.

B: Maybe you left them at work.

A: I _____ them at work. I used them to open the door and get into the house a few minutes ago.

11. A: Thanks for helping me move last Saturday.

B: My pleasure.

A: I _____ without your help.

12. A: Hi. Don't you remember me?

B: No, I'm sorry.

A: We met in a math class last year.

B: We _____ last year. I just started school two weeks ago.

5.9 Continuous Forms of Past Modals

We use continuous modals in the past to talk about a specific time in the past.

Subject	Modal	*Not*	*Have Been*	Present Participle	Complement
They	must		have been	waiting	at 8:30 P.M.
He	might		have been	sleeping	at 10:30 P.M.
You	could		have been	doing	your homework this morning.
I	should	not	have been	driving	so fast.

EXERCISE 14 Fill in the blanks with the continuous form of the modal.

EXAMPLE **A:** I was injured in a car accident. I wasn't wearing a seat belt.

B: You should ___have been wearing___ your seat belt.

1. **A:** Why didn't you finish your homework?

   B: I was watching a movie on TV last night.

   A: You should _____ your homework instead.

2. **A:** I wasted so much time when I was young. I didn't take my studies

   seriously.

   B: But you had a good education.

   A: I know. But I could _____ English instead of

   playing soccer every day after school.

3. **A:** I tried to call you a few hours ago but there was no answer.

   B: I was home. I must _____ a shower when you called.

4. **A:** What do you think of last night's rainstorm?

   B: I didn't hear it. I must _____.

   A: How could you sleep through so much thunder?

   B: I'm a heavy sleeper.

(continued)

5. A: I went to your house last Saturday, but you didn't answer the door.
I thought you were going to be home.

    B: I often work on my car on Saturdays. I might _____

        on my car when you arrived. Did you look in the garage?

    A: No. I didn't think of it.

6. (*teacher to student*)

    T: Peter, can you answer question number six?

    S: I'm sorry. I wasn't listening. I was thinking of something else.
What was the question?

    T: You should _____.

Summary of Lesson 5

Modals

Must

Meaning	Present/Future	Past
Legal obligation	I **must go** to court next week.	I **had to go** to court last week.
Urgency	I **must talk** to the doctor right now!	
Strong necessity	I **must study** for the test next week.	I **had to study** for the test last month.
Prohibition	You **must not tell** a lie in court.	
Deduction; conclusion	He's wearing a coat inside. He **must be** cold.	I can't find my keys. There's a hole in my pocket. I **must have lost** them.

Should

Meaning	Present/Future	Past
Advice	You **should buy** a new car next year.	You **should have bought** a new car last year.
Mistakes (in past)	You **shouldn't eat** fatty foods.	I **shouldn't have eaten** so many potato chips last night.

Can/Could

Meaning	Present/Future	Past
Ability	I **can speak** English now.	I **could speak** German when I was a child.
Acceptability	You **can wear** jeans to class every day.	You **could have worn** jeans to the party last night.
Permission/ prohibition	We **can use** a dictionary to write a composition. We **can't use** our books during a test.	We **could use** a dictionary to write the last composition. We **couldn't use** a dictionary during the last test.
Suggestion	To learn about computers, you **can take** a course, or you **could buy** a book and teach yourself.	
Possibility	Mary isn't here today. She **could be** sick.	Mary wasn't here yesterday. She **could have been** sick.
Direction not taken		I **could have gone** to Canada, but I decided to come to the U.S.
Impossibility; disbelief		**A:** I voted for President Obama in 2008. **B:** You **couldn't have voted** for Obama. You weren't a citizen in 2008.

May/Might

Meaning	Present/Future	Past
Permission	You **may use** a dictionary during the test.	
Possibility	I **may have** a job interview next week. I'm still not sure. The teacher isn't here. She **might be** sick.	Simon is wearing a suit to class. He **may have had** a job interview this morning. The teacher wasn't here yesterday. She **might have been** sick.

Ought To

Meaning	Present/Future	Past
Advice	She **ought to buy** a new car soon.	She **ought to have bought** a new car last year. (*rare*)

Related Expressions

Have To

Meaning	Present/Future	Past
Necessity (personal or legal)	I **have to study** now. I **have to go** to court next week.	I **had to study** yesterday. I **had to go** to court last week.
Lack of necessity	My job is close to my home. I **don't have to drive**. I can walk.	My last job was close to my home. I **didn't have to drive**. I could walk.

Have Got To

Meaning	Present/Future	Past
Necessity	I**'ve got to go** to court next week.	

Be Able To

Meaning	Present/Future	Past
Ability	She **is able to play** chess now.	She **was able to play** chess when she was a child.

Be Allowed To / Be Permitted To

Meaning	Present/Future	Past
Permission	We **are not allowed to talk** during a test.	We **were not allowed to talk** during the last test.
	You **are not permitted to park** at a bus stop.	You **were not permitted to park** on this street yesterday because the city was cleaning the streets.

Be Supposed To

Meaning	Present/Future	Past
Expectation	My brother **is supposed to arrive** at 10 P.M.	My brother **was supposed to arrive** at 10 P.M., but his plane was delayed.
	The weatherman said it **is supposed to rain** tomorrow.	The weatherman said it **was supposed to rain** yesterday, but it didn't.
	I**'m supposed to help** my brother move on Saturday.	I **was supposed to help** my brother move last Saturday, but I got sick.
	You **are supposed to wear** your seat belt.	He **was supposed to wear** his seat belt, but he didn't.

Had Better

Meaning	Present/Future	Past
Warning	You**'d better take** an umbrella, or you'll get wet.	

Editing Advice

1. After a modal, always use a base form.

   have
   He could ~~has~~ gone to the party.

2. To form the past of a modal, use *have* + past participle.

   have eaten
   I shouldn't ~~ate~~ so much before I went to bed last night.

3. Don't use *of* after a modal to express past. Use *have*.

   have
   You should ~~of~~ gone to bed earlier last night.

4. Don't confuse *couldn't have* + past participle and *couldn't* + base form.

   find
   Last night when I got home, I couldn't ~~have found~~ a parking space.

5. Use the correct form for the past participle.

   gone
   He should have ~~went~~ to the doctor when he felt the pain in his chest.

6. Don't forget the **d** in *supposed to*. Don't forget the verb *be*.

   d
   You were suppose ˄ to meet me after class yesterday.

   was
   ˄ I supposed to work last Saturday, but I got sick.

7. *Can* is never used for the past.

   couldn't drive
   He ~~can't drove~~ his car this morning because the battery was dead.

Editing Quiz

Some of the shaded words and phrases have mistakes. Find the mistakes and correct them. If the shaded words are correct, write *C*.

I had a terrible day yesterday. I was supposed to be ~~C~~ at work early, but I
(example)

couldn't start
~~can't started~~ my car in the morning. The battery was dead. I
(example)

must had forgotten to turn off the lights the night before. I saw a neighbor
(1)

of mine and asked him to help, but he can't stopped because he was in a
(2)

hurry. He had to attend an important meeting. I stopped another neighbor
(3)

and asked for help, but she couldn't have helped me because she was
(4)

taking her kids to school. I stopped a third neighbor and said, "Do you

remember when I helped you push your car last winter?" He answered,

"It couldn't have been me. I just moved here last month. It must of been
(5)   *(6)*

someone else." He must thought I was crazy.
(7)

I was suppose to arrive at work at 8 A.M. but I didn't arrive until
(8)

10:30. I should have took the subway to work. It might have been a
(9)   *(10)*

lot easier.

Lesson 5 Test/Review

PART 1 **A husband (H) and wife (W) are driving to a party and are lost. They are arguing in the car. Fill in the blanks to complete this conversation.**

W: We're lost. And we don't even have a map. You should

_____**have taken**_____ a map.
(example)

H: I didn't think we were going to need one. I must _____
(1)

a wrong turn.

W: I think you were supposed to make a right turn at the last intersection, but you turned left. We should _____ for directions (2) the last time we stopped for gas.

H: You know I don't like to ask for directions.

W: Let's use the cell phone and call the Allens and ask them how to get to their house.

H: Let's see. I thought I had the cell phone in my pocket. I can't find it. I must _____ it at home. (3)

W: No, you didn't leave it at home. I've got the phone here in my purse. Oh, no. You forgot to recharge the battery. You should _____ it last night. (4)

H: Why is it my fault? You could _____ it too. (5)

W: Well, we'll just have to look for a pay phone. Do you have any change?

H: I only have dollar bills.

W: You should _____ some change with you. (6)

H: Again, it's my fault.

W: Watch out! You could _____ that other car! (7)

H: I wasn't going to hit that car. I didn't come anywhere close to it.

W: I don't know why we're going in our car anyway. The Petersons offered us a ride. We could _____ with them. (8)

H: You should _____ with the Petersons and I should (9) _____ home. I could _____ (10) (11) the football game today instead of listening to you complain!

Fill out the following form. Print in black ink. Mail or fax the application to:

Ms. Judy Lipton
P.O. Box 32X
Chicago, IL 60640
FAX number: 312-555-4321

Applications must be submitted by November 15.

Name _____*Wilson*_____ _____*Jack*_____ _____*N*_____
　　　　(last)　　　　　　　　　(first)　　　　　　　(middle initial)

Address _____*5040 N. Albany Ave.*_____
City _____*Chicago*_____ State _____*IL*_____ Zip code _____
Telephone ( ) _____*539-2756*_____
E-mail address (optional) _____*jnwilson00@e*mail.com*_____ Sex _____*M*_____
Date of birth _____*18*_____ _____*2*_____ _____*69*_____ (You must be at least 18.)
　　　　　　　　(month)　　(day)　　(year)
Social Security number _____*549*_____ . _____*62*_____ . _____*71XX*_____

Educational background:

		Date graduated	Degree or major
High School	*Roosevelt*	*1897*	
College			
Graduate School			

Employment history (Please start with your present or last job.)

Company	Position	Dates	Supervisor	Reason for leaving
Apex	*stock boy*	*5/88–3/94*	*R. Wilinot*	*personal*
Smith, Inc.	*warehouse*	*5/94–12/01*	*M. Smith*	*pay*
Olson Co.	*loading dock*	*1/02–present*	*B. Adams*	

Do not write in the shaded box. For office use only.

> Rec'd. by _____*J.W.*_____
> Amer. cit. _____*yes*_____
> Doc. checked _____*?*_____
> Transcripts received _____*yes*_____

The Immigration Act of 1986 requires all successful applicants to present documents to prove U.S. citizenship or permanent residence with permission to work in the U.S.

This company is an Equal Opportunity Employer. Race, religion, nationality, marital status, and physical disability will not influence our decision to hire. _____*Catholic*_____

I certify that these answers are true.

Signature: _____*Jack N. Wilson*_____ Date: _____*November 13*_____

EXAMPLE   He didn't read the instructions carefully. He should
_____ **have read** _____ them more carefully.

1. He wrote his application with a pencil. He was supposed to

_____.

2. He didn't write his zip code. He should _____ his

zip code.

3. He forgot to include his area code. He should _____ it.

4. He included his e-mail address. He didn't have to

_____ it.

5. He wrote the day (18) before the month (2). He should

_____.

6. He wrote that he graduated from high school in 1897. He couldn't

_____ in 1897. That's more than 100 years ago! He

must _____ 1987.

7. He didn't fill in any college attended. He might not

_____ college.

8. He said that he left his first job for personal reasons. He might

_____ because he didn't like his boss.

9. He didn't fill in his reason for leaving his last job. He should

_____.

10. He wrote his first job first. He was supposed to _____.

11. He wrote in the shaded box. He wasn't supposed to

_____. He must not _____ the

directions very carefully.

12. He included his religion. He wasn't supposed to _____

it. He must not _____ the sentence about religion.

13. He printed his name on the bottom line. He was supposed to

_____.

14. He mailed the application, but he could _____

instead.

15. For today's date, he wrote only the month and day. He should

_____ the year too.

PART 3

Fill in the blanks with the past of the modal or expression in parentheses ( ).

After Alan (A) has waited for two hours for his friend Bill (B) to arrive for dinner, Bill finally arrives.

A: Why are you so late? You _____**were supposed to**_____ be here two hours ago.
(example: be supposed to)

B: I'm sorry. I got lost and I _____ your house.
(1 can't/find)

A: You _____ a road map.
(2 should/take)

B: I did, but I _____ it while I was driving.
(3 can/not/read)

I _____ a wrong turn.
(4 must/make)

A: Where did you get off the highway?

B: At Madison Street.

A: That's impossible. You _____ off at Madison Street.
(5 can/not/get)
There's no exit there.

B: Oh. It _____ Adams Street, then.
(6 must/be)

A: But Adams Street is not so far from here.

B: I know. But I had a flat tire after I got off the highway.

A: Did you call for a tow truck?

B: I _____ for a tow truck because I'm a member of a
(7 can/call)

motor club. But I thought it would take too long. So I changed the

tire myself.

A: But you're over two hours late. How long did it take you to change

the tire?

B: It _____ about 15 minutes, but then
(8 might/take)

I _____ home, take a shower, and change clothes.
(9 have to/go)
I was so dirty.

A: You _____ me.
(10 should/call)

B: I wanted to, but I _____ the paper where I had your
(11 can/not/find)

phone number. I _____ it while I was changing the tire.
(12 must/lose)

A: Well, thank goodness you're here now. But you'll have to eat dinner

alone. I got hungry and _____ for you.
(13 can/not/wait)

Expansion

Classroom Activities

1 **A student will read one of the following problems out loud to the class. The student will pretend that this is his or her problem. Other students will ask for more information and give advice about the problem. Try to use past and present modals.**

Problem A My mother-in-law came to the U.S. last May. She stayed with us for three months. I told my husband that he had to find another apartment for her. He didn't want to. I finally said to my husband, "Tell her to leave, or I'm leaving." So he helped her move into her own apartment. Now my husband is mad at me. Do you think I did the right thing?

Problem B My wife gave me a beautiful watch last Christmas. While I was on a business trip in New York last month, I left my watch in my hotel room. A few days later, I called the hotel, but they said that no one reported finding a watch. So far, I haven't told my wife that I lost the watch. What should I do?

Problem C A very nice American family invited me to dinner last night. The wife worked very hard to make a beautiful dinner. I'm not used to eating American food and thought it tasted awful. But I ate it so I wouldn't hurt their feelings. They invited me to dinner again next week. What can I do about the food?

Problem D *Write your own problem, real or imaginary.*

2 **Fill out the application on page 180 of Lesson Four. Make some mistakes on purpose. Find a partner and exchange books with him or her. Tell each other about the mistakes using modals.**

EXAMPLE   For "sex" you wrote M. You're a woman, so you should have written F.

Talk About It

1 **The following excerpt from a poem by John Greenleaf Whittier is about regret. Discuss the meaning of the poem.**

> For all sad words of tongue or pen,
> The saddest are these: "It might have been!"

2 **Talk about the election process in your native country. How is the leader chosen?**

3 **Talk about how the media influences our decisions in voting or buying.**

Write
About It

❶ Write about a mistake you once made. Tell about what you should have done to avoid the problem.

❷ Write a short composition about another direction your life could have taken. What made you decide not to go in that direction?

❸ The assassinations of Abraham Lincoln and John F. Kennedy were great American tragedies. Write about the tragic death of a famous person.

❹ Write about how a tragedy occurred and what was done (or not done) to solve this problem.

EXAMPLE

Hurricane Katrina

In our English class, we read an article about Hurricane Katrina in New Orleans. The mayor told residents to leave before the hurricane struck. Everyone should have left immediately, but many people stayed . . .

 For more practice using grammar in context, please visit our Web site.

Appendices

Appendix A

Noncount Nouns

There are several types of noncount nouns.

Group A: Nouns that have no distinct, separate parts. We look at the whole.

milk	juice	bread	electricity
oil	yogurt	meat	lightning
water	pork	butter	thunder
coffee	poultry	paper	cholesterol
tea	soup	air	blood

Group B: Nouns that have parts that are too small or insignificant to count.

rice	hair	sand
sugar	popcorn	corn
salt	snow	grass

Group C: Nouns that are classes or categories of things. The members of the category are not the same.

money or cash (nickels, dimes, dollars)	mail (letters, packages, postcards, flyers)
furniture (chairs, tables, beds)	homework (compositions, exercises, readings)
clothing (sweaters, pants, dresses)	jewelry (necklaces, bracelets, rings)

Group D: Nouns that are abstractions.

love	happiness	nutrition	patience	work	nature
truth	education	intelligence	poverty	health	help
beauty	advice	unemployment	music	fun	energy
luck/fortune	knowledge	pollution	art	information	friendship

Group E: Subjects of study.

history	grammar	biology
chemistry	geometry	math (mathematics*)

*__Note:__ Even though *mathematics* ends with *s*, it is not plural.

(continued)

Notice the quantity words used with count and noncount nouns.

Singular Count	Plural Count	Noncount
a tomato	tomatoes	coffee
one tomato	**two** tomatoes	**two cups of** coffee
	some tomatoes	**some** coffee
no tomato	**no** tomatoes	**no** coffee
	any tomatoes (with questions and negatives)	**any** coffee (with questions and negatives)
	a lot of tomatoes	**a lot of** coffee
	many tomatoes	**much** coffee (with questions and negatives)
	a few tomatoes	**a little** coffee
	several tomatoes	**several** cups of coffee
	How many tomatoes?	**How much** coffee?

The following words can be used as either count nouns or noncount nouns. However, the meaning changes according to the way the nouns are used.

Count	Noncount
Oranges and grapefruit are **fruits** that contain a lot of vitamin C.	I bought some **fruit** at the fruit store.
Ice cream and butter are **foods** that contain cholesterol.	We don't need to go shopping today. We have a lot of **food** at home.
He wrote a **paper** about hypnosis.	I need some **paper** to write my composition.
He committed three **crimes** last year.	There is a lot of **crime** in a big city.
I have 200 **chickens** on my farm.	We ate some **chicken** for dinner.
I don't want to bore you with all my **troubles.**	I have some **trouble** with my car.
She went to Puerto Rico three **times.**	She spent a lot of **time** on her project.
She drank three **glasses** of water.	The window is made of bulletproof **glass.**
I had a bad **experience** during my trip to Paris.	She has some **experience** with computer programming.
I don't know much about the **lives** of my grandparents.	**Life** is sometimes happy, sometimes sad.
I heard a **noise** outside my window.	Those children are making a lot of **noise.**

Appendix B

Uses of Articles

Overview of Articles

Articles tell us if a noun is definite or indefinite.

	Count		Noncount
	Singular	**Plural**	
Definite	**the** book	**the** books	**the** coffee
Indefinite	**a** book	**(some/any)** books	**(some/any)** coffee

Part 1. Uses of the Indefinite Article

A. To classify a subject

Examples	Explanation
Chicago is **a** city. Illinois is **a** state. Abraham Lincoln was **an** American president. What's that? It's **a** tall building.	• Use *a* before a consonant sound. • Use *an* before a vowel sound. • You can put an adjective before the noun.
Chicago and Los Angeles are cities. Lincoln and Washington were American presidents. What are those? They're tall buildings.	Do not use an article before a plural noun.

B. To make a generalization about a noun

Examples	Explanation
A dog has sharp teeth. **Dogs** have sharp teeth. **An elephant** has big ears. **Elephants** have big ears.	Use the indefinite article (*a/an*) + a singular count noun or no article with a plural noun. Both the singular and plural forms have the same meaning.
Coffee contains caffeine. **Milk** is white. **Love** makes people happy. **Money** can't buy **happiness**.	Do not use an article to make a generalization about a noncount noun.

(continued)

Appendix B / Uses of Articles **AP3**

C. To introduce a new noun into the conversation

Examples	Explanation
I have **a cell phone**. I have **an umbrella**.	Use the indefinite article *a/an* with singular count nouns.
Count: I have **(some) dishes**. Do you have **(any) cups**? I don't have **(any) forks**. **Noncount:** I have **(some) money** with me. Do you have **(any) cash** with you? I don't have **(any) time**.	Use *some* or *any* with plural nouns and noncount nouns. Use *any* in questions and negatives. *Some* and *any* can be omitted.
There's **an elevator** in the building. Are there **any restrooms** on this floor? There isn't **any money** in my checking account.	*There* + a form of *be* can introduce an indefinite noun into a conversation.

Part 2. Uses of the Definite Article

A. To refer to a previously mentioned noun

Examples	Explanation
There's **a dog** in the next apartment. **The dog** barks all the time.	We start by saying *a dog*. We continue by saying *the dog*.
We bought **some grapes**. We ate **the grapes** this morning.	We start by saying *some grapes*. We continue by saying *the grapes*.
I need **some sugar**. I'm going to use **the sugar** to bake a cake.	We start by saying *some sugar*. We continue by saying *the sugar*.
Did you buy **any coffee?** Yes. **The coffee** is in the cabinet.	We start by saying *any coffee*. We continue by saying *the coffee*.

B. When the speaker and the listener have the same reference

Examples	Explanation
The boy is shoveling snow. **The toys** are broken. **The money** on the table is mine.	The object is present, so the speaker and listener have the same object in mind.
a. **The teacher** is writing **on the board** in **the classroom**. b. **The president** is talking about taxes. c. Please turn off **the lights** and shut **the door** and **the windows** before you leave **the house**.	a. Students in the same class have things in common. b. People who live in the same country have things in common. c. People who live in the same house have things in common.
The house on the corner is beautiful. I spent **the money you gave me**.	The listener knows exactly which one because the speaker defines or specifies which one.

C. When there is only one in our experience

Examples	Explanation
The sun is bigger than **the moon**. There are many problems in **the world**.	The *sun*, the *moon*, and the *world* are unique objects. There is only one in our immediate experience.
Write your name on **the top** of the page. Sign your name on **the back** of the check.	The page has only one top. The check has only one back.
The Amazon is **the longest** river in the world. Alaska is **the biggest** state in the U.S.	A superlative indicates that there is only one.

(continued)

D. With familiar places

Examples	Explanation
I'm going to **the store** after work. Do you need anything? **The bank** is closed now. I'll go tomorrow.	We use *the* with certain familiar places and people—*the bank, the zoo, the park, the store, the movies, the beach, the post office, the bus, the train, the doctor, the dentist*—when we refer to the one that we habitually visit or use.

Language Notes:
1. Omit *the* after a preposition with the words *church, school, work,* and *bed*.
   He's **in church**.
   I'm going **to school**.
   They're **at work**.
   I'm going **to bed**.
2. Omit *to* and *the* with *home* and *downtown*.
   I'm going **home**.
   Are you going **downtown** after class?

E. To make a formal generalization

Examples	Explanation
The shark is the oldest and most primitive fish. **The bat** is a nocturnal animal.	To say that something is true of all members of a group, use *the* with singular count nouns.
The computer has changed the way people deal with information. **The cell phone** uses radio waves.	To talk about a class of inventions, use *the*.
The heart is a muscle that pumps blood to the rest of the body. **The ear** has three parts: outer, middle, and inner.	To talk about an organ of the body in a general sense, use *the*.

Language Note:
For informal generalizations, use *a* + a singular noun or no article with a plural noun.

Compare:
   The computer has changed the way we deal with information.
   A computer is expensive.
   Computers are expensive.

Part 3. Special Uses of Articles

No Article	Article

Personal names:
    John Kennedy
    George Bush
	The whole family:
	    the Kennedys
	    the Bushes

Title and name:
    Queen Elizabeth
    Pope Benedict
	Title without name:
	    the Queen
	    the Pope

Cities, states, countries, continents:
    Cleveland
    Ohio
    Mexico
    South America
	Places that are considered a union:
	    the United States
	    the former Soviet Union
	Place names: the _____ of _____
	    the Republic of China
	    the District of Columbia

Mountains:
    Mount Everest
    Mount McKinley
	Mountain ranges:
	    the Himalayas
	    the Rocky Mountains

Islands:
    Coney Island
    Staten Island
	Collectives of islands:
	    the Hawaiian Islands
	    the Philippines

Lakes:
    Lake Superior
    Lake Michigan
	Collectives of lakes:
	    the Great Lakes
	    the Finger Lakes

Beaches:
    Palm Beach
    Pebble Beach
	Rivers, oceans, seas, canals:
	    the Mississippi River
	    the Atlantic Ocean
	    the Dead Sea
	    the Panama Canal

Streets and avenues:
    Madison Avenue
    Wall Street
	Well-known buildings:
	    the Willis Tower
	    the Empire State Building

Parks:
    Central Park
    Hyde Park
	Zoos:
	    the San Diego Zoo
	    the Milwaukee Zoo

Seasons:
    summer   fall   spring   winter
    Summer is my favorite season.
Note: After a preposition, *the* may be used.
    In (the) winter, my car runs badly.
	Deserts:
	    the Mojave Desert
	    the Sahara Desert

(continued)

No Article	Article

Directions:
    north   south
    east   west
	Sections of a piece of land:
	    the Southwest (of the U.S.)
	    the West Side (of New York)

School subjects:
    history   math
	Unique geographical points:
	    the North Pole the Vatican

Name + *college* or *university*:
    Northwestern University
    Bradford College
	The University/College of _____
	    the University of Michigan
	    the College of DuPage County

Magazines:
    Time   *Sports Illustrated*
	Newspapers:
	    the *Tribune* the *Wall Street Journal*

Months and days:
    September
    Monday
	Ships:
	    the *Titanic*
	    the *Queen Elizabeth II*

Holidays and dates:
    Mother's Day
    July 4 (month + day)
	The day of month:
	    the fifth of May
	    the Fourth of July

Diseases:
    cancer   AIDS
    polio   malaria
	Ailments:
	    a cold a toothache
	    a headache the flu

Games and sports:
    poker
    soccer
	Musical instruments, after *play*:
	    the drums the piano
	Note: Sometimes *the* is omitted.
	    She plays (the) drums.

Languages:
    French
    English
	The _____ language:
	    the French language
	    the English language

Last month, year, week, etc. = the one before this one:
    I forgot to pay my rent last month.
    The teacher gave us a test last week.
	The last month, the last year, the last week, etc. = the last in a series:
	    December is the last month of the year.
	    Summer vacation begins the last week in May.

In office = in an elected position:
    The president is in office for four years.
	In the office = in a specific room:
	    The teacher is in the office.

In back/in front:
    She's in back
    of the car.
	In the back/in the front:
	    He's in the back of the bus.

Appendix C

The Verb *GET*

Get has many meanings. Here is a list of the most common ones:

- get something = receive
  I got a letter from my father.

- get + (to) place = arrive
  I got home at six. What time do you get to school?

- get + object + infinitive = persuade
  She got him to wash the dishes.

- get + past participle = become

get acquainted	get worried	get hurt	get engaged
get lost	get bored	get married	get accustomed to
get confused	get divorced	get used to	get scared
get tired	get dressed		

  They got married in 1989.

- get + adjective = become

get hungry	get sleepy	get rich	get dark	get nervous
get angry	get well	get old	get upset	get fat

  It gets dark at 6:30.

- get an illness = catch
  While she was traveling, she got malaria.

- get a joke or an idea = understand
  Everybody except Tom laughed at the joke. He didn't get it.
  The boss explained the project to us, but I didn't get it.

- get ahead = advance
  He works very hard because he wants to get ahead in his job.

- get along (well) (with someone) = have a good relationship
  She doesn't get along with her mother-in-law.
  Do you and your roommate get along well?

- get around to something = find the time to do something
  I wanted to write my brother a letter yesterday, but I didn't get around to it.

- get away = escape
  The police chased the thief, but he got away.

- get away with something = escape punishment
  He cheated on his taxes and got away with it.

(continued)

- get back = return
  He got back from his vacation last Saturday.

- get back at someone = get revenge
  My brother wants to get back at me for stealing his girlfriend.

- get back to someone = communicate with someone at a later time
  The boss can't talk to you today. Can she get back to you tomorrow?

- get by = have just enough but nothing more
  On her salary, she's just getting by. She can't afford a car or a vacation.

- get in trouble = be caught and punished for doing something wrong
  They got in trouble for cheating on the test.

- get in(to) = enter a car
  She got in the car and drove away quickly.

- get out (of) = leave a car
  When the taxi arrived at the theater, everyone got out.

- get on = seat yourself on a bicycle, motorcycle, horse
  She got on the motorcycle and left.

- get on = enter a train, bus, airplane
  She got on the bus and took a seat in the back.

- get off = leave a bicycle, motorcycle, horse, train, bus, airplane
  They will get off the train at the next stop.

- get out of something = escape responsibility
  My boss wants me to help him on Saturday, but I'm going to try to get out of it.

- get over something = recover from an illness or disappointment
  She has the flu this week. I hope she gets over it soon.

- get rid of someone or something = free oneself of someone or something undesirable
  My apartment has roaches, and I can't get rid of them.

- get through (to someone) = communicate, often by telephone
  She tried to explain the harm of eating fast food to her son, but she couldn't get through to him.
  I tried to call my mother many times, but her line was busy. I couldn't get through.

- get through (with something) = finish
  I can meet you after I get through with my homework.

- get together = meet with another person
  I'd like to see you again. When can we get together?

- get up = arise from bed
  He woke up at six o'clock, but he didn't get up until 6:30.

Appendix D

Gerund and Infinitive Patterns

1. Verb + Infinitive

> They need **to leave**.
> I learned **to speak** English.

agree	claim	know how	seem
appear	consent	learn	swear
arrange	decide	manage	tend
ask	demand	need	threaten
attempt	deserve	offer	try
be able	expect	plan	volunteer
beg	fail	prepare	want
can afford	forget	pretend	wish
care	hope	promise	would like
choose	intend	refuse	

2. Verb + Noun/Object Pronoun + Infinitive

> I want you **to leave**.
> He expects me **to call** him.

advise	convince	hire	require
allow	dare	instruct	select
appoint	enable	invite	teach
ask	encourage	need	tell
beg	expect	order	urge
cause	forbid	permit	want
challenge	force	persuade	warn
choose	get	remind	would like
command	help*		

*Note: After *help*, *to* is often omitted: "He helped me (to) move."

(continued)

3. Adjective + Infinitive

They are happy **to be** here.
We're willing **to help** you.

afraid	disturbed	lucky	sorry
ashamed	eager	pleased	surprised
amazed	foolish	prepared	upset
careful	fortunate	proud	willing
content	free	ready	wrong
delighted	glad	reluctant	
determined	happy	sad	
disappointed	likely	shocked	

4. Verb + Gerund

I enjoy **dancing**.
She delayed **going** to the doctor.

admit	detest	miss	resent
advise	discuss	permit	resist
anticipate	dislike	postpone	risk
appreciate	enjoy	practice	stop
avoid	finish	put off	suggest
can't help	forbid	quit	tolerate
complete	imagine	recall	understand
consider	keep (on)	recommend	
delay	mention	regret	
deny	mind	remember	

5. Expressions with *Go* + Gerund

He **goes fishing** every Saturday.
They **went shopping** yesterday.

go boating	go hiking	go sightseeing
go bowling	go hunting	go skating
go camping	go jogging	go skiing
go dancing	go sailing	go swimming
go fishing	go shopping	

6. Preposition + Gerund

Verb + Preposition + Gerund
   We talked about **moving**.
   I look forward to **having** my own apartment.

adjust to	concentrate on	forget about	refrain from
argue about	depend on	insist on	succeed in
believe in	(dis)approve of	look forward to	talk about
care about	dream about	object to	think about
complain about	feel like	plan on	worry about

Adjective + Preposition + Gerund
   I'm fond of **traveling**.
   She's not accustomed to **eating** alone.

accustomed to	famous for	interested in	sure of
afraid of	fond of	lazy about	surprised at
appropriate for	good at	proud of	tired of
ashamed of	grateful to . . . for	responsible for	upset about
concerned about	guilty of	sorry about	used to
excited about	(in)capable of	suitable for	worried about

Verb + Object + Preposition + Gerund
   I thanked him for **helping** me.
   I apologized to him for **forgetting** his birthday.

accuse . . . of	devote . . . to	prevent . . . from	suspect . . . of
apologize to . . . for	forgive . . . for	prohibit . . . from	thank . . . for
blame . . . for	keep . . . from	stop . . . from	warn . . . about

(continued)

Gerund After Preposition in Certain Expressions

Who's in charge of **collecting** the papers?
What is your reason for **coming** late?

impression of	in favor of	in the middle of	requirement for
in charge of	instead of	need for	technique for
in danger of	interest in	reason for	the point of

7. Noun + Gerund

He has difficulty **speaking** English.
She had a problem **finding** a job.
She spent three weeks **looking** for an apartment.

Use a gerund after the noun in these expressions:

have a difficult time	have a hard time
have difficulty	have a problem
have experience	have trouble
have fun	spend time/money
have a good time	there's no use

8. Verb + Gerund or Infinitive (with little or no difference in meaning)

They like **to sing**.
They like **singing**.

I started **to read**.
I started **reading**.

attempt	intend
begin	like
can't stand	love
continue	neglect
deserve	prefer
hate	start
hesitate	

Appendix E

Verbs and Adjectives Followed by a Preposition

Many verbs and adjectives are followed by a preposition.

accuse someone of
(be) accustomed to
adjust to
(be) afraid of
agree with
(be) amazed at/by
(be) angry about
(be) angry at/with
apologize for
approve of
argue about
argue with
(be) ashamed of
(be) aware of
believe in
blame someone for
(be) bored with/by
(be) capable of
care about
care for
compare to/with
complain about
concentrate on
(be) concerned about
consist of
count on
deal with
decide on
depend on/upon
(be) different from
disapprove of
(be) divorced from
dream about/of
(be) engaged to
(be) excited about

(be) familiar with
(be) famous for
feel like
(be) fond of
forget about
forgive someone for
(be) glad about
(be) good at
(be) grateful to someone for
(be) guilty of
(be) happy about
hear about
hear of
hope for
(be) incapable of
insist on/upon
(be) interested in
(be) involved in
(be) jealous of
(be) known for
(be) lazy about
listen to
look at
look for
look forward to
(be) mad about
(be) mad at
(be) made from/of
(be) married to
object to
(be) opposed to
participate in
plan on
pray to
pray for

(be) prepared for/to
prevent (someone) from
prohibit (someone) from
protect (someone) from
(be) proud of
recover from
(be) related to
rely on/upon
(be) responsible for
(be) sad about
(be) satisfied with
(be) scared of
(be) sick of
(be) sorry about
(be) sorry for
speak about
speak to/with
succeed in
(be) sure of/about
(be) surprised at
take care of
talk about
talk to/with
thank (someone) for
(be) thankful (to someone) for
think about/of
(be) tired of
(be) upset about
(be) upset with
(be) used to
wait for
warn (someone) about
(be) worried about
worry about

Appendix F

Direct and Indirect Objects

> **The order of direct and indirect objects depends on the verb you use. It also can depend on whether you use a noun or a pronoun as the object.**

Group 1 Pronouns affect word order. The preposition used is *to*.

Patterns: He gave a present to his wife. (DO to IO)
He gave his wife a present. (IO/DO)
He gave it to his wife. (DO to IO)
He gave her a present. (IO/DO)
He gave it to her. (DO to IO)

Verbs:	bring	lend	pass	sell	show	teach
	give	offer	pay	send	sing	tell
	hand	owe	read	serve	take	write

Group 2 Pronouns affect word order. The preposition used is *for*.

Patterns: He bought a car for his daughter. (DO for IO)
He bought his daughter a car. (IO/DO)
He bought it for his daughter. (DO for IO)
He bought her a car. (IO/DO)
He bought it for her. (DO for IO)

Verbs:	bake	buy	draw	get	make
	build	do	find	knit	reserve

Group 3 Pronouns don't affect word order. The preposition used is *to*.

Patterns: He explained the problem to his friend. (DO to IO)
He explained it to her. (DO to IO)

Verbs:	admit	introduce	recommend	say
	announce	mention	repeat	speak
	describe	prove	report	suggest
	explain			

Group 4 Pronouns don't affect word order. The preposition used is *for*.

Patterns: He cashed a check for his friend. (DO for IO)
He cashed it for her. (DO for IO)

Verbs:	answer	change	design	open	prescribe
	cash	close	fix	prepare	pronounce

Group 5 Pronouns don't affect word order. No preposition is used.

Patterns: She asked the teacher a question. (IO/DO)
She asked him a question. (IO/DO)

Verbs:	ask	charge	cost	wish	take (with time)

Appendix G

Spelling and Pronunciation of Verbs

Spelling of the -s Form of Verbs

Rule	Base Form	-s Form
Add -s to most verbs to make the -s form.	hope eat	hopes eats
When the base form ends in *ss*, *zz*, *sh*, *ch*, or *x*, add -es and pronounce an extra syllable, /əz/.	miss buzz wash catch fix	misses buzzes washes catches fixes
When the base form ends in a consonant + *y*, change the *y* to *i* and add -es.	carry worry	carries worries
When the base form ends in a vowel + *y*, do not change the *y*.	pay obey	pays obeys
Add -es to *go* and *do*.	go do	goes does

Three Pronunciations of the -s Form		
We pronounce /**s**/ if the verb ends in these voiceless sounds: /**p t k f**/.	hope—hopes eat—eats	pick—picks laugh—laughs
We pronounce /**z**/ if the verb ends in most voiced sounds.	live—lives grab—grabs read—reads	run—runs sing—sings borrow—borrows
When the base form ends in *ss*, *zz*, *sh*, *ch*, *x*, *se*, *ge*, or *ce*, we pronounce an extra syllable, /əz/.	miss—misses buzz—buzzes wash—washes watch—watches	fix—fixes use—uses change—changes dance—dances
These verbs have a change in the vowel sound.	do/**du**/—does/**dʌz**/	say/**seɪ**/—says/**sɛz**/

(continued)

Spelling of the *-ing* Form of Verbs

Rule	Base Form	*-ing* Form
Add *-ing* to most verbs. **Note:** Do not remove the *y* for the *-ing* form.	eat go study carry	eating going studying carrying
For a one-syllable verb that ends in a consonant + vowel + consonant (CVC), double the final consonant and add *-ing*.	p l a n | | | C V C s t o p | | | C V C s i t | | | C V C g r a b | | | C V C	planning stopping sitting grabbing
Do not double the final *w*, *x*, or *y*.	show mix stay	showing mixing staying
For a two-syllable word that ends in CVC, double the final consonant only if the last syllable is stressed.	refér admít begín rebél	referring admitting beginning rebelling
When the last syllable of a multi-syllable word is not stressed, do not double the final consonant.	lísten ópen óffer límit devélop	listening opening offering limiting developing
If the word ends in a consonant + *e*, drop the *e* before adding *-ing*.	live take write arrive	living taking writing arriving

Spelling of the Past Tense of Regular Verbs

Rule	Base Form	-ed Form
Add -ed to the base form to make the past tense of most regular verbs.	start kick	started kicked
When the base form ends in e, add -d only.	die live	died lived
When the base form ends in a consonant + y, change the y to i and add -ed.	carry worry	carried worried
When the base form ends in a vowel + y, do not change the y.	destroy stay	destroyed stayed
For a one-syllable word that ends in a consonant + vowel + consonant (CVC), double the final consonant and add -ed.	s t o p | | | C V C p l u g | | | C V C	stopped plugged
Do not double the final w or x.	sew fix	sewed fixed
For a two-syllable word that ends in CVC, double the final consonant only if the last syllable is stressed.	occúr permít	occurred permitted
When the last syllable of a multi-syllable word is not stressed, do not double the final consonant.	ópen háppen devélop	opened happened developed

Pronunciation of Past Forms that End in -ed

The past tense with -ed has three pronunciations.			
We pronounce a /t/ if the base form ends in these voiceless sounds: /p, k, f, s, š, č/.	jump—jumped cook—cooked	cough—coughed kiss—kissed	wash—washed watch—watched
We pronounce a /d/ if the base form ends in most voiced sounds.	rub—rubbed drag—dragged love—loved bathe—bathed use—used	charge—charged glue—glued massage—massaged name—named learn—learned	bang—banged call—called fear—feared free—freed stay—stayed
We pronounce an extra syllable /əd/ if the base form ends in a /t/ or /d/ sound.	wait—waited hate—hated	want—wanted add—added	need—needed decide—decided

Appendix H

Capitalization Rules

- The first word in a sentence: **My** friends are helpful.

- The word "I": My sister and **I** took a trip together.

- Names of people: **J**ulia **R**oberts; **G**eorge **W**ashington

- Titles preceding names of people: **D**octor (**D**r.) **S**mith;
  President **L**incoln; **Q**ueen **E**lizabeth; **M**r. **R**ogers; **M**rs. **C**arter

- Geographic names: the **U**nited **S**tates; **L**ake **S**uperior; **C**alifornia; the
  Rocky **M**ountains; the **M**ississippi **R**iver

  NOTE: The word "the" in a geographic name is not capitalized.

- Street names: **P**ennsylvania **A**venue (**A**ve.); **W**all **S**treet (**S**t.);
  Abbey **R**oad (**R**d.)

- Names of organizations, companies, colleges, buildings, stores, hotels:
  the **R**epublican **P**arty; **H**einle **C**engage; **D**artmouth **C**ollege; the
  University of **W**isconsin; the **W**hite **H**ouse; **B**loomingdale's; the **H**ilton
  Hotel

- Nationalities and ethnic groups: **M**exicans; **C**anadians; **S**paniards;
  Americans; **J**ews; **K**urds; **E**skimos

- Languages: **E**nglish; **S**panish; **P**olish; **V**ietnamese; **R**ussian

- Months: **J**anuary; **F**ebruary

- Days: **S**unday; **M**onday

- Holidays: **C**hristmas; **I**ndependence **D**ay

- Important words in a title: *Grammar in Context*; *The Old Man and the
  Sea*; *Romeo and Juliet*; *The Sound of Music*

  NOTE: Capitalize "the" as the first word of a title.

Appendix I

Plural Forms of Nouns

REGULAR NOUN PLURALS				
Word Ending	**Example Noun**	**Plural Addition**	**Plural Form**	**Pronunciation**
Vowel	bee banana	+ s	bees bananas	/z/
ch, sh, x, s, ss	church dish box bus class	+ es	churches dishes boxes buses classes	/əz/
Voiceless consonants	cat lip month	+ s	cats lips months	/s/
Voiced consonants	card pin	+ s	cards pins	/z/
Vowel + *y*	boy day	+ s	boys days	/z/
Consonant + *y*	lady story	*y* + ies	ladies stories	/z/
Vowel + *o*	video radio	+ s	videos radios	/z/
Consonant + *o*	potato hero	+ es	potatoes heroes	/z/
Exceptions: photos, pianos, solos, altos, sopranos, autos, and avocados				
f or *fe*	leaf knife	*f* + ves	leaves knives	/z/
Exceptions: beliefs, chiefs, roofs, cliffs, chefs, and sheriffs				

(continued)

IRREGULAR NOUN PLURALS

Singular	Plural	Explanation
man woman tooth foot goose	men women teeth feet geese	Vowel change (**Note:** The first vowel in *women* is pronounced /I/.)
sheep fish deer	sheep fish deer	No change
child person mouse	children people (OR persons) mice	Different word form
	(eye)glasses jeans belongings pajamas clothes pants/slacks goods scissors groceries shorts	No singular form
alumnus cactus radius stimulus syllabus	alumni cacti (OR cactuses) radii stimuli syllabi (OR syllabuses)	*us → i*
analysis crisis hypothesis oasis parenthesis thesis	analyses crises hypotheses oases parentheses theses	*is → es*
appendix index	appendices (OR appendixes) indices (OR indexes)	*ix → ices* OR *→ ixes* *ex → ices* OR *→ exes*
bacterium curriculum datum medium memorandum criterion phenomenon	bacteria curricula data media memoranda criteria phenomena	*um → a* *ion → a* *on → a*
alga formula vertebra	algae formulae (OR formulas) vertebrae	*a → ae*

Appendix J

Metric Conversion Chart

Length

When You Know	Symbol	Multiply by	To Find	Symbol
inches	in	2.54	centimeters	cm
feet	ft	30.5	centimeters	cm
feet	ft	0.3	meters	m
yards	yd	0.91	meters	m
miles	mi	1.6	kilometers	km
Metric:				
centimeters	cm	0.39	inches	in
centimeters	cm	0.03	feet	ft
meters	m	3.28	feet	ft
meters	m	1.09	yards	yd
kilometers	km	0.62	miles	mi

Note:
12 inches = 1 foot
3 feet / 36 inches = 1 yard

Area

When You Know	Symbol	Multiply by	To Find	Symbol
square inches	in²	6.5	square centimeters	cm²
square feet	ft²	0.09	square meters	m²
square yards	yd²	0.8	square meters	m²
square miles	mi²	2.6	square kilometers	km²
Metric:				
square centimeters	cm²	0.16	square inches	in²
square meters	m²	10.76	square feet	ft²
square meters	m²	1.2	square yards	yd²
square kilometers	km²	0.39	square miles	mi²

(continued)

Weight (Mass)

When You Know	Symbol	Multiply by	To Find	Symbol
ounces	oz	28.35	grams	g
pounds	lb	0.45	kilograms	kg
Metric:				
grams	g	0.04	ounces	oz
kilograms	kg	2.2	pounds	lb
Note: 1 pound = 16 ounces				

Volume

When You Know	Symbol	Multiply by	To Find	Symbol
fluid ounces	fl oz	30.0	milliliters	mL
pints	pt	0.47	liters	L
quarts	qt	0.95	liters	L
gallons	gal	3.8	liters	L
Metric:				
milliliters	mL	0.03	fluid ounces	fl oz
liters	L	2.11	pints	pt
liters	L	1.05	quarts	qt
liters	L	0.26	gallons	gal

Temperature

When You Know	Symbol	Do this	To Find	Symbol
degrees Fahrenheit	°F	Subtract 32, then multiply by $\frac{5}{9}$	degrees Celsius	°C
Metric:				
degrees Celsius	°C	Multiply by $\frac{9}{5}$, then add 32	degrees Fahrenheit	°F

Sample temperatures

Fahrenheit	Celsius
0	− 18
10	−12
20	−7
32	0
40	4
50	10
60	16
70	21
80	27
90	32
100	38
212	100

Appendix K

Comparative and Superlative Forms

Comparative and Superlative Forms

	Simple	Comparative	Superlative
One-syllable adjectives and adverbs*	tall fast	taller faster	the tallest the fastest
Two-syllable adjectives that end in y	easy happy	easier happier	the easiest the happiest
Other two-syllable adjectives	frequent active	more frequent more active	the most frequent the most active
Some two-syllable adjectives have two forms.**	simple common	simpler more simple commoner more common	the simplest the most simple the commonest the most common
Adjectives with three or more syllables	important difficult	more important more difficult	the most important the most difficult
-ly adverbs	quickly brightly	more quickly more brightly	the most quickly the most brightly
Irregular adjectives and adverbs	good/well bad/badly far little a lot	better worse farther less more	the best the worst the farthest the least the most

Language Notes:

1.*Exceptions to one-syllable adjectives:

| bored | more bored | the most bored |
| tired | more tired | the most tired |

2.**Other two-syllable adjectives that have two forms:
   handsome, quiet, gentle, narrow, clever, friendly, angry, polite, stupid

The Superlative Form

Subject	Verb	Superlative Form + Noun	Prepositional Phrase
Alaska	is	the biggest state	in the U.S.
California	is	the most populated state	in the U.S.

The Comparative Form

Subject	Linking Verb[1]	Comparative Adjective	*Than*	Noun/Pronoun
She	is	taller	than	her sister (is).
She	seems	more intelligent	than	her sister.
Subject	**Verb Phrase**	**Comparative Adverb**	***Than***	**Noun/Pronoun**
I	speak English	more fluently	than	my sister (does).
I	sleep	less	than	you (do).

Comparisons with Nouns

Subject	Verb	Comparative Word + Noun	*Than*	Noun/Pronoun
I	work	fewer hours	than	you (do).
I	have	more time	than	you (do).

Equality or Inequality with Adjectives and Adverbs

Subject	Linking Verb	*As*	Adjective	*As*	Noun/Pronoun
She	isn't	as	old	as	her husband (is).
She	looks	as	pretty	as	a picture.
Subject	**Verb Phrase**	***As***	**Adverb**	***As***	**Noun/Pronoun**
She	speaks English	as	fluently	as	her husband (does).
He	doesn't work	as	hard	as	his wife (does).

[1]The linking verbs include *be, look, seem, feel, taste, sound,* and *seem.*

(continued)

Equality or Inequality with Quantities

Subject	Verb	*As Many/Much*	Noun	*As*	Noun/Pronoun
She	works	as many	hours	as	her husband (does).
Milk	doesn't have	as much	fat	as	cream (does).

Subject	Verb	*As Much As*	Noun/Pronoun		
Chicken	doesn't cost	as much as	meat (does).		
I	don't drive	as much as	you (do).		

Equality or Inequality with Nouns

Pattern A Subject	Verb	*The Same*	Noun	*As*	Noun/Pronoun
She	wears	the same	size	as	her mother (does).
She	isn't	the same	height	as	her brother (is).

Pattern B Subject & Subject	Verb	*The Same*	Noun
She and her mother	wear	the same	size.
She and her brother	aren't	the same	height.

Similarities Using *Like/Alike*

Pattern A Subject	Linking Verb	*Like*	Noun/Pronoun
Sugar	looks	like	salt.
Regular coffee	tastes	like	decaf.

Pattern B Subject & Subject	Linking Verb	*Alike*
Sugar and salt	look	alike.
Regular coffee and decaf	taste	alike.

Glossary of Grammatical Terms

- **Adjective** An adjective gives a description of a noun.

    It's a *tall* tree.   He's an *old* man.   My neighbors are *nice*.

- **Adverb** An adverb describes the action of a verb, an adjective, or another adverb.

    She speaks English *fluently*.   I drive *carefully*.
    She speaks English *extremely* well.   She is *very* intelligent.

- **Adverb of Frequency** An adverb of frequency tells how often the action happens.

    I *never* drink coffee.   They *usually* take the bus.

- **Affirmative** means *yes*.

- **Apostrophe '** We use the apostrophe for possession and contractions.

    My *sister's* friend is beautiful.   Today *isn't* Sunday.

- **Article** The definite article is *the*. The indefinite articles are *a* and *an*.

    I have *a* cat.   I ate *an* apple.   *The* teacher came late.

- **Auxiliary Verb** Some verbs have two parts: an auxiliary verb and a main verb.

    He *can't* study.   We *will* return.

- **Base Form** The base form, sometimes called the "simple" form, of the verb has no tense. It has no ending (*-s* or *-ed*): *be, go, eat, take, write*.

    I didn't *go* out.   We don't *know* you.   He can't *drive*.

- **Capital Letter** A B C D E F G . . .

- **Clause** A clause is a group of words that has a subject and a verb. Some sentences have only one clause.

    She speaks Spanish.

    Some sentences have **a main clause** and a **dependent clause**.

MAIN CLAUSE	DEPENDENT CLAUSE **(reason clause)**
She found a good job	because she has computer skills.
MAIN CLAUSE	DEPENDENT CLAUSE **(time clause)**
She'll turn off the light	before she goes to bed.
MAIN CLAUSE	DEPENDENT CLAUSE **(if clause)**
I'll take you to the doctor	if you don't have your car on Saturday.

(continued)

- **Colon :**

- **Comma ,**

- **Comparative Form** A comparative form of an adjective or adverb is used to compare two things.

    My house is *bigger* than your house.
    Her husband drives *faster* than she does.

- **Complement** The complement of the sentence is the information after the verb. It completes the verb phrase.

    He works *hard*.   I slept *for five hours*.   They are *late*.

- **Consonant** The following letters are consonants: *b, c, d, f, g, h, j, k, l, m, n, p, q, r, s, t, v, w, x, y, z*.

    NOTE: *y* is sometimes considered a vowel, as in the world *syllable*.

- **Contraction** A contraction is made up of two words put together with an apostrophe.

    He's my brother.   *You're* late.   They *won't* talk to me.
    (*He's = he is*)   (*You're = you are*)   (*won't = will not*)

- **Count Noun** Count nouns are nouns that we can count. They have a singular and a plural form.

    1 pen — 3 pens   1 table — 4 tables

- **Dependent Clause** See **Clause**.

- **Direct Object** A direct object is a noun (phrase) or pronoun that receives the action of the verb.

    We saw *the movie*.   You have *a nice car*.   I love *you*.

- **Exclamation Mark !**

- **Frequency Words** Frequency words are *always, usually, generally, often, sometimes, rarely, seldom, hardly ever, never*.

    I *never* drink coffee.   We *always* do our homework.

- **Hyphen –**

- **Imperative** An imperative sentence gives a command or instructions. An imperative sentence omits the word *you*.

    Come here.   *Don't* be late.   Please *sit* down.

- **Infinitive** An infinitive is *to* + base form.

    I want *to leave*.   You need *to be* here on time.

- **Linking Verb** A linking verb is a verb that links the subject to the noun or adjective after it. Linking verbs include *be, seem, feel, smell, sound, look, appear, taste*.

    She *is* a doctor.   She *seems* very intelligent.   She *looks* tired.

- **Modal** The modal verbs are *can, could, shall, should, will, would, may, might, must.*

  They *should* leave.   I *must* go.

- **Negative** means no.

- **Nonaction Verb** A nonaction verb has no action. We do not use a continuous tense (*be* + verb *-ing*) with a nonaction verb. The nonaction verbs are: *believe, cost, care, have, hear, know, like, love, matter, mean, need, own, prefer, remember, see, seem, think, understand, want,* and sense-perception verbs.

  She *has* a laptop.   We *love* our mother.   You *look* great.

- **Noncount Noun** A noncount noun is a noun that we don't count. It has no plural form.

  She drank some *water.*   He prepared some *rice.*
  Do you need any *money?*   We had a lot of *homework.*

- **Noun** A noun is a person (*brother*), a place (*kitchen*), or a thing (*table*). Nouns can be either count (*1 table, 2 tables*) or noncount (*money, water*).

  My *brother* lives in California.   My *sisters* live in New York.
  I get *advice* from them.   I drink *coffee* every day.

- **Noun Modifier** A noun modifier makes a noun more specific.

  fire department   *Independence* Day   *can* opener

- **Noun Phrase** A noun phrase is a group of words that form the subject or object of the sentence.

  A *very nice woman* helped me at registration.
  I bought *a big box of cereal.*

- **Object** The object of the sentence follows the verb. It receives the action of the verb.

  He bought *a car.*   I saw *a movie.*   I met *your brother.*

- **Object Pronoun** Use object pronouns (*me, you, him, her, it, us, them*) after the verb or preposition.

  He likes *her.*   I saw the movie. Let's talk about *it.*

- **Parentheses** ( )

- **Paragraph** A paragraph is a group of sentences about one topic.

- **Participle, Present** The present participle is verb + *-ing.*

  She is *sleeping.*   They were *laughing.*

- **Period** .

- **Phrase** A group of words that go together.

  Last month my sister came to visit.
  There is a strange car *in front of my house.*

(continued)

- **Plural** Plural means more than one. A plural noun usually ends with *-s*.

  She has beautiful *eyes*.   My *feet* are big.

- **Possessive Form** Possessive forms show ownership or relationship.

  Mary's coat is in the closet.   *My brother* lives in Miami.

- **Preposition** A preposition is a short connecting word: *about, above, across, after, around, as, at, away, back, before, behind, below, by, down, for, from, in, into, like, of, off, on, out, over, to, under, up, with.*

  The book is *on* the table.   She studies *with* her friends.

- **Pronoun** A pronoun takes the place of a noun.

  I have a new car. I bought *it* last week.
  John likes Mary, but *she* doesn't like *him*.

- **Punctuation** Period . Comma , Colon : Semicolon ; Question Mark ? Exclamation Mark !

- **Question Mark** ?

- **Quotation Marks** " "

- **Regular Verb** A regular verb forms its past tense with *-ed*.

  He *worked* yesterday.   I *laughed* at the joke.

- **-s Form** A present tense verb that ends in *-s* or *-es*.

  He *lives* in New York.   She *watches* TV a lot.

- **Sense-Perception Verb** A sense-perception verb has no action. It describes a sense. The sense-perception verbs are: *look, feel, taste, sound, smell.*

  She *feels* fine.   The coffee *smells* fresh.   The milk *tastes* sour.

- **Sentence** A sentence is a group of words that contains a subject[2] and a verb (at least) and gives a complete thought.

  SENTENCE: She came home.
  NOT A SENTENCE: When she came home

- **Simple Form of Verb** The simple form of the verb, also called the base form, has no tense; it never has an *-s*, *-ed*, or *-ing* ending.

  Did you *see* the movie?   I couldn't *find* your phone number.

- **Singular** Singular means one.

  She ate a *sandwich*.   I have one *television*.

- **Subject** The subject of the sentence tells who or what the sentence is about.

  My sister got married last April. *The wedding* was beautiful.

---

[2]In an imperative sentence, the subject *you* is omitted: *Sit down. Come here.*

- **Subject Pronouns** Use subject pronouns (*I, you, he, she, it, we, you, they*) before a verb.

  They speak Japanese.   *We* speak Spanish.

- **Superlative Form** A superlative form of an adjective or adverb shows the number one item in a group of three or more.

  January is the *coldest* month of the year.
  My brother speaks English the *best* in my family.

- **Syllable** A syllable is a part of a word that has only one vowel sound. (Some words have only one syllable.)

  change (one syllable)   after (af·ter = two syllables)
  look (one syllable)   responsible (re·spon·si·ble = four syllables)

- **Tag Question** A tag question is a short question at the end of a sentence. It is used in conversation.

  You speak Spanish, *don't you?*   He's not happy, *is he?*

- **Tense** A verb has tense. Tense shows when the action of the sentence happened.

  SIMPLE PRESENT: She usually *works* hard.
  FUTURE: She *will work* tomorrow.
  PRESENT CONTINUOUS: She *is working* now.
  SIMPLE PAST: She *worked* yesterday.

- **Verb** A verb is the action of the sentence.

  He *runs* fast.   I *speak* English.

  Some verbs have no action. They are linking verbs. They connect the subject to the rest of the sentence.

  He *is* tall.   She *looks* beautiful.   You *seem* tired.

- **Vowel** The following letters are vowels: *a, e, i, o, u.* Y is sometimes considered a vowel (for example, in the word *mystery).*

Alphabetical List of Irregular Verb Forms

Base Form	Past Form	Past Participle	Base Form	Past Form	Past Participle
be	was/were	been	find	found	found
bear	bore	born/borne	fit	fit	fit
beat	beat	beaten	flee	fled	fled
become	became	become	fly	flew	flown
begin	began	begun	forbid	forbade	forbidden
bend	bent	bent	forget	forgot	forgotten
bet	bet	bet	forgive	forgave	forgiven
bid	bid	bid	freeze	froze	frozen
bind	bound	bound	get	got	gotten
bite	bit	bitten	give	gave	given
bleed	bled	bled	go	went	gone
blow	blew	blown	grind	ground	ground
break	broke	broken	grow	grew	grown
breed	bred	bred	hang	hung	hung[3]
bring	brought	brought	have	had	had
broadcast	broadcast	broadcast	hear	heard	heard
build	built	built	hide	hid	hidden
burst	burst	burst	hit	hit	hit
buy	bought	bought	hold	held	held
cast	cast	cast	hurt	hurt	hurt
catch	caught	caught	keep	kept	kept
choose	chose	chosen	know	knew	known
cling	clung	clung	lay	laid	laid
come	came	come	lead	led	led
cost	cost	cost	leave	left	left
creep	crept	crept	lend	lent	lent
cut	cut	cut	let	let	let
deal	dealt	dealt	lie	lay	lain
dig	dug	dug	light	lit/lighted	lit/lighted
dive	dove/dived	dove/dived	lose	lost	lost
do	did	done	make	made	made
draw	drew	drawn	mean	meant	meant
drink	drank	drunk	meet	met	met
drive	drove	driven	mistake	mistook	mistaken
eat	ate	eaten	overcome	overcame	overcome
fall	fell	fallen	overdo	overdid	overdone
feed	fed	fed	overtake	overtook	overtaken
feel	felt	felt	overthrow	overthrew	overthrown
fight	fought	fought	pay	paid	paid

[3]*Hanged* is used as the past form to refer to punishment by death. *Hung* is used in other situations: She *hung* the picture on the wall.

Base Form	Past Form	Past Participle	Base Form	Past Form	Past Participle
plead	pled/pleaded	pled/pleaded	sting	stung	stung
prove	proved	proven/proved	stink	stank	stunk
put	put	put	strike	struck	struck/stricken
quit	quit	quit	strive	strove	striven
read	read	read	swear	swore	sworn
ride	rode	ridden	sweep	swept	swept
ring	rang	rung	swell	swelled	swelled/swollen
rise	rose	risen	swim	swam	swum
run	ran	run	swing	swung	swung
say	said	said	take	took	taken
see	saw	seen	teach	taught	taught
seek	sought	sought	tear	tore	torn
sell	sold	sold	tell	told	told
send	sent	sent	think	thought	thought
set	set	set	throw	threw	thrown
sew	sewed	sewn/sewed	understand	understood	understood
shake	shook	shaken	uphold	upheld	upheld
shed	shed	shed	upset	upset	upset
shine	shone/shined	shone/shined	wake	woke	woken
shoot	shot	shot	wear	wore	worn
show	showed	shown/showed	weave	wove	woven
shrink	shrank/shrunk	shrunk/shrunken	wed	wedded/wed	wedded/wed
shut	shut	shut	weep	wept	wept
sing	sang	sung	win	won	won
sink	sank	sunk	wind	wound	wound
sit	sat	sat	withdraw	withdrew	withdrawn
sleep	slept	slept	withhold	withheld	withheld
slide	slid	slid	withstand	withstood	withstood
slit	slit	slit	wring	wrung	wrung
speak	spoke	spoken	write	wrote	written
speed	sped	sped			
spend	spent	spent			
spin	spun	spun			
spit	spit	spit			
split	split	split			
spread	spread	spread			
spring	sprang	sprung			
stand	stood	stood			
steal	stole	stolen			
stick	stuck	stuck			

Note:
The past and past participle of some verbs can end in -ed or -t.

burn	burned or burnt
dream	dreamed or dreamt
kneel	kneeled or knelt
learn	learned or learnt
leap	leaped or leapt
spill	spilled or spilt
spoil	spoiled or spoilt

Map of the United States of America

AL	Alabama	HI	Hawaii	MA	Massachusetts	NM	New Mexico	SD	South Dakota
AK	Alaska	ID	Idaho	MI	Michigan	NY	New York	TN	Tennessee
AZ	Arizona	IL	Illinois	MN	Minnesota	NC	North Carolina	TX	Texas
AR	Arkansas	IN	Indiana	MS	Mississippi	ND	North Dakota	UT	Utah
CA	California	IA	Iowa	MO	Missouri	OH	Ohio	VT	Vermont
CO	Colorado	KS	Kansas	MT	Montana	OK	Oklahoma	VA	Virginia
CT	Connecticut	KY	Kentucky	NE	Nebraska	OR	Oregon	WA	Washington
DE	Delaware	LA	Louisiana	NV	Nevada	PA	Pennsylvania	WV	West Virginia
FL	Florida	ME	Maine	NH	New Hampshire	RI	Rhode Island	WI	Wisconsin
GA	Georgia	MD	Maryland	NJ	New Jersey	SC	South Carolina	WY	Wyoming
								DC*	District of Columbia

*The District of Columbia is not a state. Washington, D.C., is the capital of the United States.
Note: Washington, D.C., and Washington state are not the same.

Index

vs. past continuous tense, 104

with past perfect continuous
tense, 119

with past perfect tense, 112

vs. past perfect tense, with *when*,
114

vs. present perfect tense, 16,
25, 30

questions with *when*, 25

of regular verbs, 6

with repetition, 30

in *since* clauses, 13

with wishes, 438–439

Simple present tense, 344,
438–439

in future sentences, 344

with general present, 344

in time clauses, 334

with wishes, 438–439

Since

with present perfect continuous
tense, 21

with present perfect tense, 13

with reasons, 330

with time, 330, 335

Since/ever since, 13

So

to replace noun clauses, 370

to show result, 349

vs. *so that*, 330

So . . . that, 353

So far with present perfect tense,
27

So few . . . that, 353

So little . . . that, 353

So many . . . that, 353

So much . . . that, 353

So that, 330

Still with contrast, 340

Stop with infinitive or gerund,
306

Subject(s)

gerunds as, 297, 305

infinitive phrases as, 290–291,
305

Subject questions

with modals, 138

with passive voice, 61

Such . . . that, 353

Suggestions with modals, 161

T

Take with infinitives, 290, 291

Tell

reporting imperatives with,
394

vs. *say*, 391

Tense(s)

in future, 334, 430

with passive voice, 61

past tenses, 98, 125

past continuous tense, 98,
100–108, 125

past perfect tense, 98, 109–110,
111–112, 114, 121–122,
125, 438–439

past perfect continuous tense,
118–124, 125

present perfect tense, 4–20, 25,
27, 30, 33, 34, 38, 41, 44,
46, 98, 121–122, 125, 335

present perfect continuous
tense, 20–21, 43, 46, 98,
121–122, 125

rule of sequence of, 389–390

exceptions to, 394

in *if* clauses, 434

with noun clauses, 399, 403

simple past tense, 6–7, 13, 16,
25, 30, 34, 98, 101–102,
104, 112, 114, 119, 125,
403, 430, 438–439

That

to introduce noun clauses,
370

as object of relative clauses,
235

omission of in adjective clauses,
353, 370

with preposition in adjective
clauses, 238

as relative pronoun in adjective
clauses, 232, 235, 236, 244,
245, 258

as subject of adjective clauses,
232

Therefore, 349

Time clauses

changed to participial phrases,
338

with past continuous tense,
102

Time expressions, 334–335

Time words

with participial phrases, 338

in reported speech, 390

To

before indirect object, 69

as preposition, not part of
infinitive, 300

to show purpose, 289, 330

Too before infinitives, 293

Too much/too many before
infinitives, 293

Transitive vs. intransitive verbs, 73

Try with infinitive or gerund,
306

U

Unless, 344

Unless clauses, with unreal
conditions, 419

Unreal conditions

past, 434

present, 419

vs. real conditions, 430

Until, 334

Up to now with present perfect
tense, 27

Urgency

base form after expressions of,
374

with *must*, *have to*, and *have got
to*, 142

noun clauses after expressions
of, 374

Used to

negative of, 310

vs. *be used to/get used to*, 310

V

Verb(s)

action, 21

auxiliary, after *wish*, 438–439

causative, 284

continuous, with modals, 174

followed by gerunds, 302, 304

followed by infinitives, 278

followed by noun clauses, 370

followed by prepositions, 304

gerunds and infinitives after,
differences in meaning,
306

intransitive vs. transitive, 73

irregular forms of, AP34–35

nonaction, 21, 43, 119

prepositions after, 299

pronunciation of, AP17–19

with reported speech, 391

Photo Credits